Police Work: A Career Survival Guide, 2/e *is a must-read for every police officer in this nation, as well as anyone contemplating a career in law enforcement. It provides an honest, straightforward, and total insight of what police officers can do to achieve excellence.*

Ed Nowicki
Founding Executive Director
American Society of Law Enforcement Trainers
Founding Executive Director
International Law Enforcement Educators and Trainers Association

OTHER BOOKS BY NEAL E. TRAUTMAN, PH.D.

How to Be a Great Cop

The Cutting Edge of Police Integrity

How to Protect Your Kids from Internet Predators

Law Enforcement Training

Law Enforcement In-Service Training Programs

Law Enforcement—The Making of a Profession

A Study of Law Enforcement

Landing a Law Enforcement Job

The Internet Safety Workbook

POLICE WORK

A Career Survival Guide

SECOND EDITION

NEAL E. TRAUTMAN, PH.D.

PEARSON

Prentice
Hall

Upper Saddle River, New Jersey 07458

Library of Congress Cataloging-in-Publication Data

Trautman, Neal E.
  Police work : a career survival guide/Neal E. Trautman—2nd ed.
    p. cm.
  Rev. ed. of: How to be a great cop. c2002.
  Includes bibliographical references.
  ISBN 0-13-113311-X
    1. Police—Vocational guidance—United States.   2. Law enforcement—Vocational guidance—United States.   I. Trautman, Neal E. How to be a great cop.   II. Title.

HV8143.T725 2005
363.2′023′73′—dc22

2004044654

Executive Editor: Frank Mortimer, Jr.
Assistant Editor: Korrine Dorsey
Production Editor: Janet Bolton
Production Liaison: Brian Hyland
Director of Manufacturing and
  Production: Bruce Johnson
Managing Editor: Mary Carnis
Manufacturing Buyer: Cathleen Peterson

Manufacturing Manager: Ilene Sanford
Copyediting/Proofreading: Maine
  Proofreading Services
Cover Designer: Carey Davies
Cover Image: Ramin Talaie, CORBIS
Composition: Integra
Printing and Binding: Phoenix Color

Pearson Education LTD
Pearson Education Singapore, Plc. Ltd
Pearson Education, Canada, Ltd
Pearson Education–Japan
Pearson Education, Upper Saddle River, New Jersey

Pearson Education Australia PTY, Limited
Pearson Education North Asia Ltd
Pearson Educaçion de Mexico, S.A. de C.V.
Pearson Education Malaysia, Plc. Ltd

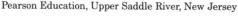

10 9 8 7 6 5 4 3 2 1
ISBN 0-13-113311-X

To Dad

The author wishes to acknowledge sincere gratitude to his wife, Robin, for her untiring effort and endless love.

CONTENTS

3

CHARACTER OF GREAT COPS   119

4

COPS AND THE JUDICIAL SYSTEM   142

5

SURVIVING THE STREET   181

6

EMOTIONALLY SURVIVING   220

7

FOREWORD

It takes a special kind of person to be a police officer. They must remain alert during hours of monotonous patrol, yet react quickly when need be, switch instantly from a state of near somnambulism to an adrenaline-filled struggle for survival, and learn their patrol area so well they can recognize what's out of the ordinary. It takes initiative, effective judgment, and imagination in coping with a complex situation, family disturbance, potential suicide, robbery in progress, gory accident, or natural disaster. Officers must be able to size up a situation instantly and react properly, perhaps with a life or death decision.

Officers need the initiative to perform their functions when their supervisor is miles away, yet they must be able to be part of a strike force team under the direct command of a superior. They must take charge in chaotic situations, yet avoid alienating those involved. They must be able to identify, single out, and placate an agitator trying to precipitate a riot. They must have curiosity tempered with tact and be skilled in questioning a traumatized victim or a suspected perpetrator. They must be brave enough to face an armed criminal, yet tender enough to help a woman deliver a baby. They must maintain a balanced perspective in the face of constant exposure to the worst side of human nature, yet be objective in dealing with special interest groups. And if that isn't enough, officers must be adept in a variety of psychomotor skills: operating a vehicle in normal and emergency situations; firing weapons accurately in adverse conditions; and strength in applying techniques to defend themselves while apprehending a suspect with a minimum of force.

Then, when it's all over, they must be able to explain what happened—in writing—to someone who wasn't there, in such a way that there's no opportunity for misunderstanding and to document their actions so they can relate their reasons years later.

Bill Clede
Retired Officer and Trainer
Member, American Society of Law Enforcement Trainers
Charter member, International Association
of Law Enforcement Firearms Instructors
Technical Editor, *Law and Order Magazine*
Author of Police Textbook

PREFACE

Law enforcement—it is one of America's greatest, yet most difficult, professions.
A heritage of pride. A history of tradition.

This book is for people who thrive on overcoming obstacles and working hard for a good cause. Whether you have yet to be sworn in, are on the street right now, or have become a seasoned cop, you should have a thirst for knowledge. *Police Work: A Career Survival Guide*, 2/e shares the insights and experiences of those who have "been there." It talks about reality and the things that are important in an officer's life.

Chapter 1 focuses on the history of law enforcement. Everyone benefits from the insight that only experience can deliver. When you understand police tradition, you'll better understand yourself, your fellow officers, and the future of policing. It provides recent statistics about both crime and law enforcement agencies.

Chapter 2 is about greed, honesty, temptation, and pride and the choices that must be made between them. It's about ethics and honor. It doesn't preach but "talks straight" about things that may ruin your career and life. The chapter delivers recent research reports on the police culture and excessive use of force.

Chapter 3 responds to the question of what it takes to have a great law enforcement career. It begins with the official and "real life" qualifications of officers. Highlights include personal control, discipline, wisdom, caring, positive attitude, hard work, supporting others, and staying educated. You have to work hard to have the "right stuff."

Chapter 4 discusses interacting with the judicial system. Some of the subjects reviewed include the law, American justice, prosecution, courts, civil suits, plea bargaining, defense attorneys, and legal terms. If you learn how to make the most of the legal frustrations with which our criminal justice system confronts you,

you will have enough knowledge to do your job and save yourself a lot of grief. Recent FBI crime statistics and a profile of jails and prisons are included.

Chapter 5 discusses surviving the street, including strategies and techniques of the nation's leading survival trainers. Mental conditioning is emphasized. Practical, realistic techniques can make a difference when you need them. The chapter provides important information on anticipating danger, understanding physiological changes in a crisis, and analyzing shoot-outs. Details about officers who have been killed in the line of duty are given.

Emotional survival is often overlooked in police work. Officers suffer serious medical problems or die from stress-related difficulties more often than attacks from guns or knives. Chapter 6 sheds light on these issues. It examines why people become cops, the natural changes in emotions anyone can expect, and how to manage police stress. In addition, it offers information on dealing with angry citizens, your spouse, and children; the truth about exercise; and special concerns of veteran officers. Recent research findings about the anger and frustrations that officers experience toward their own agency give readers valuable insights into the reality of police work.

Chapter 7 discusses why it is important for an officer to be physically fit. It presents helpful information on physical exams, stretching, choosing the right exercises, nutrition, and eating habits. Contemporary, researched facts on physical activity, nutrition, and sports are presented.

Appendices A-D provide information on law enforcement training organizations and related associations; and state training councils and police standards commissions. Contact information for more than two hundred important organizations is included. Understanding the facts, figures, and statistics about the operations of contemporary law enforcement is a priceless tool for any officer to achieve greatness. Every chapter has been written to cover specific subjects with reasonable thoroughness. The underlying premise is that most people have the ability to be successful. The extent of their commitment determines whether they will achieve greatness. To be a great cop, attitude and commitment are everything.

ACKNOWLEDGMENTS

The author acknowledges his appreciation to the following law enforcement authorities for their thoughtful comments:

Julian Allen, Ph.D.	Major, Academy Director, Harrison County Sheriff's Office, Gulfport, Mississippi
Vincent Benincasa	Hesser College, Manchester, New Hampshire
Robert Brode	College of the Canyons Santa Clarita, California
John Buckovich	Richmond Police Department Richmond, Virginia
Gary Bullard	Executive Director, Northern Virginia Criminal Justice Academy
Bill Clede	Law Enforcement Author
Timothy M. Dees	Law Enforcement Trainer and Author
Louis M. Dekmar	Chief, La Grange, Georgia, Police Department
Lee D. Donohue, Sr.	Chief of Police, Honolulu Police Department
Gordon Graham	Captain, California Highway Patrol, National Police Trainer
Paul Harvey	National Media Commentator
Donald Keith	Assistant Director, Mississippi Police Corps, University of Southern Mississippi
John Linn, Ph.D.	Criminal Justice Department, Altoona College, Penn State University

J. Dale Mann	Georgia Law Enforcement Academy
William A. May, Jr., Ph.D.	Major, Louisville Fire/Police Department, Louisville, Kentucky
Richard Mears	Professor, Department of Criminal Justice, University of Maine
Ed Nowicki	Executive Director, International Law Enforcement Educators and Trainers Association
Richard Pennington	Chief of Police, Atlanta Police Department
Lon Pepper	Chief of Police, Greenville, Mississippi
Ed Sanow	Editor, *Law and Order* Magazine
Neil Strobel	Chief of Police, Merrill, Wisconsin
Kevin Thom	Director, Division of Criminal Investigation, Office of Attorney General, State of South Dakota
David Thompson	Chief of Police, Atlantic Beach, Florida
J. E. Tillman	Chief, North Las Vegas Police Department
August Vollmer	"Dean" of Modern Policing

ORGANIZATIONS

Federal Bureau of Investigation

National Institute of Ethics

Police Executive Research Forum, International Association of Chiefs of Police (IACP)

International Association of Directors of Law Enforcement Standards and Training (IADLEST)

U.S. Department of Justice, Bureau of Justice Statistics

About the Author

Neal Trautman directs both the Global Institute of Law Enforcement Supervision at the University of Southern Mississippi and the National Institute of Ethics. He has delivered 56 law enforcement conference presentations, written 51 articles, and instructed 366 police leadership seminars. Neal Trautman has been the:

- *Chair*, Ethics Committee, American Society of Law Enforcement Trainers,
- *Board of Directors*, International Police Ethics Network,
- *Chair*, Ad Hoc Ethics Training Committee, International Association of Chief's of Police,
- *Co-chair*, Police Image and Ethics Committee, International Association of Chief's of Police,
- *Chair*, Professional Development Committee, American Society of Law Enforcement Trainers,
- *National Chairman*, National Commission on Law Enforcement Integrity,
- *Chairman*, *Law and Order* Magazine "Roundtable Inquirey" on Administrator Misconduct,
- *Member*, National Advisory Committee, National Criminal Justice Assessment Program, Bureau of Justice Assistance, National Institute of Justice,
- *President*, International Association of Ethics Trainers, and is currently on the
- *Board of Directors*, International Law Enforcement Educators and Trainers Association

Abraham Lincoln was raised in poverty.

Franklin Roosevelt was brutally struck down with childhood polio.

Elementary school teachers told Albert Einstein he was "retarded."

Glenn Cunningham, who broke the world record in the one-mile run, was told by doctors when he was a child that he would never walk again.

The most important aspect of courage is never giving up ... when it's important.

I shall not pass through this world but once. Any good, therefore, that I can do let me do it now. Let me not defer or neglect it, for I shall not pass this way again.

Unknown Author

It is my belief what it takes to be a great cop is: When sworn into office, the sacred Oath is taken, is held to its highest regard through their entire law enforcement career and even beyond. The badge worn is not just a piece of metal, but a symbol of the public's trust that will not be compromised, under any circumstances.

Officers must perform and adhere to the department's core beliefs of integrity, fairness and service. Integrity, dedicated to maintaining the highest moral and ethical standards, through the principles of pride, honesty, trust and courage. Fairness, dedicated to treating citizens with dignity, respect and equality. Service, committed to developing a well-trained, highly motivated and courteous officer to serve the community and the organization with pride and professionalism.

Officers must possess the ability to forge partnerships with diverse communities for the purpose of building confidence and accountability to the public they serve.

They must continue their academic education for upward mobility in their organization and to keep abreast of the latest police policies, practices and techniques in modern law enforcement. Their knowledge of today's policing must go beyond a single jurisdiction, but expand into how other law enforcement agencies, throughout the United States and abroad, are progressing.

The job of today's law enforcement official is difficult because of the many responsibilities he or she is required to perform daily. They are the men and women in policing who have gone beyond the normal scope of their performance and truly exemplify the meaning of law enforcement.

Richard Pennington
Chief of Police
Atlanta Police Department

Compassion. The really great cops that I know—the ones that I really respect—are very compassionate people. They really care about others. Sure, some seem to be pretty crusty on the outside after twenty years of watching man's inhumanity to his fellow man. But deep down inside, under that cover, there's a person who really cares. That's what keeps them going after twenty years. They still wear the badge and put on the uniform each day, going to work really believing that they're going to help at least one person today. At least one person today will be alive, or somehow be better off because of something that they did. That quality comes from within. It can't be taught at any academy or in-service class. It doesn't show up on any written or oral exam. But it's there. The cops that don't have it aren't as good as they could be. It's the one thing that separates the good cops from the great cops. A really great cop keeps that compassion for their entire career.

William May, Jr.
Major
Louisville Fire/Police Department
Louisville, KY

Keep away from people who try to belittle your ambitions. Small people always do that, but the really great make you feel that you, too, can become great.

Mark Twain

My mother taught me very early to believe I could achieve any accomplishment I wanted to. The first was to walk without braces.

Wilma Rudolph
Four-Time Olympic Gold Medalist

COPS THEN AND NOW

A police officer is expected . . . to have the wisdom of Job, the kindness of the Good Samaritan, the strategy of Alexander, the faith of Daniel, the diplomacy of Lincoln, the tolerance of the Carpenter of Nazareth, and finally, an intimate knowledge of every brand of the natural, biological, and social sciences. If he had all of these he might be a good policeman.

In loving memory of the late August Vollmer
"Dean" of Modern Policing

Cops—so many things to so many people. To a crime victim they may be heroes. The next person may call them incompetent fools. A small child may look at them with admiration. A teenager may glare at them with arrogance or hatred.

Every experienced street cop has felt the frustration of having to deal with the same "lowlife" over and over. Yet they are expected to take it all in stride and be ready to handle the next call with wisdom, courage, and patience. Sometimes they make serious yet honest mistakes, and few will be able to forgive themselves.

What type of person would choose to face daily animosity and ridicule? Who would want to work the long, miserable hours of midnight shift, stand in the rain or cold and direct traffic, or live with the discomfort of wearing a bulletproof vest during the summer? Who would want to live with the glares and snide remarks from motorists stopped for traffic violations? Veteran officers know and understand the peculiar kind of isolation that cops feel when walking uniformed into a restaurant or being identified as cops at a party.

Why do people become law enforcement officers? They usually are sincere, enthusiastic, and driven by good intentions, but above all, they simply want to help others. These feelings will probably change to some degree as the years pass, as enthusiasm and sincerity gradually mix with frustration or cynicism. With good leadership, though, cops' dedication to duty can resist disintegrating into apathy and arrogance.

This book is dedicated to the principles for which thousands of officers have died. The highest ideals of law enforcement must become ingrained in all officers, so that those who die will not do so in vain. Loyalty, dedication, and integrity cannot be the brunt of jokes or be taken lightly—serving others is the foundation of good policing.

EVOLUTION OF POLICE

When aspiring military officers begin their careers, they spend considerable time studying the tradition and history of the American military. In this and many other disciplines, the wisdom and insight acquired by understanding the past is invaluable. A deep sense of pride and tradition creates sincerity and understanding of purpose.

Police departments, unfortunately, rarely appreciate the value of such training programs. Pride, dedication, and comradeship could be developed by understanding the sacrifices made by former officers. Such an appreciation of the past could become the foundation for building the future.

Beginnings—Early 1900s

Prior to 1900 law enforcement left a lot to be desired. Some cities began to pass laws that replaced lazy and incompetent night watchmen with officers. Although this was a considerable improvement, police protection usually consisted of merely a single constable who worked during the day.

As cities grew, the number of officers increased accordingly. Yet graft (illegal or unfair gain) and corruption were widespread throughout the political arena, and political interference manipulated a chief's authority to appoint, assign, or dismiss officers. There were no employment standards. Fairness within the workplace was often nonexistent. Lack of employment procedures combined with political favoritism caused extremely low morale.

Lack of employment requirements also resulted in a relatively low salary. Officers wore no uniforms, and the numbers on their copper badges were the only means of identification. Officers carried a 33-inch nightstick as their only weapon of defense and political favoritism continued to flourish.[1]

During these early days, a few farsighted individuals realized that officers could become proficient with special training. One individual, August Vollmer, town marshal and later chief of police of Berkeley, California, knew that patrolmen must recognize criminal acts and the elements for securing convictions. He believed that officers must understand how and when to use force. Further, Vollmer understood the grave responsibilities placed on law enforcement.

In the early 1900s many officers voiced their dissatisfaction with work conditions. The famous Boston Police Strike of September 9, 1919, originated from union settlement. By the turn of the century local police unionization had begun. The Boston union had requested permission to affiliate with the American Federation of Labor. The police commissioner refused and suspended several officers for their union activities. The union reacted by voting to strike. Thousands of officers walked off their assignments, sending Boston residents into panic.

After eight deaths, nearly a hundred injuries, and in excess of $1 million in property damage, President Wilson expressed the nation's sentiment. He stated, "A strike of policemen of a great city, leaving that city at the mercy of an army of thugs, is a crime against civilization. In my judgment the obligation of a policeman is as sacred and direct as the obligation of a soldier. He is a public servant, not a private employee, and the whole honor of the community is in his hands. He has no right to prefer any private advantage to public safety."[2]

Roaring '20s

Police professionalism was struggling during the 1920s and 1930s, and social unrest was placing tremendous demands on law enforcement. In addition to the passage of the Eighteenth Amendment, which prohibited the manufacture, sale, and import of liquor, the Volstead Act of 1919 made provisions for enforcement of the Eighteenth Amendment.

Prohibition was repealed in 1933, but until then, it created a great deal of difficulty for the officers who were required to enforce it.

The majority of citizens ignored Prohibition laws, and the police became extremely unpopular. Graft, political influence, and corruption among the police force substantially increased because officers were frustrated.

A large percentage of the population frequently offered bribes to police officers. As Prohibition continued to be unpopular, a general feeling of apathy toward police authority and the belief that officers could be "bought" resulted in extremely low morale and self-respect within police departments.

America's response to the turmoil, lawlessness, and corruption of the 1920s was the creation of a presidential commission commonly referred to as the Wickersham Commission. It scrutinized virtually every aspect of the criminal judicial system. An assortment of recommendations and suggestions were developed. Many recommendations were directed toward law enforcement management and operations.

Throughout history, most law enforcement agencies have attempted to hire only high-caliber applicants. New recruits help create an agency's image. Unfortunately, America's law enforcement image suffered a setback as a result of manpower shortages during World War I. The lack of manpower resulted in unqualified and poorly skilled individuals entering the ranks.

Police recruitment was difficult in this era. Years later we still live with some of the personnel procedures created decades ago. Police personnel selection today lacks uniformity throughout the nation. Further, a definite relationship exists between the quality of officers hired and the quality of performance within an agency. If agencies fail to develop a thorough, effective hiring process, officers with character flaws will be hired. As a result, corruption is likely to occur when such officers face the temptations that a law enforcement career presents.

Many attempts have been made to develop consistent police professionalism. As an example, a civil service merit system was established to provide an avenue to escape political sponsorship and manipulation. This system rewarded merit and provided a means to deal appropriately with the problems of graft and corruption. However, experience has shown that civil service frequently protects the inept and lazy. It sometimes becomes counterproductive to professionalism by preventing the termination of those who should be terminated.

Growth and Struggle—1930s, 1940s, and 1950s

Higher education began to flourish in the 1930s. The University of Chicago offered police-related courses as part of its undergraduate curriculum. San Jose College began a two-year criminal justice associate degree in 1930. In 1932 J. Edgar Hoover continued his relentless pursuit of professionalism by developing the *Law Enforcement Bulletin*. Its initial purpose was to promote the advancement of police service through professionalism. To this day, it continues to offer realistic and practical assistance.

The International Association of Chiefs of Police created a safety division within Northwestern University during 1935. The division provided field services, promoted traffic safety, and conducted valuable research. During the same year, Michigan State University began to require courses such as physics and chemistry in its police curriculum.

The Federal Bureau of Investigation's National Academy was established in 1935. The academy has played a crucial role in upgrading police service. It has trained thousands of administrative and supervisory officers for all levels of law enforcement.

The 1940s and early 1950s was an era of only mediocre professional advancement. The International Association of Chiefs of Police conducted a survey, which indicated that officers throughout the nation were dissatisfied with their working conditions. Unsatisfactory working hours, salary, pension, and other employment benefits resulted in the formation and operation of 44 police unions by 1956.[3]

The quality of any law enforcement agency is dependent upon the quality of its personnel. Likewise, all cops want to have partners they can count on. Partners grow to know each other and often become good friends. One does not have to be a chief to understand that the most capable rookies will probably develop into reliable, confident officers.

Revolution—1960s

Unlike the '40s and '50s, the 1960s was a time when municipal police forces were subjected to a tide of criticism. Student unrest exploded in the streets as our nation's colleges protested social conditions and the war in Vietnam. Civil rights demonstrations became violent. Riots were common in some major cities. The crime rate skyrocketed. Drug addiction climbed to unprecedented heights.

During the 1960s, law enforcement across the country was ill equipped, unprepared, and poorly trained. The population had increased approximately 13 percent, and reported crimes had risen 148 percent—the front line of defense was struggling to enforce the law and maintain peace. Serious crime increased at a staggering rate: aggravated assault rose 102 percent, robbery climbed 177 percent, and rape climbed 116 percent during the decade.[4]

In 1964 J. Edgar Hoover stated, "More states need to make available police training. More universities and colleges should be initiating and increasing courses of study oriented toward the development of a police career profession. Law enforcement must raise its sights, broaden its outlook, and insist on a higher caliber of performance." Yet during the decade higher education for police was sporadic, to say the least. Fewer than 25 universities and colleges were offering any form of full-time law enforcement program.

The President's Commission on Law Enforcement report, released in 1967, was a two-year extensive study of law enforcement by more than 2,450 staff members, advisors, and consultants. It was a far-reaching collection of reports, surveys, and statistical information that is still a valuable resource today. Although the educational recommendations of the President's Commission have yet to be reached, efforts to establish higher levels of employment should continue.

Many important Supreme Court cases occurred in the 1960s. They held that the power of an officer must be regulated and misuses punished. The exclusionary rule was extended to the states through *Mapp* v. *Ohio* (1961), which was only the first of many major decisions to identify the need to prohibit police unlawfulness. *Mapp* was followed by *Escobedo* v. *Illinois* (1964), *Miranda* v. *Arizona* (1966), *Terry* v. *Ohio* (1968), and, later, *Chimel* v. *California* (1989). A rapid rise of civil liability litigation (42 USC 1983, 1987) against police misconduct also occurred during the same period. A police officer of the 1960s would be perplexed by what a professional officer of the twenty-first century faces everyday.[5]

The International City Management Association's municipal yearbook for 1968 indicated how badly police training was needed during the 1960s. The yearbook reported that police recruits received no training in 7 percent of all central city agencies, no training in 11 percent of suburban agencies, and no training in 32 percent of independent city departments. These statistics were for municipalities of 10,000 persons or more. In smaller cities, less than 50 percent of new recruits received any police basic training.[6]

No state required formal police basic training until 1959. During the 1960s the International Association of Chiefs of Police conducted a study that revealed that the typical police officer in America received less than 200 hours of formal basic training. Although the number of hours increased dramatically during the late '60s and early '70s, it is still disturbing, especially because so many other careers require more extensive training. For example, cosmetologists and barbers require several thousand hours of training, embalmers receive more than 5,000, teachers in excess of 7,000, lawyers are required to have 9,000, and physicians receive more than 11,000 hours of training.

Why do these other endeavors require so much more formal training than law enforcement? It is because these fields appreciate the fact that poorly trained personnel result in poor performance. If accreditation boards, and states, did not require members of their professions to meet high standards, their efforts would not be recognized as professional. By establishing high training standards and rigid licensing for certification, high-quality service is ensured. All facets of policing—having far more serious responsibilities than virtually any other endeavor—must make the same solemn commitment to excellence.

Professionalism—1970s

"Police professionalism" became synonymous with higher education during the 1970s. Formal college degrees brought recognition to both individual officers and their agencies. Still, the value of education was a subject of considerable debate, as many veteran officers without a college education felt that the only education of any value was learned on the street.

The '70s became a time of awareness for most agencies, and officers were subjected to an assortment of new perspectives of society. As many officers continued their education, new viewpoints and a deeper appreciation for the role of the police were developed. It became apparent that all time-honored professions demand high standards of qualification and performance. A variety of courses related to problems within the criminal justice system showed that if the police were to be considered professionals, they must comply with high standards of performance.

The '70s brought changes to both policing and the police. Officers were required to comply with many strict legal requirements and limitations. Social problems plagued the police. Crimes related to drugs and economic conditions continued. Traffic difficulties worsened.

Officers who began their careers in the early '80s recall veteran officers stating that the job was different than it was in the '70s. The veteran officers usually said it was not as much fun being a cop as it used to be. They spoke of legal restrictions that kept them from doing their job. Some resented what they referred to as "a new breed" of cop. Not only was their job changing, fellow officers were becoming more educated and had different views.

Society now demanded more of the police. Officers were required to handle more complicated human behavior and be armed with more and better coping skills. They appreciated the need to be equipped with the physical and intellectual abilities needed for regulating, directing, and controlling the broad range of circumstances they faced. In fact, overall they were expected to have the wisdom of an attorney, the counseling skills of a psychologist, the writing abilities of an author, and the physical skills of an athlete.

America's War on Crime

President Lyndon Johnson established the Commission on Law Enforcement and the Administration of Justice in 1965. The presidential commission recommended in the 1967 publication, *The Challenge of Crime in a Free Society*, that police immediately make many operational changes and work toward numerous goals. These goals and standards called for monumental changes and implementation of many new programs to further professionalize law enforcement. Although some innovative and progressive police administrators initiated similar standards and goals at the state and local levels, the impetus soon diminished. When fellow administrators did not join the movement, what had been accomplished soon faded.

The Law Enforcement Assistance Administration (LEAA) and the Omnibus Crime and Safe Streets Act were born from the presidential commission. America's "war on crime" was declared. Nearly $8 billion was directed toward the battle against crime from 1968 through 1978.[7]

When the Omnibus Crime and Safe Streets Act was passed in 1968, LEAA and the federal Office of Law Enforcement Assistance merged. The Law Enforcement Educational Program (LEEP) was established to provide financial assistance for police officers to attend colleges and universities. All across the nation, officers began to attend a variety of criminal justice and police science programs. The first year that LEEP funds were distributed was 1969; the relatively small sum of $6.5 million had been furnished. By the mid-1970s, the figure had risen to almost $40 million annually.

The social troubles of the previous decade had prompted extensive improvements within police departments. Education and training levels were advancing significantly. Fewer than 500 higher education programs participated in LEEP during its initial six months of operation, but the level of participation rose dramatically to 1,065 programs during 1975. Most college and university students participating in the program were employed by law enforcement agencies. More than 77,000 men and women attended college with LEEP funding during an average year. Grants were awarded to officers for payment of books, mandatory college fees, and university tuition.

During the latter part of the 1970s, LEEP funding gradually diminished. By the end of the program in 1981, the number of participating institutions had declined to fewer than 900. The reasoning behind such enormous federal funding was that a higher standard of education would lead to enhanced crime control. The government felt that improved working knowledge, expertise, initiative, and abilities would result in improved professionalism throughout the nation. The millions of dollars—though the subject of much debate—had a widespread, positive effect on the quality of college-level police education.

TECHNOLOGICAL ADVANCEMENT

John Naisbitt's best-selling management text, *Megatrends*, refers to society's historical "waves." The first one was agricultural in nature. Its evolution occurred over thousands of years. The second wave dealt with America's Industrial Revolution. The basis of this era was natural resources, such as gas, oil, and coal. This time span has also passed. Naisbitt described the contemporary period as the "third wave," a time when society depends on technology and information systems to offset decreased natural resources. Law enforcement finds itself both the recipient of and dependent on technology.

One of the first technological advancements in law enforcement came at the turn of the century. The Bertillon method of measurement was law enforcement's initial attempt to develop an accurate way to identify criminals. It was based on the belief that literally taking detailed measurements of various physical characteristics, such as the dimensions of the ears and nose, could serve as a positive source of identification. Although archaic compared to contemporary fingerprint analysis, it was the best that could be done in a nontechnological era. Since 1870 the Bertillon measurement method of identification was used to identify people arrested for crimes. In 1903 Will West was sentenced to Leavenworth Penitentiary. On his arrival at the penitentiary, a clerk discovered that another inmate with a similar name was already serving a life sentence there. The clerk was amazed when she realized that the two men were virtually identical in appearance. This incident destroyed the credibility of the Bertillon method and shifted tremendous significance toward fingerprint identification.

As America's technological advancements, particularly those in transportation and communication, continued, so did those in law enforcement. In the 1960s, law enforcement began to make great strides in adopting technology. Clerical functions and record systems were automated and computerized. Crime scene capabilities were enhanced. Forensic laboratories had relatively sophisticated equipment. Some agencies equipped patrol vehicles with computer-based information systems. Others had computer-assisted dispatching centers.

The National Crime Information Center (NCIC) was developed in 1965, and by 1967 it was operational across the country. This nationwide computerized information system provided officers with a means to communicate information concerning wanted persons and stolen vehicles or property. Similar state and local systems were gradually developed following the relatively successful implementation of NCIC.

In addition to educational funding, the LEAA provided millions of dollars to equip agencies across America with advanced technology. For example, in the 1960s patrol officers were armed with transmitter-receivers, allowing them to leave their vehicles without losing communications.

IN-SERVICE TRAINING

How well an officer is trained can make the difference between life and death. Yet, internal training has not been a strength of American law enforcement. Decades ago, officers were issued their badges, guns, and uniforms and then simply told to go out and put someone in jail.

The public's demand for professionalism in officers has steadily increased. The days when size and strength were the primary prerequisites for employment are long gone. The potential for a devastating civil suit accompanies officers every day, and civil law and the street accept no excuses and allow no second chances. Standards of training have never been so demanding.

Improper, outdated training—or the lack of training—is almost always a major allegation in civil suits against the police. Previously, administrators did not perceive training of officers to be justifiable, when compared to other priorities and the difficulties associated with providing it. Now, however, they pay much closer attention to training needs within their agencies.

Are chiefs and sheriffs right when they feel there are many training-related problems? Is it more difficult for a police department to conduct training than a corporation? The answers are "yes" and "yes." Major challenges are associated with in-service police training, and it is more difficult for a law enforcement agency to train its officers than for a company to train its employees.

Effective, regular in-service training is necessary in all law enforcement agencies. The benefits have been reviewed. Now we will learn about the challenges trainers face.

First, officers assigned the responsibility for training often are provided with inadequate support. Most departments today have fewer than 25 full-time officers. Budgets do not always allow for a full-time detective, a shift supervisor, or the community-oriented policing officer. It is certainly frustrating to be overworked and underpaid; yet not having the necessary knowledge or skill due to a lack of training can be devastating to an agency.

It is virtually impossible to train officers when you do not know how. In the past, few departments have understood how to develop or administer training programs, and many efforts have failed.

Second, insufficient budgets frequently have prevented the proper education of trainers and the provision of needed equipment. Each municipality has a limited revenue and tax base, and the administrators are responsible for establishing fiscal priorities. Unfortunately, employee training and development has been a low priority for many administrators.

Third, rotating shift schedules frequently used by departments create severe logistics problems. A variety of training schedules can be used to overcome this challenge. Some agencies overcome this obstacle well, primarily due to the support and cooperation of management.

Fourth, manpower shortages often interfere with training. Often there is too much work for officers to be able to "break away" for training. Most agencies feel the frustration of having too few officers.

Success is measured on two levels: the degree to which you perform your individual task of public safety; and the degree to which you rise in the ranks to a position where you have a greater impact on your organization's ability to provide public safety. To succeed on either level, you must survive. Therefore, an officer's personal safety is always job one. Never let your guard down! Secondly, remember that you are there for the convenience of the public you serve, not the other way around. Thirdly, treat the public the same as you want your own family and friends treated; fourthly, get all the training and education you can. At a minimum, it keeps you on the same level as the criminals, improves your quality of life, and improves the quality of life in your community as a whole; and finally, live by your department's rules, but always share your ideas for improvement with your supervisors. Bottom line . . . be a part of the solution, not a part of the problem.

Julian Allen, Ph.D.
Academy Director, Harrison County Sheriff's Office
Gulfport, MS

THE ROLE OF THE POLICE

Most officers see themselves as crime fighters. Retiring officers' best memories may be about high-speed pursuits, shoot-outs, fights, or chasing criminals on foot. Rookies, similarly, may enjoy "putting the bad guy in jail." However, officers' roles have become complicated. Society expects them to handle virtually any situation. Further, they must manage complicated interpersonal relationships. These internal and external influences can affect their decisions. Pressure may come from relationships with friends and family; the local media; observing departmental regulations; local citizens; and personal, ethical, and moral beliefs. A role conflict may occur when

1. Officers are confronted with expectations that are incompatible with their own beliefs.
2. Officers believe that others have different expectations about their actions.
3. Officers learn that others have different expectations for them.
4. Officers believe their role includes expectations that may be contradictory or incompatible to the role established for them.

While each person has a somewhat different impression of the nature of the police function, based primarily on personal experiences and contacts with police officers, there is a widespread popular conception of police reported by news and entertainment media. Police have come to be viewed as a group of people continually engaged in the exciting, dangerous, and competitive enterprise of apprehending and prosecuting criminals. This emphasis has led to a tendency on the part of both the public and the police to underestimate the range and complexity of the total police task. Police officers assigned to patrol duty in a large city are typically confronted with, at most, a few serious crimes in the course of a single tour of duty. Such involvement, particularly if there is some degree of danger, is viewed as real police work.

Officers, though, spend considerably more time keeping order, settling disputes, finding missing children, and managing drunks than responding to criminal conduct serious enough to call for arrest, prosecution, and correction. Officers, thus, perform a wide range of other functions, often of a highly complex nature and often involving difficult social, behavioral, and political problems.[8]

Numerous studies before and after the president's commission have reached a common conclusion: fighting crime is merely one of the roles of American police officers. The true role is a mixture of keeping the peace, serving the community, and fighting crime. Officers across the nation spend considerably more time providing community service than they do arresting criminals. Many officers prefer to think of themselves as protectors of their communities, but they are usually providers of community service.

Most citizens want their police force to do more than arrest criminals. They want to be able to call someone in the middle of the night to assist an elderly lady who has fallen out of bed. They want the police to help open their vehicles after locking the keys inside. People need the police to do these things because usually there is no other facet of society readily available and certainly none that is free. Many communities feel that their officers are always available for such tasks. However, while some departments restrict the amount of services for minor calls, the public still perceives law enforcers as public servants.

Developing a community service officer program or implementing a full community-oriented policing program is one alternative to the traditional peacekeeping, crime-fighting role of police. It requires good budgetary management. In addition, it strengthens manpower because regular officers will have more time to concentrate on more serious matters. Community service officers require less training because they do not respond to high-risk or complicated situations. Establishing this type of program is fairly easy and allows agencies to provide the best possible service to the community.

THE CONTEMPORARY COP

The 13,530 city, county, and state police agencies that reported 2001 personnel data collectively employed 659,104 officers and 279,926 civilians and provided law enforcement services to approximately 268.1 million United States inhabitants.

In 2001, law enforcement agencies employed an average of 2.5 full-time officers per 1,000 inhabitants. Cities collectively employed 2.4 officers per 1,000 residents. Suburban counties had a rate of 2.7 officers per 1,000 inhabitants; rural counties had 2.5 full-time officers per 1,000 population.

Males comprised 88.8 percent of all sworn officers, and females accounted for 62.7 percent of all civilian employees. Civilians made up 29.8 percent of the total law enforcement employee force in the Nation in 2001.[9]

Some officers today view themselves as crime fighters who have to handle menial tasks that should not be their responsibility. These officers are often frustrated by minor calls they believe are a waste of time. Although not all officers feel this way, if a substantial portion of an agency does, the department will provide a lower level of service.

Agencies must manage themselves to fit the role of providing a wide range of community services. Misdirected operations cause less efficiency and effectiveness. Obviously, the ultimate responsibility for directing a department lies with the chief administrator. Yet every officer has a responsibility to work toward the benefit of his or her community.

Contemporary Education

The constantly increasing level of formal education will help law enforcement personnel to both carry out their responsibilities and survive the challenges of a police career. The organization that has served to spearhead a national movement to advance higher education in policing is the Police Association of College Education (PACE). Led by Lou Mayo, PACE has compiled a listing of departments that require, by policy or practice, a four-year college degree for entering officers. (An asterisk indicates that extensive law enforcement experience with an AA degree is acceptable in some cases.) Where known, department website addresses are shown. For more information about PACE, go to www.police-association.org.

California

Redlands Police Department: http://www.ci.redlands.ca.us/207.html

Colorado

Arvada Police Department: http://www.arvadapd.org/

Boulder Police Department: http://www.ci.boulder.co.us/police/

Lakewood Police Department: http://www.ci.lakewood.co.us/index.cfm?&include=/PD/openingpage.cfm

Georgia

Peachtree City Police Department: http://www.peachtreecity.org/police/

Illinois

Elgin Police Department: http://www.northstarnet.org/elghome/cityelg/police_home.html

Illinois State Police: http://www.isp.state.il.us

Naperville Police Department: http://naperville.il.us/index_template.cfm?doc_id=403

Palatine Police Department: http://www.palatine.il.us/police/welcome.htm

Tinley Park Police Department: http://www.lincolnnet.net/users/lr1065k/TPPD/

Willowbrook Police Department: http://www.willowbrookil.org/police/index.html

Wilmette Police Department: http://www.wilmette.com/police

Massachusetts

Holden Police Department: http://www.holdenpd.com

Michigan

Flint Police Department: http://www.flintpolice.org

Flint Township Police Department: http://www.flinttownshippolice.org

Michigan State University Police and Public Safety: http:// www.dpps.msu.edu

Milford Police Department: http://www.milfordpolice.com

North Hills Police Department

Novi City Police Department: http://www.ci.novi.mi.us/Services/Police/Administrative/ChiefsWelcomeWithVideo.htm

Owosso Police Department

Minnesota

Burnsville Police Department: http://www.burnsville.org/government/Departments/policemain.htm

Eagan City Police Department: http://www.ci.eagan.mn.us/Employ/PD_Benefits.htm

St. Cloud Police Department: http://ci.stcloud.mn.us/Web/departments/Police/index.htm

Missouri

Richmond Heights Police Department: http://www.rejis.org/police/richmnd_pd.html

New Jersey

Cherry Hill Police Department: http://www.cherryhill-nj.com/pfe/police.asp

Dover Township Police Department: http://www.dovertwppolice.com/dover.htm

Haddon Township Police Department

Leonia Police Department

Montgomery Police Department

Montvale Police Department: http://www.montvale.org/mpd.htm

North Carolina

Gaston County Police Department: http://www.co.gaston.nc.us/gastonpd

North Dakota

*North Dakota Highway Patrol: http://www.state.nd.us/ndhp

Ohio

City of Canfield Police Department: http://www.cboss.com/ssin/canfield

Cleveland Heights Police Department

Middleburg Heights Police Department

Strongsville Police Department: http://www.strongsville.org/html/police.html

Oklahoma

Tulsa Police Department: http://www.tulsapolice.org

Oregon

Multnomah County Sheriff's Office http://www.co.multnomah.or.us/sheriff/index.html

Pennsylvania

Bethel Park Police Department: http://bethelpark.net/police_department.htm

Borough of Gettysburg Police Department: http://www.mainstreetgettysburg.org/bogwww/police/police.htm

Edinboro Police Department: http://www.erie.net/?edinboro/police.html

Rhode Island

Smithfield Police Department

South Carolina

Charleston City Police Department: http://www.charleston-pd.org

Richland County Sheriff's Department: http://www.rcsd.net

Tennessee

Johnson City Police Department

Texas

Arlington Police Department: http://www.arlingtonpd.org

Deer Park Police Department: http://www.ci.deer-park.tx.us/police/index.htm

Highland Park Police Department: http://www.hpdps.org

Wisconsin

Appleton Police Department: http://www.appleton.org/police

Langlade County Sheriff's Department: http://www.langladecounty.com/sheriffdepartmenthomepage.htm

Special Jurisdiction Departments

Arizona Game & Fish Department—Law Enforcement: http://www.gf.state.az.us

California Department of Alcoholic Beverage Control: http://www.abc.ca.gov

Colorado Department of Conservation/Wildlife

Delaware River and Bay Authority Police Department: http://www.drba.net/police/index.html

Illinois Department of Natural Resources: http://dnr.state.il.us/law3

Missouri Department of Conservation: Law Enforcement

Bergen County, New Jersey, Prosecutor's Investigators

Hudson County, New Jersey, Prosecutor's Investigators

Oklahoma Department of Wildlife Conservation Law Enforcement Division: http://www.wildlifedepartment.com/law.htm

South Carolina Department of Natural Resources—Law Enforcement Division: http://www.dnr.state.sc.us/law/index.html

Tennessee Bureau of Investigations: http://www.tbi.state.tn.us

Tennessee Wildlife Resources Agency—Law Enforcement

Texas Parks and Wildlife Department—Law Enforcement: http://www.tpwd.state.tx.us/involved/enforcement

Virginia Department of Alcoholic Beverage Control: http://www.abc.state.va.us

Washington State Department of Fish and Wildlife: http://www.wa.gov/wdfw

*West Virginia State Department of Natural Resources: http://www.dnr.state.wv.us/law/Default.htm[10]

On October 28, 2002, the FBI distributed the national press release shown in Box 1-1. It is a clear profile of the extent and types of crime that officers must face.

Continuing the "community service" attitude is easier said than done. Today's officers face more pressure than any of their predecessors. They are bombarded with increasing social, legal, and personal pressure. Many develop negative outlooks. Court decisions, community interaction, and politics—both internal and external—increase the relentless stress.

Stress affects all officers. They attempt to remain professional, yet the frustration of the judicial system and problems within agencies can be overwhelming. Further, they must face the worst of society. Sometimes dealing with human conflict, sadness, and despair can cause officers to feel powerless to uphold their responsibilities. The end result is sometimes excessive use of force, greed, or some form of unethical conduct.

Box 1-1

Crime in America

CRIME IN THE UNITED STATES, 2001

The Nation's Crime Index increased 2.1 percent in 2001 from the 2000 number, the first year-to-year increase since 1991, the Federal Bureau of Investigation reported today. However, final data released by the FBI's Uniform Crime Reporting (UCR) Program in the annual publication Crime in the United States, 2001, indicated that, when looking at 5- and 10-year trends, crime was down 10.2 percent when compared to 1997 data and down 17.9 percent when compared to 1992 statistics.

The Crime Index is composed of four violent crimes (murder and nonnegligent manslaughter, forcible rape, robbery, and aggravated assault) and three property crimes (burglary, larceny-theft, and motor vehicle theft). The Crime Index offenses plus the arson offenses form the Modified Crime Index. Index crimes serve as a measure of the level and scope of the Nation's crime experience.

In 2001, the nearly 17,000 city, county, and state law enforcement agencies that provided data to the UCR Program represented 92 percent of the total United States population as established by the Bureau of the Census. Population estimates were included for nonreporting areas. Because of the many variables that affect crime in a city, county, state, or region, data users are cautioned against comparing or ranking locales. Valid assessments are possible only with careful study and analysis of the various conditions affecting each law enforcement jurisdiction.

Crime Volume

- The estimated 11.8 million Crime Index offenses in the Nation in 2001 represented a 2.1 percent increase over the 2000 estimate.
- In 2001, estimated violent crime showed a 0.8 percent increase over the 2000 estimate. Five- and 10-year trends

Box 1-1 *(continued)*

revealed that the estimated number of violent crime offenses decreased 12.2 percent from the 1997 estimate and 25.7 percent from the 1992 estimate.

- Estimated property crime was up 2.3 percent from the prior year's estimate. Property crime trends for the 5- and 10-year periods showed a 9.9 percent decrease from the 1997 level and a 16.7 percent decrease from the 1992 level.
- Collectively, the Nation's cities reported an increase of 2.0 percent in the total number of crimes reported. Cities with populations of 250,000 to 499,999 recorded the largest increase of reported crime offenses at 4.1 percent. The smallest increase in volume (0.5 percent) occurred in cities with 1 million or more inhabitants. Suburban and rural counties had increases in the volume of crimes reported of 2.4 percent and 1.9 percent, respectively.

Crime Index Rate

- The Crime Index rate measures the total estimated volume of the seven Index offenses per 100,000 United States population. In 2001, the Crime Index rate was 4,160.5 estimated offenses per 100,000 inhabitants, 0.9 percent higher than the 2000 estimated rate. However, the rate was 15.6 percent lower than the 1997 rate and 26.5 percent lower than the 1992 rate.
- By region, the South had a Crime Index rate of 4,760.9; the West, 4,354.9; the Midwest, 3,981.1; and the Northeast, 3,006.9 offenses per 100,000 inhabitants. The Northeast was the only region to have a decrease (1.9 percent) in the Crime Index rate when compared to the previous year's rate. The West's rate increased 3.0 percent, the Midwest's rate rose 1.1 percent, and the South's rate was up 0.3 percent when compared to rates in 2000.
- Metropolitan Statistical Areas (MSAs) had a rate of 4,474.9 offenses per 100,000 inhabitants. Cities outside the Nation's MSAs recorded a rate of 4,450.4 per 100,000 population. Rural counties reported a Crime Index rate of 1,892.4 per 100,000 in population.

(continued)

Box 1-1 *(continued)*

Violent Crime

- Data reported in 2001 indicated a 0.8-percent increase in the estimated volume of violent crime from the 2000 estimate, or an estimated 1.4 million violent crimes. However, the rate of violent crime (504.4 offenses per 100,000 inhabitants) decreased 0.4 percent from the 2000 data.
- Personal weapons, such as hands, fists, and feet, were used in 31.1 percent of violent crimes. Firearms were involved in 26.2 percent of violent crimes, and knives and other cutting instruments in 14.9 percent. Other dangerous weapons were used in 27.8 percent of violent crimes reported in 2001.

Property Crime

- Both the volume and rate per 100,000 inhabitants of all property crime offenses increased in 2001. With an estimated 10.4 million offenses, the property crime total was 2.3 percent higher than the 2000 total. The estimated property crime rate of 3,656.1 per 100,000 inhabitants was 1.0 percent higher than the previous year's rate.
- The estimated dollar loss attributed to property crime (excluding arson) was $16.6 billion, a 5.6-percent increase from the 2000 estimate.

Hate Crime

- Hate crime data were provided by 11,987 law enforcement agencies. The 9,726 hate crime incidents reported in 2001 involved 11,447 separate offenses, 12,016 victims, and 9,231 known offenders.
- Of all reported single-bias incidents, 44.9 percent were motivated by racial bias, 21.6 percent were motivated by an ethnicity or national origin bias, 18.8 percent were based on a religious bias, 14.3 percent were based on a sexual-orientation bias, and 0.3 percent were based on a disability bias.
- A review of the hate crime victims showed that 64.6 percent of reported victims were targets of a hate crime against persons; 34.7 percent of victims were targets of a hate

Box 1-1 *(continued)*

crime against property. The remaining 0.6 percent of victims were targets of crimes against society.

- Intimidation accounted for 55.9 percent of hate crimes directed against persons. Destruction, damage, or vandalism was reported in 83.7 percent of hate crimes against property.

Index Crime Clearances

- Nationally, 19.6 percent of all Crime Index offenses were cleared by arrest or exceptional means in 2001. Of violent crimes, 46.2 percent were cleared, and 16.2 percent of property crimes (excluding arson) were cleared. In addition, 16.0 percent of arson offenses were cleared.
- Of all Crime Index offenses, murder was the offense most likely to be cleared—62.4 percent. Burglary had the lowest percentage (12.7 percent) of clearances among the Crime Index offenses.
- Of the Crime Index offenses cleared in 2001, 18.6 percent involved only juveniles (persons under the age of 18). Juvenile clearances accounted for 12.1 percent of the overall violent crime clearances and 21.1 percent of property crime clearances.

Arrests

- Law enforcement made an estimated 13.7 million arrests for criminal offenses (excluding traffic violations) in 2001, a 2.1-percent decline from the 2000 estimated total.
- Approximately 2.2 million of the estimated arrests involved Crime Index offenses, accounting for 16.4 percent of the total arrests. A look at the two categories of Index crime showed that violent crime arrests increased 0.1 percent, and property crime arrests decreased 1.0 percent when comparing 2000 and 2001 data.
- A review of Crime Index offense data showed that 73.8 percent of those arrested were adults. A breakdown of Index crime categories showed that 84.6 percent of arrestees for

(continued)

Box 1-1 *(continued)*

violent crime were adults as were 69.9 percent of arrestees for property crime.

- A review of violent crime arrest data by age showed that 44.2 percent of the arrestees were persons under 25 years of age, and 15.4 percent were under age 18. Arrest data for property crimes showed that 58.3 percent of those arrested were under 25 years of age, and 30.4 percent of arrestees were under age 18.

- An analysis of total arrests showed that 83.3 percent of arrestees were adults. Of total arrests nationwide, 45.9 percent involved persons under the age of 25, and 16.7 percent involved persons under the age of 18.

- An analysis of arrest data by gender showed that approximately 77.5 percent of all arrestees were male; 69.5 percent of all arrestees were white. By volume, males were most often arrested for drug abuse violations; females were most often arrested for larceny-theft offenses.

- The Nation's smallest cities, those with fewer than 10,000 inhabitants, had the highest arrest rate per 100,000 population, 6,308.4. Among cities, the lowest arrest rate (4,482.5 per 100,000 inhabitants) was reported in cities with populations of 25,000 to 49,999. Rural counties had an overall arrest rate of 3,968.3 and suburban counties a rate of 3,801.5 arrests per 100,000 inhabitants.

Murder

- An estimated 15,980 murders occurred in the United States in 2001, a 2.5-percent increase over the 2000 estimate. However, a 5-year trend reflected a 12.2-percent decline from the 1997 estimate. The rate of 5.6 murders per 100,000 population was 1.3 percent higher than the 2000 rate of 5.5, but 17.5 percent lower than the 1997 rate.

- Supplemental data such as the age, sex, and race of the victim and offender, the type of weapon used, and the circumstance of the incident were provided for 13,752 murders. Based on those reports, 76.6 percent of murder victims were male and 89.6 percent were adults (those aged 18 and over). By race,

Box 1-1 *(continued)*

49.8 percent of murder victims were white, 47.5 percent were black, and the remainder were persons of other races.

- Approximately 42.3 percent of murder victims knew their assailants. Nearly a third of all female victims were slain by a husband or boyfriend.

- Supplemental homicide data revealed that 90.3 percent of murder offenders were male, and 91.7 percent were over the age of 18. Of the incidents in which the race of the offender was known, 50.3 percent of the offenders were black, 47.2 percent were white, and 2.5 percent were of other races.

- In 2001, of murders with a single victim and a single offender, 93.6 percent of black homicide victims were killed by black offenders; 85.4 percent of white homicide victims were killed by white offenders.

- For those incidents in which the murder weapon was known, 69.5 percent were committed with a firearm. Knives or cutting instruments were employed in 14.3 percent of murders in 2001. Personal weapons, such as hands, fists, feet, etc., were used in 7.4 percent, blunt objects were used in 5.3 percent, and other dangerous weapons (e.g., poisons or explosives) were used in the remainder of the homicides.

- Twenty-eight percent of homicide victims were involved in an argument with the offender. More than 16 percent (16.6) of murders occurred in conjunction with another felony, such as robbery or arson. Circumstances were unknown in 32.4 percent of murders.

Forcible Rape

- There were an estimated 90,491 forcible rapes in the United States in 2001, an increase of 0.3 percent when compared to the 2000 estimate.

- In 2001, there were 62.2 forcible rapes per 100,000 females in the Nation, which continued a downward trend. In 2000, there were an estimated 62.7 rapes per 100,000 females. A review of 5- and 10-year trend data showed that in 1997

(continued)

Box 1-1 *(continued)*

the estimated rate was 70.3 rapes per 100,000 females; and in 1992, the estimated rate was 83.7.

Robbery

- The estimated 422,921 robberies reported in 2001 represented the first increase of this offense (up 3.7 percent) in year-to-year comparisons since 1991. The rate of robberies nationwide was 148.5 offenses per 100,000 inhabitants, a 2.4-percent increase from the 2000 rate.
- Robbery accounted for 3.6 percent of all Crime Index offenses and 29.4 percent of all violent crimes in the United States in 2001.
- Robbery resulted in an estimated $532 million loss in 2001, or an average dollar loss of $1,258. Bank robberies had the highest average loss at $4,587 per offense.
- During 2001, firearms were used in 42.0 percent of the reported robbery offenses, and strong-arm tactics were used in 39.0 percent of robberies. Offenders used knives or cutting instruments in 8.7 percent of robbery offenses; the remaining 10.4 percent involved other weapons.

Aggravated Assault

- The only Crime Index offense to show a decrease (0.5 percent) in estimated volume when compared to the 2000 estimate, aggravated assaults accounted for 63.1 percent of violent crimes in 2001, or an estimated 907,219 aggravated assault offenses.
- Five- and 10-year trends indicated that the estimated volume of aggravated assaults was down 11.3 percent from the 1997 estimate and was down 19.5 percent from the 1992 estimate.
- The rate of aggravated assaults per 100,000 inhabitants for the Nation was 318.5, which was 1.7 percent less than in 2000, 16.6 percent lower than in 1997, and 27.9 percent lower than in 1992.
- Personal weapons, such as hands, fists, and feet, were used in 27.9 percent of aggravated assaults in 2001. Firearms

Box 1-1 *(continued)*

were used in 18.3 percent of the offenses. Knives or cutting instruments were used in 17.8 percent of the incidents, and blunt objects or other dangerous weapons were used in 36.0 percent of aggravated assaults in 2001.

Burglary

* There were an estimated 2.1 million burglaries in 2001, a 2.9-percent increase from the previous year's data.
* In 2001, burglary data showed an estimated $3.3 billion in losses in the Nation with an average loss per incident of $1,545. Most burglaries (65.2 percent) were residential in nature.
* Forcible entry was involved in 63.3 percent of burglaries. Unlawful entry without the use of force comprised 30.2 percent of burglaries, and attempted forcible entry accounted for 6.5 percent.

Larceny-Theft

* There were more than 7.0 million larceny-theft offenses in 2001, an increase of 1.5 percent from the 2000 estimate.
* Larcenies accounted for 59.7 percent of all Crime Index offenses and 68.0 percent of all property crimes.
* Data reported for larceny-theft offenses showed an estimated $5.2 billion in losses nationwide. The average monetary loss per offense was $730.

Motor Vehicle Theft

* There were more than 1.2 million motor vehicle thefts in 2001, a 5.7-percent increase over the 2000 estimate. This translated into a rate of 430.6 motor vehicle thefts per 100,000 United States inhabitants.
* By vehicle type, motor vehicles were stolen at a rate of 336.9 per 100,000 inhabitants during 2001; trucks and buses were stolen at a rate of 86.5 per 100,000 persons.

(continued)

Box 1-1 *(continued)*

- Based on the more than 1.2 million motor vehicles stolen in 2001, the estimated dollar value of vehicles stolen nationwide was almost $8.2 billion. Approximately 62.0 percent of that amount was recovered. The estimated average value of stolen motor vehicles was $6,646.

Arson

- A total of 76,760 arson offenses were reported in 2001.
- For the 68,967 arson offenses for which supplemental data were provided, the average monetary value of property loss for arson was $11,098 per incident. The average loss for structural properties was $20,128, and the average loss for mobile properties was $6,974 per incident. Other property types had an average dollar loss of $1,361 per incident.
- Structural arson was the most frequently reported arson category in 2001 and accounted for 42.2 percent of the arson offense total. Mobile properties were the target of 32.5 percent of reported arson offenses, and other property types accounted for the remaining 25.4 percent.
- The offense of arson had a higher percentage of juvenile involvement than any other Index offense. Of all arson offenses cleared in 2001, 45.2 percent involved only juvenile offenders.

Terrorist Attacks of September 11, 2001

- Most of the data associated with the events of September 11, 2001, were included only in a special report published in Section V of Crime in the United States, 2001. As of the date of publication, the report revealed that:
- In all, there were 3,047 deaths as a result of the events of September 11, 2001: 2,823 homicide victims were attributed to the attacks on the World Trade Center, 184 murder victims to the Pentagon, and 40 murder victims to the airliner crash site in Somerset County, Pennsylvania.

Box 1-1 *(continued)*

- The vast majority, 99.7 percent, of victims were over age 18 in those cases when the age of the victim was known. Most victims were between the ages of 35 and 39.
- All of the offenders were white males. Four offenders were under age 22. The oldest offender was in the 30–34 age group.

Source: Federal Bureau of Investigation, *Crime in the United States, 2001* (Washington, DC: Government Printing Office, 2002).

Too much stress can harden officers' emotions. Out of necessity, officers may shield themselves from the misery that surrounds them. Unfortunately, by doing so they may sacrifice the compassion that is so essential to the performance of their duties. Suspicion and cynicism soon become psychological defenses for their actions. They also take "hardened" personalities home each day. These factors alone can make being a cop in contemporary America more dangerous mentally than physically.[11]

To an extent, officers' roles, amount of stress, and other aspects of their jobs vary from area to area. Differences exist from town to town and between zones in the same jurisdiction. Stress can come from many types of assignments, such as a long and boring stakeout, an uneventful midnight shift, or the pressures of working a high-crime district. "Survivors" learn how to take things in stride and not let the pressures of the street affect them.

THE COMMANDMENTS OF LEADERSHIP

If you do well, people will accuse you of ulterior motives.
Do well anyway.
If you are successful, you win false friends and true enemies.
Succeed anyway.
Honesty will make you vulnerable.
Be honest anyway.
The smallest men with the smallest minds can shoot down
the biggest men with the biggest ideas.
Think big anyway.
What you spend years building may be destroyed overnight.
Build anyway.

People really need help, but may attack you if you help them.
Help them anyway.
Give the world the best you've got,
knowing you may get kicked in the teeth.
Give the world the best you have anyway.

Author Unknown

LEADERSHIP

The history of police leadership has met with varied success. Chief administrators find that they have management responsibility to a municipal or county government but are accountable for leadership of a paramilitary organization.

Leadership: The process through which people motivate, direct, influence, and communicate with those they work with to get them to perform in ways that will help the organization achieve its goals.

Power: The ability to influence others in an organization. Having many levels and sources, it is exercised in many ways and has led to the development of a variety of leadership techniques and theories.

For the ethical aspect of a great cop to become a way of life, it must be supported by a strong leadership commitment and be nurtured by a leadership style that promotes respect, fairness, and honesty. Power must be used to remove the obstacles that prevent others from doing their job.

Most good cops consider their formal advancement within their department and look ahead to becoming supervisors. The quicker you start developing your skills, the better prepared you will be when it is time to take the promotional examinations.

Obviously, line supervisors are essential to integrity becoming a way of life throughout an organization. They actually translate goals and objectives into results. They can make integrity a joke or a crucial requirement of every activity. The key is to deserve and earn their respect, trust, and support. Line supervisors must be capable of carrying out various responsibilities and using several skills.

Effective Human Relations Skills

It is important for all leaders to have the ability to apply respectful and fair human relations skills. Likewise, it is important to have the ability to assess the need for specific types of leadership by understanding an organization and the necessary skills.

In a leader, personality traits that perpetuate positive human relations are essential. The degree of effective communication in any leader is influenced greatly by the relationship with fellow workers.

Generation X

The slice of American society that is generally referred to as Generation X comprises about 45 million people. They are defined as those who were born between 1965 and 1980. Baby Boomers, on the other hand, were born between 1946 and 1964 and number about twice as many within their faction. Now middle-aged and graying, the Boomers believe in staying focused on retirement, slowing down, and being optimistic and do not feel as though they have something to prove.

Generation Xers have been working with older employees for more than a decade now. Never before have segments of the American workforce had such different values, beliefs, and perspectives. Generation X often views the Boomers as stubborn and arrogant. They resent the fact that older workers are often their leaders and unfairly dominate so much of the American lifestyle. Disagreements and aggravating moments are common. The lack of teamwork, disagreements over discipline, differing views about where one's loyalty should be, and opposing work ethics beliefs are frequent.

Lynne Lancaster, who writes about generational conflict, advises that the consequences of such differences can have a big impact on workplace cultures. Recruiting, productivity, poor communication, and bitterness about all kinds of internal programs can demoralize everyone. As an example, Lancaster states "Some 70% of companies have flex-time and telework policies," she says, "but if boomer managers don't like them or don't trust working that way, they truly frustrate the purpose."[12]

Different Views

Joanna L. Krotz is a highly respected researcher and author on management and leadership. Her studies of Boomers and Xers, of course, show that both walk into work carrying loads of generational baggage. Here is how many experts I've interviewed characterize the two generations and their differences:

"Boomers tend to give themselves over to their jobs," says Claire Raines, author of *Generations at Work*. They believe in paying dues, playing by the rules, and building careers. Their feedback and guidance is indirect and considerate of people's feelings. "They're process-oriented," Raines says. "They're trained to believe that business results and relationships are intertwined."

Generation X has attitudes about the work that are very much different than those of previous generations. Basically, they distrust hierarchy. They want more relaxed arrangements. They want to be judged on merit rather than on status. They are much less loyal to their employers. They are the first generation in America to be raised on a heavy diet of employment participation and teamwork. They know computers inside and out. They like money, but they also say they want balance in their lives.[13]

Role Modeling

Supervisors act as trainers, counselors, and mentors for all employees. As a result of their constant contact with officers, they become major role models. Thus, it is vital for leaders to develop traits such as sincerity, loyalty, honesty, respect, and dedication. Their ability to influence and serve as role models is their greatest single source of power as leaders. For example, if line supervisors were unethical, it would be impossible for a company, association, or agency—let alone its officers—to be filled with integrity.

Sound Counseling Skills

Supervisors need the ability to counsel ethically in order to assist employees with a variety of professional and personal problems. These problems can be overcome through the ability to adjust to new circumstances, effective problem solving skills, and making sound ethical choices. Counseling strategies commonly used are emphasizing, suggesting, referring, reviewing, motivating, clarifying, informing, and interpreting. Leaders must convey integrity in the counseling process, regardless of situations or strategies.

Effective Motivation Skills

Supervisors must thoroughly understand the effect of motivation on employees in order to use motivation strategies that enhance successful performance. By far, the greatest motivator is helping others achieve worthwhile goals.

Leaders should emphasize enriching the work environment and positive, supportive relationships. In addition, they should remove obstacles that prevent officers from accomplishing their potential, whenever possible.

Exceptional Communication Skills

Supervisors need good reading, listening, writing, and speaking skills in order to ensure that trainees also have them. Supervisors need to be able to offer criticism constructively, disagree assertively, listen effectively, summarize messages correctly, and confirm final decisions accurately.

Communication is often a serious problem, whether within a marriage or a company of 700,000 people. Therefore, it must be given careful attention and stressed at all levels.

Effective Teaching Techniques

Supervisors should possess the instruction skills necessary to effectively teach officers. They do most of the training, yet few have ever been taught how to train. It would be ideal for supervisors to have a thorough understanding of the psychology of teaching or have the ability to enhance concentration, comprehension, and learning retention. While this is not always possible, supervisors should at least attend a "train-the-trainer" course in an effort to provide effective training.

Accurate Evaluation Skills

All leaders must accept the challenges and responsibilities associated with fairly documenting behavior. If necessary, they must also effectively correct improper behavior. Evaluation should be carried out and communicated daily and recorded in writing honestly and respectfully.

Current Knowledge

Great leaders understand the never-ending need for knowledge. They also understand the need to remain current on strategies, information, and technology in their field. For police officers, the same is true, because leaders' lack of knowledge can discredit supervisors and entire organizations.

At this point, let's pause to look at an overview of law enforcement personnel in America. Box 1-2 lists statistics regarding state and local law enforcement agencies.

Box 1-2
Law Enforcement Agencies

STATE AND LOCAL LAW ENFORCEMENT STATISTICS

Personnel

- As of June 2000, State and local law enforcement agencies had 1,019,496 full-time personnel, 11% more than the 921,978 employed in 1996. From 1996 to 2000 the number of full-time sworn personnel increased from 663,535 to 708,022.
- As of June 2000, local police departments had 565,915 full-time employees including about 441,000 sworn personnel. Sheriffs' offices had 293,823 full-time employees, including about 165,000 sworn personnel.
- From 1987 to 2000 minority representation among local police officers increased from 14.5% to 22.7%. In sheriffs' offices, minorities accounted for 17.1% of sworn personnel in 2000 compared to 13.4% in 1987.
- From 1996 to 2000, total employment by local police departments was up an average of 2.1% per year. Sheriffs' offices increased their number of employees by 3.5% per year.

Education and Training Requirements

- In 2000, 15% of local police departments and 11% of sheriffs' offices had some type of college education requirement for new officers.

Operating Expenditures

- In 2000, local police departments cost about $80,600 per sworn officer and $179 per resident to operate for the year. Sheriffs' offices cost about $107,900 per officer and $65 per resident for the year.

9-1-1 Participation

- In 2000, 89% of local police departments and 87% of sheriffs' offices participated in an emergency 9-1-1 system. About 7 in 10 local police departments and two-thirds of sheriffs' offices had enhanced 9-1-1 systems, capable of

Box 1-2 *(continued)*

automatically displaying information such as a caller's phone number, address, and special needs.

Drug Asset Forfeiture

- Collectively, local police departments received $320 million worth of cash, goods, and property from drug asset forfeiture programs during calendar year 1999. Sheriffs' offices had total receipts of $137 million.

Community Policing (as of June 30, 2000)

- Two-thirds of all local police departments and 62% of sheriffs' offices had full-time sworn personnel engaged in community policing activities.
- Local police departments had an estimated 102,598 full-time sworn personnel serving as community policing officers or otherwise regularly engaged in community policing activities, and sheriffs' offices had 16,545 full-time sworn so assigned.

Computers and Information Systems

- Twenty-eight percent of local police departments in 2000, and 33% of sheriffs' offices, used computers for inter-agency information sharing. This includes three-quarters of all local departments serving 250,000 or more residents, and more than half of all sheriffs' offices serving 100,000 or more residents.
- In 2000, 75% of local police officers and 61% of sheriffs' officers worked for an agency that used in-field computers or terminals, compared to 30% and 28% in 1990.
- In 2000, 75% of local police departments and 80% of sheriffs' offices used paper reports as the primary means to transmit criminal incident field data to a central information system, down from 86% and 87% in 1997. During the same time period, use of computer and data devices for this

(continued)

Box 1-2 *(continued)*

purpose increased from 7% to 14% in local police departments and from 9% to 19% in sheriffs' offices.

- The percentage of local police departments using computers for Internet access increased from 24% in 1997 to 56% in 2000. Among sheriffs' offices, 31% used computers for Internet access in 1997, increasing to 67% in 2000.

Video Technology and Digital Imaging

- In 2000, forty-five percent of all local police departments and 53% of all sheriffs' offices used video cameras on a regular basis. The most common use of video cameras was in patrol cars, with 37% of local police departments and 40% of sheriffs' offices using video cameras in this application.
- In 2000, forty-seven percent of sheriffs' offices, and 29% of local police departments, used digital imaging technology for mug shots; twenty-one percent of sheriffs' offices and 29% of local police departments used digital imaging technology for suspect composites; twenty-seven percent of sheriffs' offices and 11% of local police departments used digital imaging technology for fingerprints.

Police Public Contact

In a nationwide survey conducted in 1999

- Speeding was the most common reason for being pulled over, accounting for 51.2% of all traffic stops in 1999.
- The majority of drivers stopped by police felt they had been stopped for legitimate reason (84.3%).
- About one-half of 1% of the 19.3 million drivers pulled over by police in 1999 felt police had used or threatened excessive force against them.

Source: U.S. Department of Justice, *Local and State Law Enforcement Statistics* (Washington, DC: Office of Justice Programs, Bureau of Justice Statistics, U.S. Government Printing Office, 2001).

POLICE WORK: THE FUTURE

Need Is More Complex, Difficult, and Vital

Contemporary American police officers face challenges, risks, obstacles, and difficulties those of past generations could never have conceived. Today's emergency workforce must possess the skills and knowledge to interact with a multitude of religions, races, ethnic traditions, languages, and biases. Yesterday's naive officer is not equipped with the knowledge and skills required for today's first responder in an America in which the value of human life has so little meaning among gang members and terrorists.

The impact of domestic and foreign terrorism has forever changed the role of a police officer. The crucial question is whether policing will meet this unparalleled challenge with decisive, sound leadership. If so, the nucleus of any viable solution is to enhance the knowledge and proficiency of the personnel on the front lines, and we must be vastly more effective and efficient at how this is done.

Never before have the tasks of line supervisors been so complex and their expertise been so important. The International Association of Chiefs of Police (IACP) identified the work ethic and attitudes of new officers as one of the major issues facing chiefs of police in the late 1990s.[14] The IACP study documented a nationwide perception of chief administrators that recent generations of personnel are difficult to supervise. When the results of this study are combined with the new demands of homeland terrorism defense, the necessity of taking leadership training to higher levels of effectiveness and efficiency is clear.

Urgency of Homeland Terrorism

Some believe that the repeated denial of requests for police training funds by local politicians showed poor judgment and contributed to communities now being placed in unnecessary jeopardy. Regardless of a department's current training level, it is crucial that government officials do not procrastinate or impede the necessary training. Unprepared initial responders are likely to contribute to unnecessary deaths. Obstacles must be overcome and remedies implemented without delay.

It is regretful that an unprecedented catastrophe was necessary to expose insufficient training and to prompt change. History, however, is riddled with urgent needs that were only addressed after a tragedy resulted. The events of September 11, 2001, and the probability of future attacks have created an extraordinary national need to train emergency personnel immediately. The curriculum must be effective, and the instruction has to be delivered with unparalleled efficiency.

Training Funds Reduced or Eliminated

More evidence of the necessity to transform training delivery rests in the current and projected economic woes that have produced a nationwide budget crisis for state and local governments. According to the National Conference of State Legislatures, governors faced a $25.7 billion deficit in 2003, and this scenario will continue to get worse. The 39 states reporting expect a combined $68.7 billion deficit in 2004.[15]

Many state, county, and city governments grew much too fast in the 1990s. Elected officials did not plan for the possibility of an economic downturn and expanded programs that now must be cut. Some states are making serious efforts to control spending, but "others are turning to tax increases to balance their budgets. Some state officials are trying to pass the buck for their poor fiscal management by pleading for a multibillion dollar bailout from Washington. In May 2003, President Bush publicly announced to state and local officials [last week] 'Do not look to Washington for economic bailout.' "[16]

Plummeting investments revenues combined with years of overspending and tax cuts are causing severe consequences for municipal governments and their employees. All types of local government workers are being laid off and significant programs have been terminated. In California, where they faced a $34 billion deficit in 2003, 25,000 teachers from throughout the state were laid off. Teachers in Oregon agreed to work for two weeks without pay to keep public schools from closing. Firefighters across the country are standing on corners collecting cash in their boots to prevent needed fire prevention programs from shutting down.[17]

The alarming financial condition of governments is having profound repercussions for antiterrorism preparation. Such extreme budget problems mean that fire and police agencies do not have the revenue to pay for seminar fees, overtime expenses associated with internal training, or the travel costs of going away for courses. The traditional training model requires these customary expenditures. The new training paradigm does not.

Manpower Shortage Aggravates Need

Approximately 38,000 state and local jobs were eliminated nationwide in 2003. In Oregon, for example, voters recently rejected an increase in the state income tax of about 5 percent for most residents and decided to lay off 129 state troopers.[18] With no aid in sight, governments are cutting the most costly of all expenses, labor.[19] New York City is laying off 3,400 city workers to reduce an estimated $3.4 billion city deficit for fiscal 2004, and an additional 10,000 job cuts are being planned.[20]

State and local governments have gone from one set of record-breaking situations to another set of record-breaking circumstances. In the 1990s they were able to cut taxes and build reserves, but that strong economy also hid the deterioration of the states' fiscal situation. A majority of state governments are facing one of their worst fiscal crises in decades. Many are cutting spending across the board, while others are imposing hiring freezes or laying off workers.[21]

The reality of police agencies having a severe manpower deficiency will hinder the ability to deliver antiterrorism training. When departments are exceedingly understaffed, they cannot afford to send employees away for training even if there is sufficient funding to pay the expenses. Their highest priority must always be their ability to respond to emergencies. The solution, therefore, is to develop an effective way to take training to employees rather than demanding that workers travel to seminars.

Longstanding Need to Improve Education

Beyond the urgency of fighting terrorism, there has always been a need to raise the education level of public service emergency occupations. Jeremy Travis, Director of the National Institute of Justice, put the situation in perspective as he stated, "If the broader goal is better policing, and higher education becomes only one means toward that end, it would be to our advantage to look in a lot of directions to find other means, other models. So I would like to broaden our vision of the education process, and to suggest 'inventorying' and rethinking the multiple components of that process—in the way education/training is structured, in the curricula, in the way we seek to attract recruits, in the way we build leadership, in the way we 'deliver' education/training 'products,' and so on. This exploration itself has to be an ongoing process, a continuous pursuit of new methods and structures to meet new needs."[22]

Six respected national organizations and the federal courts have declared that a four-year college degree should be the minimal education level to be a police officer. The International Association of Chiefs of Police (IACP), Police Executive Research Forum (PERF), International Association of Directors of Law Enforcement Standards and Training (IADLEST), National Organization of Black Law Enforcement Executives (NOBLE), and the Police Association for College Education (PACE) have all urged that education be improved. As with agency training, one of the primary obstacles has been the feasibility of getting personnel to attend courses. Distance learning has the potential to resolve this impasse.

QUESTIONS FOR DISCUSSION

1. After the Boston Police strike of 1919, President Wilson stated, "A strike of policemen of a great city, leaving that city at the mercy of an army of thugs, is a crime against civilization. In my judgment the obligation of a policeman is as sacred and direct as the obligation of a soldier. He is a public servant, not a private employee, and the whole honor of the community is in his hands. He has no right to prefer any private advantage to public safety." Do you agree or disagree? Justify your answer.

2. "Police professionalism" became synonymous with higher education during the 1970s. Formal college degrees brought recognition to both individual officers and their agencies. Still, the value of education was a subject of considerable debate, as many veteran officers without a college education felt that the only education of any value was learned on the street. How important is a college education to the majority of officers on patrol?

3. Research confirms that officers spend considerably more time keeping order, settling disputes, finding missing children, and

managing drunks than responding to criminal conduct serious enough to call for arrest, prosecution, and correction. Is your opinion consistent with the research findings? How much is law enforcement hurt by an inaccurate image of policing?

4. In 2001, males comprised 88.8 percent of all sworn officers. What does this statistic say about women in law enforcement? What is the role female officers play now, and what role should they play in the future?

5. Generation X has attitudes about work that are very much different than those of previous generations. Basically, they distrust hierarchy. They want more relaxed arrangements. They want to be judged on merit rather than on status. They are much less loyal to their employers. They are the first generation in America to be raised on a heavy diet of employment participation and teamwork. They know computers inside and out. They like money, but they also say they want balance in their lives. Will the views of Generation X help or hurt them as police officers? What will it take for them and baby boomers to work together as a solid team?

ENDNOTES

1. George G. Lillinger and Paul F. Cromwell, Jr., *Issues in Law Enforcement* (Boston:Holbrook Press, 1975), p. 43.

2. Donald O. Schultz, *Special Problems in Law Enforcement* (Springfield, IL: Charles C Thomas, 1971), pp. 43–44.

3. Ibid., p. 45.

4. William Bopp and Donald Schultz, *Principles of American Law Enforcement and Criminal Justice* (Springfield, IL: Charles C Thomas, 1972), p. 35.

5. International Association of Directors of Law Enforcement Standards and Training Commission website (IADLEST Minimum Model Standards, Preamble June 1, 2003). www.iadlest.org/modelmin.htm

6. National Advisory Commission of Criminal Justice Standards and Goals, *Report on Police* (Washington, DC: U.S. Government Printing Office, 1973), p. 380.

7. William Bopp and Donald Schultz, *Principles of American Law Enforcement and Criminal Justice* (Springfield, IL: Charles C Thomas, 1972), p. 85.

8. The President's Commission on Law Enforcement and Administration of Justice, *Task Force Report: The Police* (Washington, DC: U.S. Government Printing Office, 1967), p. 13.

9. Federal Bureau of Investigation, Press Release, October 28, 2002.

10. Lou Mayo, Police Association of College Education website Police Agencies that Require a Four-year Degree for New Officers (accessed June 1, 2003). www.police-association.org.

11. Paul Harvey, "What Are Policemen Made of?" *The Los Angeles Times Website*, 1986. www.sover.net/~tmartin/Paul.htm.

12. Jay A. Conger, "How 'Gen X' Managers Manage," London Business School, 1998.

13. Claire Raines, *Generations at Work: Managing the Clash of Veterans, Boomers, Xers, and Nexters in Your Workplace*, American Management Association, 2000.

14. Bill Burger, Michael Cosgrove, Neal Trautman, "Ethics Training in Law Enforcement," Ethics Training Subcommittee, Internataional Association of Chiefs of Police, Ad Hoc Committee on Police Image and Ethics, http://www.theiacp.org

15. Patrick McMahon, "State Services Fall with Economy. Washington State's Debates over Budget Cuts Mirror Struggle Across Nation," *USA TODAY*, January 31, 2003. A3.

16. ABC News, *Good Morning America*, April 24, 2003.

17. Ibid.

18. Patrick McMahon, "State Services Fall with Economy" Washington State's Debates over Budget Cuts Mirror Struggle Across Nation," *USA TODAY*, January 31, 2003. A3

19. ABC News, *Good Morning America*, April 24, 2003.

20. Ibid.

21. Richard Yamarone, "Add The Economy To The List Of War Wounded," http://www.nightlybusiness.org/transcript/2003/transcript032703.html, 3-27-2003

22. Jeremy Travis, during an address at the Forum on the Police and Higher Education, Washington DC, February 10, 1995.

chapter **2**

INTEGRITY VERSUS CORRUPTION

The best and the worst people I have ever known were cops. There is something about police work that brings out extremes in people.

Tim M. Dees
Law Enforcement Trainer and Author
Board of Directors, American Society of Law Enforcement Trainers

---

Mediocrity is, in general terms, the opposite of professionalism. Great cops do not settle for mediocre careers or convince themselves that they are professional when they are not. They should rise above mediocrity and reassess their view of professionalism.

Professionalism is easy to recognize but extremely hard to define. Professionals possess particular personality traits and a professional attitude in an uncompromising pursuit of excellence.

Professionals, no matter what their endeavors, have a certain uniqueness in their attitudes. They take pride in the quality of their work, whether or not they are being observed or evaluated. Great cops, likewise, reflect this same trait.

Having this type of attitude has absolutely nothing to do with a particular occupation or endeavor. A professional attitude cannot be awarded, adjudicated, or bestowed. Many people within various occupations and endeavors demand to be referred to as professionals. Often these same individuals are too busy climbing a self-serving ladder of success to be sincere in their efforts to improve their organization. Apathy and a general insincerity toward work are just not compatible with being professional.

Professionals display uncommon tenacity when others give up. Their positive view and untiring devotion pull them through adversity. The greatest individuals in America have always had this attitude, but it cannot be taught. It requires a positive outlook, confidence, self-esteem, and courage. In fact, when people act, think, and work like professionals, they truly must be professionals.

Ethics is a code or system of conduct and values with moral obligations and duties that define how to act. It is the training area needed most in many professions. Values are the basic beliefs that also guide actions and attitudes.

Most professions typically have done a poor job in preparing employees to make challenging ethical decisions on the job. This is incredible, especially in law enforcement, considering virtually every substantiated scandal and many civil suits have resulted from an unethical decision made by the parties involved.

> *Gaining access to a police agency to collect information on high-risk topics is a difficult prospect. There are many administrators who do not trust researchers and do not want their data scrutinized. I have had success with police administrators because I have been honest and ethical with them and with the data I have been allowed to collect. It is not the results that seem to bother the police officials as much as it is the process. I have always been careful to be accurate and check my work several times before reporting it to the police agency. And that is a key: always keep the chief aware of any findings before they are released. Honesty and communication are the key elements to success in police research. Progressive chiefs want to know if they have problems but they want to know before anyone else knows so the problem can be addressed and fixed.*

Geoffrey P. Alpert, Professor and Chair
Department of Criminology and Criminal Justice

CORRUPTION

To dedicated officers, reading a newspaper headline such as "Police Officer Indicted During Drug Probe" is devastating. Every profession has members who violate moral, ethical, or professional standards of conduct. When the individual in question is a police officer, however, the offense seems even worse. Perhaps this is because no other occupation is afforded so much authority and responsibility. Citizens have practically given police officers the right to be judge, jury, and executioner. They expect high standards and offer little sympathy for ineptness or corruption.

Like the general public, "good" cops do not tolerate internal corruption. Law enforcement cannot prevent some officers from "going bad." Still, past and current levels of graft and corruption cannot be tolerated, and agencies must give no compassion to officers who have yielded to temptation. As standard policy across America, substantial offenses should result in automatic termination following due process.

It is essential to gain insight as to how departments can prevent problems of graft and corruption. We must learn from past mistakes and attempt to achieve unyielding, high standards for the future. The future is certain; what we make of it is not.

Study: Miami Police Department

One way to protect future standards is to examine how some departments have become infiltrated with corruption. As an example, more than 70 Miami police officers were arrested between 1980 and the end of 1986. Chief Clarence Dickson of the Miami department wrote "Paranoia and suspicion has run rampant through the police department and city hall, to the extent that free verbal expression cannot be exchanged without fear that the halls, telephones, desks, walls, and offices of everyone who is part of the decision-making process are illegally bugged.

The inside of the Miami Police Department is filled with suspicion and uneasiness. Officers must live with the fact that they neither respect nor trust many fellow officers. Some officers have conducted major drug dealing. Others have been charged with murder. The Special Investigation Section has found $150,000 missing from its safe. Several hundred pounds of marijuana are also missing."[1]

The purpose here is not to examine isolated incidences of officers who have gone astray but to inspect what went wrong with the organization. Our inquiry should be taken in the context of learning to safeguard against further similar tragedies. The extracts throughout this section are provided to alert you to the thought processes and consequences of corruption within law enforcement.

Demoralized, ashamed, sickened, scared, and frustrated are accurate words for how some Miami officers have felt. Who's to blame? Certainly the officers having committed unethical, immoral, or illegal acts. Yet what about supervisors who take part in or allow conversations that demean or ridicule administrators?

Aren't top-level managers who conveniently remain unaware of low morale or dissension within departments also to blame? Aren't they responsible for taking quick and decisive steps to correct department-wide apathy? Could administrators be to blame for sweeping internal policies that are blatantly unfair? Could local politicians be guilty of political interference or persuasion that demoralizes the rank and file?

The nightmare within the Miami force also involved racial and ethnic tension. White, African-American, and Hispanic officers were openly angry and distrustful of one another. Separate bulletin boards for the various groups were displayed in the hallways. Some groups alleged that other groups hampered investigations of them. In addition, resentment over hiring practices and promotions further tore fellow officers apart.

By responding to public pressures created by two devastating riots during a 10-year period, the city attempted to revolutionize the police department. Some officers believed that the unprecedented recruitment and affirmative action efforts were beneficial, and others thought they were harmful. Within two years, however, the department was transformed: a police force that had once been dominated by white males was suddenly one in which white males comprised only one-third of the force. Now two out of five Miami officers were Hispanic, women accounted for approximately 11 percent of the force, and almost one in five officers was African-American. It had also increased in size from 650 officers to 1,050.

If an agency has a majority of officers who are minorities, it does not mean the agency will be ineffective. The manner of the transformation is what went wrong. Such staggering changes did not occur without a price. Many veteran officers were convinced that they stood little chance for promotion. To them it appeared that efforts were being made to hire and promote only minorities. Thus, veteran officers at all levels became discouraged by the changes.

In January 1984, Chief Ken Harms was fired by black city manager Howard Gary. Like most veteran officers, Chief Harms became frustrated when interdepartmental policies suddenly changed.

White officers who were irate over the number of minorities being promoted bombarded Harms. At the same time, the city manager demanded he promote more minorities. In a war in which there are no winners, Harms, a good cop, lost.

Herbert Breslow replaced Ken Harms as chief of police. Breslow was quick to follow the city manager's recommendations to double his number of top administrators by including more African-Americans and Hispanics and a woman in the top echelon. Several civic leaders and politicians applauded the promotions, feeling that the department had finally come close to reaching the "recommended" integrated level of top administration.

However, there was ample reason to be angry over the promotions: seven officers were promoted from sergeant to major. In doing so, many lieutenants and captains were overlooked. Internal and political contacts appeared to be the overriding criteria necessary for these promotions. One of the promoted officers had been a leader in the African-American benevolent association. Another was a former head of the Fraternal Order of Police. One female officer was the organizer of the women's officer group.[2] The message was clear. If you were going to get anywhere within the department, it was who you knew that was going to get you there. Loyalty, dedication, and hard work were nice, but they didn't help you climb the ladder of success. Affirmative action, being the right color or sex, playing politics well, or having friends in influential places had become the essential ingredients for success.

What could have been done to prevent the devastating political influence? Does the same thing happen in other governmental entities?

By January of 1985 Chief Breslow had been fired. Once again city politicians had forced the chief's termination. Clarence Dickson, an African-American, replaced Breslow as the new chief of police. Though many problems occurred under Dickson's reign, the rank and file generally believed that the department's internal problems were not his fault. The early 1980s was a period of incredible pressure and tension. First, there was the wave of Mariel immigrants (those who came to southern Florida in the early 1980s from the city of Mariel in western Cuba). Second came the Liberty City riots. The riots had been ignited by the acquittal of five white metro officers who were accused of murdering an African-American man. Because Miami continued to experience a very high violent crime rate, it was a logical conclusion that the city needed more police officers. Theoretically, the hiring of more minorities should have helped to improve racial tensions, but once again, the problem was the way they were hired and promoted.

Although personnel officials claim that hiring standards were never lowered, the force grew from 650 officers to 1,050 within two years. Every experienced chief of police or sheriff knows that hiring low-quality officers will result in low-quality performance. The consequences of superficial or indiscriminate hiring practices can be crippling.

During the early and mid-1980s, the Miami Police Department had a dark, unethical element within it. Fellowship and comradeship were replaced with animosity, resentfulness, and distrust. Some citizens marked many dedicated officers with the label of "corrupt cop." Even so, there is no reason the Miami police can't rebuild. A "culture change" must replace distrust with respect and unity. Management must become totally committed to sincere, "people-oriented leadership."[3]

2003 Update: Miami Police Department

The headline in the *Miami Daily Business Review* on April 11, 2003, read "Judge in Miami Cops Case Opens Door to Civil Suits." In this article, reporter Dan Christensen accurately conveyed how little the true problems of the Miami Police Department were dealt with throughout the 1990s: "In all, Miami has paid more than $20 million since 1990 to resolve more than 110 federal and state lawsuits alleging brutality, misconduct or unnecessary death caused by city officers."[4]

Study: New York City Police Department/ Knapp Commission

The Knapp Commission, directed by Whitman Knapp as chair, conducted a monumental investigation into alleged corruption within the New York City Police Department. Mayor John Lindsey appointed the five-man commission in May 1970, and they completed a grueling, thorough investigation. Their findings can help others to understand why some officers yield to temptation; after all, every unethical act reflects on dedicated cops everywhere.

The commission was responsible for three things:

1. To investigate input of corruption from the commission's formation.
2. To evaluate New York City Police Department procedures concerning the investigation of corruption and to determine

whether the procedures were adequate and followed with rapid and fair enforcement.

3. To recommend improvements for departmental procedures.[5]

The commission soon was able to determine the extent of corruption, and its findings were disturbing. Uniformed officers received regular payoffs from a variety of businesses and individuals. Detectives were routinely conducting shakedowns of individuals. Vice officers often received individual payoffs. Plainclothes officers frequently received semiweekly or monthly collections of payoffs from gambling organizations. Lastly, the assortment of bribes and payoffs was received from not only first-level officers but sergeants and lieutenants as well. The percentage of corrupt officers still was relatively small, though the publicity surrounding the commission did not emphasize that.

Following seemingly endless reviews of incidents, reports, transcriptions, and testimony, the commission reached many conclusions. Many observers felt that underlying the commission's logic was the premise that officers who become corrupt are simply "rotten apples" and little can be done to stop them. The commission actually concluded the opposite. It concluded that a department trying to maintain a good public image frequently promotes the "rotten apple" theory. Instead, it stressed that managers should promote a realistic attitude toward corruption. Further, they should be honest, open, and factual in order to enhance the department's credibility and ability to deal with the causes of corruption.[6]

Contrary to the idea that corruption is difficult to prevent because a few "rotten apples" will be hired from time to time, the commission determined that corruption can be curtailed by eliminating situations that expose officers to corruption. Open and honest internal communication also is crucial. Developing an atmosphere of trust, camaraderie, and loyalty is absolutely essential.

The commission also made several more recommendations. Informal arrest quotas should be eliminated. Officers should always be reimbursed for legitimate expenses. Thorough hiring practices must be conducted. Personnel records should be centralized. Internal affairs divisions must operate effectively. Lastly, relentless prosecution of officers who have succumbed to graft and corruption must occur, and internal investigation and outside assistance, when appropriate, should be used for investigation and prosecution. Above all, there should never be leniency.[7]

Facts About Bad Cops

In 1996, without a lot of fanfare, the directors of Peace Officer Standards and Training Commissions and Councils throughout the nation were busy creating more work for themselves. With an untiring commitment, they researched data concerning all the officers within their state who had been formally disciplined by a member commission or council between 1990 and 1995. When the statistics were compiled, they were forwarded to the National Institute of Ethics so that nationwide analysis, conclusions, and recommendations could be developed.

Every state, in some way or another, responded—a 100 percent response rate. Such nationwide involvement has the potential to yield priceless new knowledge that can lead to preventing the devastation associated with brutality, corruption, and scandal. These facts could make training and leadership much more effective and efficient. A summary of the 85-page report appears in Box 2-1.

Box 2-1

The National Law Enforcement Officer Disciplinary Research Project Report

It is the mission of the National Law Enforcement Officer Disciplinary Research Project to identify ways to prevent officer misconduct within law enforcement, based upon an extensive, accurate needs assessment.

Goals

1. Develop an effective survey instrument.
2. Obtain a response from 100% of the states.
3. Receive a written response of usable data from 50% of states.
4. Ensure validity and reliability of survey findings.
5. Analyze the submitted data.
6. Develop leadership and training conclusions and recommendations.
7. Communicate findings throughout the nation.

Box 2-1 *(continued)*

INTRODUCTION

The importance of this research is profound for two reasons. First is the fact that ethics is our greatest training and leadership need. The second reason is that never before has there been a national law enforcement ethics-needs assessment that has focused on documented misconduct and the officers who committed the misconduct.

FINDINGS

Number of Officers Disciplined by State Commissions/Councils

Findings The total number of law enforcement officers having gone through the decertification process from 1990 through 1995 is 3,884. Of this number, 502 cases were dismissed, leaving 3,382 officers. Of the 3,382 officers, 2,296 officers were totally decertified. The term decertification means that the state in which an officer works has completed a process through which the state takes the officer's legal right to be a law enforcement officer away from the concerned officer. The person can no longer be an officer anywhere in that state.

When the number of cases dismissed (502) and cases still pending (278) are subtracted from the total number of 3,884 cases, we learn that there have been 3,104 cases where some form of discipline has been rendered. Below is a summary.

Discipline Action	*Number of Cases*	*Percentage of Cases*
Revocation	2,296	59.1%
Case Dismissed	502	12.9%
Suspension	320	8.2%
Cases Still Pending	278	7.2%
Initial Certification Denied	244	6.3%
Probation	203	5.2%
Reprimand	41	1.1%

(continued)

Box 2-1 *(continued)*

Conclusions

1. The procedures which allow for the decertification of officers vary tremendously throughout the nation.
2. Decertification procedures should be standardized throughout the country.
3. State and nationwide systems for identifying officers who have been decertified should be developed and maintained.

Reasoning for Conclusions Some people should never be hired as law enforcement officers, because they have committed crimes or other unethical acts. Although the best solution is a hiring process effective enough that they are eliminated from consideration, the decertification process is the next best solution.

Many problems exist with contemporary decertification. Several states do not decertify officers. Many decertify for different reasons and in a variety of ways. Since there is no nationwide, standardized format used to track decertification data, many states had only data related to particular sections of the survey. This caused the survey sampling size to vary from topic to topic.

Age

Findings The average age of an officer who was the subject of this research was 32.

Conclusions The focus of the majority of contemporary law enforcement ethics training has been on academy, FTO training, or executive development. The fact that the average officer who has been decertified is 32 has reprioritized where the focus of ethics training should be—the officer with 5–10 years' experience.

Working within an organizational culture of disrespect and unfairness for several years can prompt officers to commit unethical acts.

Reasoning for Conclusions Many administrators and trainers presume that new officers are the most likely to give in to the temptations of anger, lust, greed, or peer pressure. As a result, ethics training has focused on new officers.

Box 2-1 *(continued)*

Sex

Findings   The study revealed that of those officers who were the subject of this research, 93% were male and 7% were female.

Conclusions   The percentages of decertified officers who are male and female is generally consistent with the overall percentages of male and female officers within the entire law enforcement profession.

Findings indicate that the female officers are slightly less likely to commit misconduct.

Reasoning for Conclusions   According to the Source Book of Criminal Justice Statistics, 1995, as of October 31, 1994, males comprised 90.5% of sworn, full-time officers throughout the nation. Females accounted for 9.5%.

Race/Ethnicity

Findings   The study revealed that of those officers who were the subject of this research:

> 73% were Caucasian
> 19% were African American
> 8% were Hispanic

Conclusions   The percentage of Caucasian officers who have been processed for decertification throughout the nation is 8% less than the overall percentage of Caucasian officers within the work force.

The percentage of African American officers who have been processed for decertification is 8% higher than the overall percentage of African American officers within the work force.

The percentage of Hispanic officers who commit unethical acts is slightly less than the overall percentage of Hispanic officers within the work force.

Reasoning for Conclusions   According to the U.S. Department of Justice, Bureau of Justice Statistics, 1996, the race and ethnicity of full-time officers in local police departments is White/80.9%, Black/11.3% and Hispanic/6.2%.

(continued)

Box 2-1 *(continued)*

Education Level

Findings The study revealed that of those officers who were the subject of this research:

    70% had a high school degree
    11% had a GED
    10% had an A.A./A.S. degree
    9% had a B.A./B.S. degree

Conclusions The study concluded that there were no substantial differences of officers who were the subject of this research compared to the national education levels of the overall population of law enforcement officers. This could not be verified by confirmed statistics, however.

Number of Employments

Findings The study revealed that officers who were the subject of this research averaged 2.16 previous employments.

Conclusions The number of previous employments of officers who have been processed for decertification is not significantly different than the normal career changes of officers throughout the work force. This could not be verified by confirmed statistics, however.

Employment Status

Findings The study determined that of those officers who were the subject of this research, 92% are full-time, sworn officers, 5% are part-time, and 3% are auxiliary officers.

Type of Officer

Findings The study determined that the types of officers who were the subject of this research were comprised as follows:

    56% were city officers, although they comprise 66% of the work force
    33% were county deputies, although they comprise 25% of the work force

Box 2-1 *(continued)*

11% were state officers, although they comprise 8% of the work force

Conclusions The percentage of municipal officers who have been processed for decertification throughout the nation is 10% less than the overall percentage of municipal officers within the work force.

The percentage of sheriff deputies who have been processed for decertification throughout the nation is 8% greater than the overall percentage of sheriff deputies within the work force.

The percentage of state officers who have been processed for decertification throughout the nation is 3% greater than the overall percentage of state officers within the work force.

Reasoning for Conclusions According to the Bureau of Justice Statistics, Local Police Departments, NCJ-148822, Washington DC, 1996, there are 622,913 city, county, and state law enforcement officers in America.

Of this number, approximately:

66%, or 415,224, are city police officers

25%, or 155,815, are sheriff deputies

8%, or 51,874, are state police officers

Rank

Findings The study determined that 85% of officers who have been processed for decertification between 1990 and 1995 were patrol officers, deputies, or troopers.

Conclusions From the perspective of rank or position within a law enforcement agency, the rank of patrol officer, deputy, or trooper accounts for a disproportionately high number of officers who commit unethical acts.

In-service ethics training should target patrol officers as a high-priority focus.

Reasoning for Conclusions From the perspective of rank, the percentages of officers ultimately processed for decertification

(continued)

Box 2-1 *(continued)*

between 1990 and 1995 resulting from misconduct is presented below.

Patrolman	59%
Deputy	22%
Sergeant	5%
Trooper	4%
Detective	3%
Special Agent	3%
Captain, Chief, Sheriff, Lieutenant	1% for each group
Assistant Chief, Major, Wildlife Officer	each less than 1%

Years Sworn

Findings The study revealed that officers who were processed for decertification from 1990 through 1995 had an average of 7.2 years of sworn service when the decertification was initiated.

Conclusions   Officers most likely to commit unethical acts are not rookies, but those with 5 to 10 years of service.

Reasoning for Conclusions   The fact that officers processed for decertification had an average of 7.2 years of sworn service is consistent with the fact that the average age of these officers is 32. This is a single, yet vital, fact from which ethics training can become more effective.

Offenses Charged

Findings The four most frequent crimes committed by officers who have been processed for decertification are making false statements/reports (19.92%), larceny (12.12%), sex offenses other than rape (9.48%), battery (9.15%). These four offenses comprise 51% of the crimes for which officers have been decertified. Other than filing false statements/reports, virtually all other offenses committed by the concerned officers can be grouped into four groups:

Box 2-1 *(continued)*

Greed	(25.47%)
Larceny	(12.12%)
Fraud/Forgery	(5.03%)
Sale of Cocaine	(3.08%)
Sale of Cannabis	(1.36%)
Robbery	(1.19%)
Bribery	(1.19%)
Stolen Property	(1.11%)
Gambling	(.41%)
Anger	(19.69%)
Battery	(9.15%)
Excessive Use of Force	(5.05%)
Weapon Offense	(4.02%)
Family Offense	(1.47%)
Lust	(12.74%)
Sexual Offenses Other than Rape	(9.48%)
Sexual Battery/Rape	(2.77%)
Morals/Decency Crimes	(.49%)
Peer Pressure	(12.76%)
Driving Under the Influence	(5.08%)
Drugs Other than Cocaine and Cannabis	(4.64%)
Cocaine Drug Test	(1.68%)
Cannabis Drug Test	(1.36%)

Top Ten Offenses for Which Officers Are Decertified:

1. False Statements/Reports	19.92%
2. Larceny	12.12%
3. Sex Offenses Other than Rape	9.48%
4. Battery	9.15%
5. Driving Under the Influence	5.08%
6. Excessive Use of Force	5.05%
7. Fraud/Forgery	5.03%

(continued)

Box 2-1 *(continued)*

8. Drugs Other than Cannabis/Cocaine	4.64%
9. Weapon Offenses	4.02%
10. Cocaine—Possession or Sale	3.08%

Conclusions   Research should begin immediately to determine the root causes for the excessive number of false statements or reports that are committed.

Individual agencies should conduct their own ethics training needs assessments, focusing on the motivations of anger, lust, greed, and peer pressure.

Individual agencies should conduct their own leadership needs assessments, focusing on the motivations of anger, lust, greed, and peer pressure.

Academies, FTO programs, in-service training, leadership training, civilian training, and job-specific training should focus on anger, lust, greed, peer pressure, and falsifying records.

Reasoning for Conclusions   Understanding training and leadership needs, both for professions and specific organizations, is crucial for effective training and leadership. It is very unlikely that training and leadership can be as effective if the needs of the agency are not known. Conducting a training needs assessment should be the first step in the development of any training program. The value of this research is that it is a nationwide needs assessment for law enforcement ethics training and leadership.

RECOMMENDATIONS TO STOP BAD COPS

1. Standardize decertification terminology and procedures throughout the country. The lack of a single standardized process makes effective nationwide tracking of officers who have been totally decertified very difficult.

2. Develop and maintain state and nationwide systems for identifying officers who have been decertified as a means for preventing decertified officers from being hired unknowingly by agencies.

3. Identify a group of International Association of Law Enforcement Standards and Training members who are

Box 2-1 *(continued)*

willing to assist states seeking to develop or enhance decertification.

4. Continue to track and analyze decertification statistics so that we can continue to become more effective at preventing misconduct.

RECOMMENDATIONS FOR LEADERSHIP

1. Orchestrate a positive organizational culture within the patrol division—an extremely high priority.
2. Hold all levels of leadership accountable for being role models for integrity.
3. National and state sheriff's associations, state POST commissions, and law enforcement academies should assist state and county law enforcement agencies in providing state-of-the-art executive development ethics training.
4. State police administrators and particularly sheriffs throughout the country should implement contemporary leadership solutions to prevent misconduct.

    The state of the art for preventing officer misconduct is comprised of three steps:

    - Maintain a leadership style driven by respect and dignity for all employees.
    - Implement ethical dilemma simulation training to anchor an ethical decision-making process into the long-term memory of officers.
    - Implement a comprehensive administrative process that prevents misconduct.

5. Administrators must embrace and support their Field Training Officer programs.

    Field training officers create the culture of patrol divisions and individual patrol shifts. If FTOs are cynical, bitter, resentful, or unethical, they will consistently develop new officers with the same outlook. On the other hand, if FTOs

(continued)

Box 2-1 *(continued)*

are the end result of effective FTO selection, training, compensation, recognition, and leadership, they will likely create a patrol culture of positive, motivated officers.

6. Administrators should conduct an ethics needs assessment to determine the integrity-related needs of their organization.

The first step for preventing unethical acts is to determine your ethics-related needs. Identifying your needs should then be the basis for immediate and future training and leadership initiatives.

RECOMMENDATIONS FOR TRAINING

1. Develop effective in-service ethics training that is focused on the 5–10 year patrol officer.

The majority of contemporary law enforcement ethics training focus has been on academy, FTO training, or executive development. The fact that the average officer who has been decertified is 32 years of age has reprioritized where the focus of ethics training should be: the officer with 5–10 years' experience.

2. Address the ethical perspectives of the topic.
3. Develop ethical dilemma simulation training about the most common offenses committed by officers.

Source: Neal E. Trautman, "The National Law Enforcement Officer Disciplinary Research Project," The National Institute of Ethics, June 8, 1998, pp. 1–10.

HONESTY

Everyone agrees that honesty is a worthy principle. Every major religion preaches it, schools teach it, civil litigation enforces it, and businesses, governments, and individuals claim that they practice it.

Yet honesty is frequently ignored. Self-serving interests often rule out the choice to do the right thing. Few endeavors offer more temptations to be dishonest than law enforcement. Some officers finding an open door to a business at 0315 hours may be tempted to steal. Others may find it difficult to answer questions honestly during a deposition if the answer would make them look bad.

In a profession representing integrity, pride, protection, and service to others, why is there a problem with officers being dishonest? Unfortunately, it has become part of our culture in major and minor ways. For some, the "American way" includes cheating on your taxes, lying to avoid awkward situations, and copying seemingly harmless examples of dishonesty set by role models. All professions must embed honesty in their operations and workforce.

> *Cops are expected to be loyal, but their loyalty is often misplaced. At the outset of their careers, they swear loyalty to the Constitution, to the laws of their state, and to the communities they serve. Later on, they are told that other loyalties are expected—to other cops, to certain supervisors and administrators, to some unwritten code of conduct. These are not necessarily bad things, until they conflict with that first loyalty—the one that they formally swore to, the one that is binding. There's a reason that one came first. Putting it second, or even farther down the list, is a betrayal of their office, and the public trust.*
>
> Tim M. Dees
> Law Enforcement Trainer and Author

ETHICAL PERCEPTIONS

Historically, regardless of the profession, some organizations have reacted to individual acts of misconduct or devastating scandals by holding employees accountable for their actions following a violation.

Others have knowingly ignored the constant lack of integrity by some employees, fearing that addressing the problem might ultimately result in negative publicity. Thus, they knowingly let it continue.

In the worst cases, supervisors become driven by the hope that employees and the community will not learn about internal misdeeds. Meanwhile, an internal climate of dishonesty is perpetuated by the role-modeling of deceitfulness and bitter internal politics. Ignoring it allows it to continue.

Good administrators and law enforcement leaders are inherently driven by their own integrity and honor. It is their personal role-modeling of honesty and respect toward others that molds a culture of dignity, integrity, and honor in those they manage or lead. Their leadership style prevents misconduct and maintains integrity within an organization.

The 1990s witnessed a revolution of knowledge of and ability to prevent unethical acts. Most of the elements that comprise the current state of the art focus on prevention rather than reaction after careers have been destroyed and reputations have been lost. Ethics has been law enforcement's greatest training need since the mid-1980s.

Prior to this time, law enforcement's most significant need was firearms training. For decades, instructors had been anchoring the wrong survival responses into officers' long-term memory during firearms training. Because research had not been conducted prior to the mid-1970s, firearms instructors did not know that they were sometimes anchoring detrimental behavior into the long-term memory of officers. As an example, after firing several rounds at targets during firearms training, officers were usually required to throw the empty shell casings into a bucket behind them. As a result, this response was anchored deeply into their long-term memory. This means that in a real shooting these same officers may take the time to throw the empty casing into a non-existent bucket. This response caused some officers to be killed or injured. The only reason this unfortunate situation changed was that the FBI in Quantico, Virginia, conducted a training needs assessment and literally determined how officers were dying. The results of this study changed firearms training forever. Armed with this vital new knowledge, trainers and corporations developed discretionary dilemma video training systems. The result has been dramatically improved firearms training.

Similarly, identical improvements have been made with ethics training. This is fortunate, because virtually none of the 16,000 agencies across the nation had provided any in-service ethics training prior to the 1980s.

With the exception of dying in the line of duty, nothing is more devastating to an officer's personal life, a leader's career, or an agency's respect than allegations of unethical conduct. Such allegations are the basis for many civil suits filed against law enforcement.

Many officers commit suicide as a result. Each year two to three times the number of officers who die in the line of duty commit suicide. Some do so because they made a foolish three- to five-second decision that would potentially ruin their lives, and they feel as though they have lost their career, dignity, respect, and retirement.

Such split-second, poor decisions—when facing moments of anger, lust, greed, or peer pressure—can destroy the future of good people. Thus, it is crucial that we help each other maintain a strong, positive, and ethical mental outlook.

EXCUSES

Some people believe that abiding by a strict, professional code of ethics is an unrealistic goal. Others feel that although high ideals and integrity are worthy objectives to seek, they remain impractical in real life. They claim that officers will never be able to follow exceedingly high ethical standards because their values were already programmed by an unethical society. This thought is sometimes used as an excuse by corrupt officers who say it is all right to steal, lie, or cheat because the rest of society does it.

People who believe high ideals and ethical standards cannot be met by America's police officers are mistaken. They have not felt the brotherhood and camaraderie of dedicated street cops. Sincere cops are bound together in their moral convictions by the sweat and blood spent in years on the street. Their loyalties are to ethical principles supported by pride and guts. Their language is theirs alone. Unlike the few weak individuals among them, they neither search for nor need excuses. Their actions are above the temptations of money, lust, or drugs.

Officers who use self-serving excuses or do things morally or ethically wrong do so because their character is weak. There is little difference in why a child lies and why officers try to justify unethical acts by using deceit to explain their actions. A weakness of character caused them not to accept responsibility for their own actions.

Professionalism is tarnished every time an officer is intentionally misleading. Excuses are easy to think of. The officer who "fixes" a ticket merely says he was mistaken. Those who accept gratuities and favors from local businesses usually claim there is no harm in taking gifts.

After all, businessmen are simply trying to support their local police department. In reality, such businessmen frequently expect to receive special treatment in return.

In 1984, Miami police officer Carlos Pedrera was accused of committing criminal acts. During his corruption trial in 1987, Pedrera testified that he went from committing small-time rip-offs of cocaine smugglers to making more than $1 million in two boat-yard drug deals. At the time of his testimony, Pedrera was facing 20 years in prison. He testified against three former Miami officers accused of a cocaine-related murder. When the U.S. attorney asked Pedrera why he did these things, Pedrera answered simply, "I needed the money."

Excuses such as "I needed the money" or the acceptance of gifts and favors from local businesses as "signs of their appreciation" are nothing more than a cop-out. Vice detectives or other officers who have sex with hookers try to justify it by telling themselves they did not hurt anyone. Investigators who commit perjury may be trying to make themselves look good or convict someone they dislike. They might feel that "the scumbag deserves it."

Nothing is complicated about officers who cheat, steal, or lie. All of them realize that what they are doing is wrong, but their character is not strong enough to avoid it.

While ethics education and training will help a great deal, another solution is to not hire weak individuals to begin with. Officers who give in to daily temptations should not be cops. Therefore, hiring practices must be strengthened so that agencies can detect character weaknesses.

CODE OF ETHICS

Principles provide guidance, direction, and vision. For law enforcement, an example of such principles is the Law Enforcement Code of Ethics. A sense of professional responsibility can come from understanding the reasons this code of ethics was established.

Most people respect the regulations set to assist their professional life. A clear understanding and appreciation of the responsibilities needed to achieve professionalism can lay the foundation for a strong tomorrow. The first step in developing an appreciation is to know the Code of Ethics, and sincere reflection can help to understand its value.

In 1956 a committee of the Peace Officers Research Association of California drafted a code of ethics. After it was edited by a committee of the California Peace Officers Association, it was adopted that same year. It gradually became accepted throughout the nation as the Law Enforcement Code of Ethics. It was adopted by the International Association of Chiefs of Police in 1957. The code is provided in Box 2-2.

Box 2-2

Law Enforcement Code of Ethics

As a law enforcement officer, my fundamental duty is to serve mankind; to safeguard lives and property; to protect the innocent against deception, the weak against oppression or intimidation, and the peaceful against violence or disorder; and to respect the constitutional rights of all men to liberty, equality and justice.

I will keep my private life unsullied as an example to all; maintain courageous calm in the face of danger, scorn or ridicule; develop self-restraint; and be constantly mindful of the welfare of others. Honest in thought and deed in both my personal and official life, I will be exemplary in obeying the laws of the land and the regulations of my department. Whatever I see of a confidential nature of that which is confided to me in my official capacity will be kept ever secret unless revelation is necessary in the performance of my duty.

I will never act officiously or permit personal feelings, prejudices, animosities or friendships to influence my decisions. With no compromise for crime in the relentless prosecution of criminals, we will enforce the law courteously and appropriately without fear or favor, malice, or ill will, never employing unnecessary force or violence and never accepting gratuities. I recognize the badge of an officer as a symbol of public faith, and I accept it, as a public trust to be held so long as I am true to the ethics of police service. I will constantly strive to achieve these objectives, ideals, and dedication of myself before God to my chosen profession ... law enforcement.

Source: International Association of Chiefs of Police.

OATH OF HONOR—THE NEW MOVEMENT

As the effort to incorporate ethics training fully within law enforcement begins, it will be important to heighten the visibility and awareness of ethics across the profession. A public affirmation to adhering to the current code of ethics and the adoption of an oath of honor will have to be undertaken along with role-modeling and mentoring—powerful vehicles for changing behavior.

To be successful at enhancing integrity within an organization, leaders must ensure that ethical mentoring and role-modeling is consistent, frequent, and visible. Therefore, the committee from the California Peace Officers Association wholeheartedly supported the creation of a symbolic iteration and public affirmation in order to attest a commitment to ethical conduct. After numerous drafts and conferences, the following Law Enforcement Oath of Honor was recommended in 1997 as the International Association of Chiefs of Police's (IACP's) symbolic statement of commitment to ethical behavior. The oath reads:

> *On my honor,*
> *I will never betray my badge,*
> *my integrity, my character, or the public trust.*
> *I will always have*
> *the courage to hold myself*
> *and others accountable for our actions.*
> *I will always uphold the constitution and community I serve.*

An oath is a solemn pledge one makes and intends to follow. Before officers take the Law Enforcement Oath of Honor, it is important that they understand what it means.

Honor is one's word given as a guarantee.

Betray is the breaking of faith with the public trust.

Badge is the symbol of office.

Integrity is adherence to a code of honesty, in both private and public life.

Character is the set of qualities that distinguish an individual.

Public trust is a charge of duty imposed in faith toward those being served.

Courage is the strength to withstand unethical pressure, fear, or danger.

Accountable is being answerable and responsible to the oath.

Community is the jurisdiction and citizens served.

Because the oath is brief it can be constantly referred to and reinforced during conversations with FTOs and line supervisors and used in the following manner:

- Referred to by administrators while communicating with others.
- Placed on the back of academy students' name cards, so that they can refer to it as needed.
- Placed visibly in all police academies and law enforcement agencies.
- Enlarged and framed so that all academy students can see it.
- Recited at all official police ceremonies and gatherings.
- Printed on equipment labels.
- Used as a backdrop in citizen's meetings and news media events.

The oath reconfirms the significance of integrity within agencies. It helps bring the entire profession together to show that the vast majority of law enforcement officers are good, decent individuals willing to step forward to stop unethical acts by any members of the profession.[8]

POLICE ETHICS

Great cops require deep and abiding sincerity, in addition to sensible action. Therefore, another priceless document in the law enforcement profession is the Canon of Police Ethics, in Box 2-3, which provides ethical direction and guidance. Topics include indi-

---

Box 2-3

Canon of Police Ethics

Article 1. Primary Responsibility of Job

The primary responsibility of the police service and of the individual officer is the protection of the people of the United States through the upholding of their laws; chief among these is the Constitution of the United States and its amendments. The law

(continued)

Box 2-3 *(continued)*

enforcement officer always represents the whole of the community and its legally expressed will and is never the arm of any political party or clique.

Article 2. Limitations of Authority

The first duty of a law enforcement officer, as upholder of the law, is to know its bounds upon him in enforcing it. Because he represents the legal will of the community, be it local, state or federal, he must be aware of the limitations and proscriptions which the people, through the law, have placed upon him. He must recognize the genius of the American system of government, which gives to no man, groups of men, or institution, absolute power, and he must insure that he, as a prime defender of that system, does not pervert its character.

Article 3. Duty to be Familiar with the Law and with Responsibilities of Self and Other Public Officials

The law enforcement officer shall assiduously apply himself to the study of the principles of the laws which he is sworn to uphold. He will make certain of his responsibilities in the particulars of their enforcement, seeking aid from his superiors in matters of technicality or principle when these are not clear to him; he will make special effort to fully understand his relationship to other public officials, including other law enforcement agencies, particularly on matters of jurisdiction, both geographically and substantively.

Article 4. Utilization of Proper Means to Gain Proper Ends

The law enforcement officer shall be mindful of his responsibility to pay strict heed to the selection of means in discharging the duties of his office. Violations of law or disregard for public safety and property on the part of an officer are intrinsically wrong; they are self-defeating in that they instill in the public mind a like disposition. The employment of illegal means, no matter how worthy the end, is certain to encourage disrespect for the law and its officers. If the law is to be honored, those who enforce it must first honor it.

Box 2-3 *(continued)*

Article 5. Cooperation with Public Officials in the Discharge of Their Authorized Duties

The law enforcement officer shall cooperate fully with other public officials in the discharge of authorized duties, regardless of party affiliation or personal prejudice. He shall be meticulous, however, in assuring himself of the propriety, under the law, of such actions and shall guard against the use of his office or person, whether knowingly or unknowingly, in any improper or illegal action. In any situation open to question, he shall seek authority from his superior officer, giving him a full report of the proposed service or action.

Article 6. Private Conduct

The law enforcement officer shall be mindful of his special identification by the public as an upholder of the law. Laxity of conduct or manner in private life, expressing either disrespect for the law or seeking to gain special privilege, cannot but reflect upon the police officer and the police service. The community and the service require that the law enforcement officer lead the life of a decent and honorable man. Following the career of a policeman gives no man special prerequisites. It does give the satisfaction and pride of following and furthering an unbroken tradition of safeguarding the American republic. The officer who reflects upon this tradition will not degrade it.

Article 7. Conduct Toward the Public

The law enforcement officer, mindful of his responsibility to the whole community, shall deal with individuals of the community in a manner calculated to instill respect for its laws and its police service. The law enforcement officer shall conduct his official life in a manner such as will inspire confidence and trust. Thus, he will be neither overbearing nor subservient, as no individual citizen has an obligation to stand in awe of him nor a right to command him. The officer will give service where he can and require compliance with the law. He will do neither from personal preference nor prejudice but rather as a duly appointed officer of the law discharging his sworn obligation.

(continued)

Box 2-3 *(continued)*

Article 8. Conduct in Arresting and Dealing with Law Violators

The law enforcement officer shall use his powers of arrest strictly in accordance with the law and with due regard to the rights of the citizen concerned. His office gives him no right to prosecute the violator or to mete out punishment for the offense. He shall, at all times, have a clear appreciation of his responsibilities and limitations regarding detention of the violator; he shall conduct himself in such a manner as will minimize the possibility of having to use force. To this end he shall cultivate a dedication to the service of the people and the equitable upholding of their laws whether in the handling of law violators or in dealing with the law-abiding.

Article 9. Gifts and Favors

The law enforcement officer, representing government, bears the heavy responsibility of maintaining, in his own conduct, the honor and integrity of all government institutions. He shall, therefore, guard against placing himself in a position in which any person can expect special consideration or in which the public can reasonably assume that special consideration is being given. Thus, he should be firm in refusing gifts, favors, or gratuities, large or small, which can, in the public mind, be interpreted as capable of influencing his judgment in the discharge of his duties.

Article 10. Presentation of Evidence

The law enforcement officer shall be concerned equally in the prosecution of the wrongdoer and the defense of their innocence. He shall ascertain what constitutes evidence and shall present such evidence impartially and without malice. In so doing, he will ignore social, political, and all other distinctions among the person involved, strengthening the tradition of the reliability and integrity of an officer's word. The law enforcement officer shall take special pains to increase his perception and skill of observation, mindful that in many situations his is the sole impartial testimony to the facts of a case.

Box 2-3 *(continued)*

Article 11. Attitude Toward Profession

The law enforcement officer shall regard the discharge of his duties as a public trust and recognize his responsibility as a public servant. By diligent study and sincere attention to self-improvement he shall strive to make the best possible application of science to the solution of crime and, in the field of human relationships, strive for effective leadership and public influence in matters affecting public safety. He shall appreciate the importance and responsibility of his office, and hold police work to be an honorable profession rendering valuable service to his community and his country.

Source: International Association of Chiefs of Police, "The Patrol Operation," Washington, DC, 1970.

vidual conduct, limitations of authority, primary responsibility, duty to serve, and attitude.

The high standards put forth in codes of ethics are not always translated into practice in police culture. The National Institute of Justice published a report in 2000 with findings regarding police culture, which is shown in Box 2-4.

Box 2-4

Measuring the Police Culture

ISSUES AND FINDINGS

Discussed in this Brief: Research exploring police officers' understanding of agency rules concerning police misconduct and the extent of their support for these rules. The survey also considered officers' opinions about appropriate punishment for misconduct, their familiarity with the expected disciplinary threat, their perceptions of disciplinary fairness, and their willingness to report misconduct. The results of this survey have important implications for researchers and policymakers, as well as for police practitioners.

(continued)

Box 2-4 *(continued)*

Key Issues

Until recently, most studies of police corruption were based on a traditional administrative approach—one that views the problem of corruption primarily as a reflection of the moral defects of individual police officers. This research, however, is based on the organizational theory of police corruption, which emphasizes the importance of organizational and occupational culture.

Researchers asked officers in 30 U.S. police agencies for their opinions about various hypothetical cases of police misconduct, thereby avoiding the resistance that direct inquiries about corrupt behavior would likely provoke. The survey measured how seriously officers regarded police corruption, how willing they were to report it, and how willing they were to support punishment. By analyzing officers' responses to the survey questions, researchers were able to rank the police agencies according to their environments of integrity. The capacity to measure integrity in this way is especially significant for police administrators, who, this research suggests, may be able to influence and cultivate environments of integrity within their agencies.

Key Findings

Based on officers' responses to questions relating to 11 hypothetical case scenarios involving police officers engaged in a range of corrupt behavior, the following findings emerged:

- In assessing the 11 cases of police misconduct, officers considered some types to be significantly less serious than others.
- The more serious the officers perceived a behavior to be, the more likely they were to think that more severe discipline was appropriate, and the more willing they were to report a colleague who had engaged in such behavior.
- Police officers' evaluations of the appropriate and expected discipline for various types of misconduct were very similar; the majority of police officers regarded the expected discipline as fair.

Box 2-4 *(continued)*

- A majority of police officers said that they would not report a fellow officer who had engaged in what they regarded as less serious misconduct (for example, operating an off-duty security business; accepting free gifts, meals, and discounts; or having a minor accident while driving under the influence of alcohol).
- At the same time, most police officers indicated that they would report a colleague who stole from a found wallet or a burglary scene, accepted a bribe or kickback, or used excessive force on a car thief after a foot pursuit.
- The survey found substantial differences in the environment of integrity among the 30 agencies in the sample.
- Target audience: Criminal justice researchers and policy-makers, legislators, police administrators, police officers, and educators.

As the history of virtually every police agency attests, policing is an occupation that is rife with opportunities for misconduct. Policing is a highly discretionary, coercive activity that routinely takes place in private settings, out of the sight of supervisors, and in the presence of witnesses who are often regarded as unreliable. Corruption—the abuse of police authority for gain—is one type of misconduct that has been particularly problematic. The difficulties of controlling corruption can be traced to several factors: the reluctance of police officers to report corrupt activities by their fellow officers (also known as "The Code," "The Code of Silence," or "The Blue Curtain"), the reluctance of police administrators to acknowledge the existence of corruption in their agencies, the benefits of the typical corrupt transaction to the parties involved, and the lack of immediate victims willing to report corruption.

Until recently, police administrators viewed corruption primarily as a reflection of the moral defects of individual police officers. They fought corruption by carefully screening applicants for police positions and aggressively pursuing morally defective officers in an attempt to remove them from their positions before their corrupt behavior had spread through the agency. This administrative/individual approach,

(continued)

Box 2-4 *(continued)*

sometimes called the "bad apple" theory of police corruption, has been subject to severe criticism in recent years.

This Research in Brief summarizes a study that measured police integrity in 30 police agencies across the United States. The study was based on an organizational/occupational approach to police corruption. Researchers asked officers for their opinions about 11 hypothetical cases of police misconduct and measured how seriously officers regarded police corruption, how willing they were to support its punishment, and how willing they were to report it. The survey found substantial differences in the environments of integrity among the agencies studied. The more serious the officers considered a behavior to be, the more likely they were to believe that more severe discipline was appropriate, and the more willing they were to report a colleague for engaging in that behavior.

CONTEMPORARY APPROACHES TO CORRUPTION

Pioneered by Herman Goldstein,[1] contemporary theories of police corruption are based on four organizational and occupational dimensions. Each is described below.

Organizational Rules

The first dimension concerns how the organizational rules that govern corruption are established, communicated, and understood. In the United States, where police agencies are highly decentralized, police organizations differ markedly in the types of activities they officially prohibit as corrupt behavior. This is particularly true of marginally corrupt behavior, such as off-duty employment and acceptance of favors, small gifts, free meals, and discounts. Further complicating the problem, the official policy of many agencies formally prohibits such activities while their unofficial policy, supported firmly but silently by supervisors and administrators, is to permit and ignore such behavior so long as it is limited in scope and conducted discreetly.

Prevention and Control Mechanisms

The second dimension of corruption emphasized in contemporary approaches is the wide range of mechanisms that police

Box 2-4 *(continued)*

agencies employ to prevent and control corruption. Examples include education in ethics, proactive and reactive investigation of corruption, integrity testing, and corruption deterrence through the discipline of offenders. The extent to which agencies use such organizational anticorruption techniques varies greatly.

The Code

The third dimension of corruption, inherent in the occupational culture of policing, is The Code or The Blue Curtain that informally prohibits or discourages police officers from reporting the misconduct of their colleagues. The parameters of The Code—precisely what behavior it covers and to whom its benefits are extended—vary among police agencies. For example, The Code may apply to only low-level corruption in some agencies and to the most serious corruption in others. Furthermore, whom and what The Code covers can vary substantially not only among police agencies but also within police agencies. Particularly in large police agencies, the occupational culture of integrity may differ substantially among precincts, service areas, task forces, and work groups.

Public Expectations

The fourth dimension of police corruption that contemporary police theory emphasizes is the influence of the social, economic, and political environments in which police institutions, systems, and agencies operate. For example, some jurisdictions in the United States have long, virtually uninterrupted traditions of police corruption. Other jurisdictions have equally long traditions of minimal corruption, while still others have experienced repeated cycles of scandal and reform. Such histories indicate that public expectations about police integrity exert vastly different pressures on police agencies in different jurisdictions. These experiences also suggest that public pressures to confront and combat corruption may be successfully resisted.

(continued)

Box 2-4 *(continued)*

METHODOLOGICAL CHALLENGES TO THE STUDY
OF POLICE CORRUPTION

Although many theories can be applied to the study of police corruption, the contemporary organizational/occupational culture theory has an important advantage over the traditional administrative/individual bad-apple theory: The organizational/occupational approach is much more amenable to systematic, quantitative research.

Corruption is extremely difficult to study in a direct, quantitative, and empirical manner. Because most incidents of corruption are never reported or recorded, official data on corruption are best regarded as measures of a police agency's anticorruption activity, not the actual level of corruption. Even with assurances of confidentiality, police officers are unlikely to be willing to report their own or another officer's corrupt activities.

Unlike the administrative/individual approach, an organizational/occupational culture approach to the study of police integrity involves questions of fact and opinion that can be explored directly, without arousing the resistance that direct inquiries about corrupt behavior are likely to provoke. Using this approach, it is possible to ask nonthreatening questions about officers' knowledge of agency rules and their opinions about the seriousness of particular violations, the punishment that such violations would warrant or actually receive, and their estimates of how willing officers would be to report such misconduct.

Moreover, sharply different goals and visions of police integrity characterize these two approaches to understanding corruption. The administrative/individual theory of corruption envisions the police agency of integrity as one from which all morally defective individual officers have been removed and in which vigilance is maintained to prevent their entry or emergence. By contrast, the organizational/occupational culture theory envisions the police agency of integrity as one whose culture is highly intolerant of corruption.

Methodologically, the consequences of these two visions are critical. For example, although it may be possible to use an administrative/individual approach to measure the level of corrupt behavior, the number of morally defective police officers,

Box 2-4 *(continued)*

and an agency's vigilance in discovering misconduct, the obstacles to doing so are enormous. Using an organizational/occupational culture approach, by contrast, modern social science can easily measure how seriously officers regard misconduct, how amenable they are to supporting punishment, and how willing they are to tolerate misconduct in silence.

In an effort to measure the occupational culture of police integrity, a systematic, standardized, and quantitative survey questionnaire was designed and pretested. The survey sought information in key areas that constitute the foundation of an occupational/organizational culture theory of police integrity. At the same time, the survey responses could be used to satisfy certain basic informational needs of practical police administration. The survey attempted to answer the following questions:

- Do officers in this agency know the rules governing police misconduct?
- How strongly do they support those rules?
- Do officers know what disciplinary threat they face if they violate those rules?
- Do they think the discipline is fair?
- How willing are they to report misconduct?

For a more detailed description of the survey methodology and samples, see Survey Design and Methodology. The actions taken to enhance the legitimacy of the survey results are discussed in Validity of Survey Responses.

SURVEY RESULTS

The results of the survey show that the more serious a particular behavior was considered by police officers, the more severely they thought it should and would be punished, and the more willing they were to report it. The extraordinarily high rank-order correlation among the responses to the survey questions suggests that all six integrity-related questions measured the same phenomenon—the degree of police intolerance for corrupt behavior.

(continued)

Box 2-4 *(continued)*

Offense Seriousness

The 11 case scenarios fall into 3 categories of perceived serious-ness. Four cases were not considered very serious by police respondents: Case 1, off-duty operation of a security system business; Case 2, receipt of free meals; Case 4, receipt of holiday gifts; and Case 8, coverup of a police accident that involved driving under the influence of alcohol (DUI). The majority of police respondents, in fact, reported that the operation of an off-duty security system business (Case 1) was not a violation of agency policy. Respondents considered four other cases of misconduct to be at an intermediate level of seriousness: Case 10, the use of excessive force on a car thief following a foot pursuit; Case 7, a supervisor who offers a subordinate time off during holidays in exchange for tuning up his personal car; Case 9, acceptance of free drinks in exchange for ignoring a late bar closing; and Case 6, receipt of a kickback. Respondents regarded the remain-ing three cases—those that involved stealing from a found wallet (Case 11), accepting a money bribe (Case 3), and stealing a watch at a crime scene (Case 5)—as very serious offenses.

Discipline

In general, police officers thought that the four cases they regarded as not very serious warranted little or no discipline. Officers thought that the four cases involving an intermediate level of seriousness merited a written reprimand or a period of suspension, and that the three very serious cases merited dismissal.

To measure how officers perceived the fairness of disci-pline, the scores on the "discipline would receive" scale were subtracted from the scores on the "discipline should receive" scale. A difference of zero was interpreted to mean that the respondent thought the discipline was fair. If the difference was greater than zero (positive), the respondent thought that the discipline was too lenient. Conversely, if the difference was less than zero (negative), the respondent thought that the discipline was too harsh.[2] In 7 of the 11 cases, the overwhelming majority of police officers in the sample thought that the discipline that would be imposed was in the "fair" range. But in the remaining

Box 2-4 *(continued)*

four cases, including three that officers considered not serious—Case 2 (accepting free meals and discounts on the beat), Case 4 (accepting holiday gifts), Case 8 (coverup of police DUI), and Case 10 (excessive force on car thief)—more than 20 percent of police officers believed that the discipline administered by their agencies would be too harsh.

Parameters of The Code

An examination of the parameters of The Code of Silence, as revealed in the responses of police officers in the sample, indicated that the majority would not report a police colleague who had engaged in behavior described in the four scenarios considered the least serious. At the same time, a majority indicated that they would report[3] a fellow police officer who had engaged in behavior they deemed to be at an intermediate or high level of seriousness.

AGENCY CONTRASTS IN THE CULTURE OF INTEGRITY

Measurements of the inclination of U.S. police to resist temptations to abuse the rights and privileges of their occupation are likely to prove useful for academic, historical, and cross-cultural studies of police.[4] For police administrators, however, measurements of the culture of integrity of individual police agencies are more relevant than national averages, which often mask significant differences among agencies.

To uncover these differences and allow comparisons to be made, a system was devised for ranking the responses of officers in each agency. To determine an agency's overall ranking on how its officers perceived the seriousness of a particular offense, the mean score of all responses by officers in that agency to each of the 11 case scenarios was compared to the mean scores of the remaining 29 agencies. The agency was then awarded 3 points if its mean score placed it among the top 10 agencies on any question, 2 points if it scored in the middle 10, and 1 point if it scored among the lowest 10. These scores were then totaled for all 11 case scenarios. Using this scaling system, an agency's score on its officers' perceptions of the seriousness of the offenses could

(continued)

Box 2-4 *(continued)*

range from 11 (if it ranked in the lowest third of agencies on all 11 cases) to 33 (if it ranked among the highest third of agencies on all 11 cases).[5]

These summary scores formed the basis for placing agencies in rank order from 1 to 30 (with 1 being the highest integrity rating), making it possible to say that an agency ranked "n out of 30" in its officers' perceptions of offense seriousness. This procedure was used to calculate a summary score and an integrity ranking for each agency's responses to each of the six questions about offense seriousness, discipline that should and would be received, and willingness to report the offense.

The Environment of Integrity in Two Agencies

To illustrate how environments of integrity differ across U.S. police agencies, it is useful to contrast the responses of officers from two of the agencies in the sample. Agency 2, which ranked 8th in integrity of the 30 agencies surveyed, and Agency 23, which ranked in a 5-way tie for 24th place, are both large municipal police agencies. Agency 2 has a national reputation for integrity, is extremely receptive to research, and is often promoted as a model of innovation. Agency 23 has a long history of scandal, and its reputation as an agency with corruption problems persists despite numerous reform efforts. Although a local newspaper once dubbed Agency 23 "the most corrupt police department in the country," six other agencies in the sample appear to have integrity environments that are as poor or worse.

In both agencies, the correlation of the scores' rank ordering among the categories was very high, as it was for all 30 agencies surveyed. For every agency, the mean rank order of officers' responses to the six integrity-related questions was nearly identical. Furthermore, the rank ordering of the scenarios differed little among the agencies.

Although differences in the rank ordering of the scenarios were minimal, both within and between the two agencies, discrepancies in the agencies' absolute scores reflected significant differences. Estimates of offense seriousness were consistently higher for Agency 2 than for Agency 23. The differences were especially large (between 0.5 and 1.0 on a 5-point scale) for three

Box 2-4 *(continued)*

scenarios: Case 6 (auto repair shop kickback), Case 9 (drinks to ignore late bar closing), and Case 10 (excessive force on car thief). Police officers from Agency 2 evaluated each of these cases as substantially more serious than did officers from Agency 23.

The mean scores for discipline indicate that, in almost every case, police officers in Agency 2 not only expected more severe discipline than did officers in Agency 23, but they also thought that more severe discipline was appropriate. The differences in perceptions of discipline were especially great for the most serious types of corruption, such as the scenarios described in Case 3 (bribe from speeding motorist), Case 5 (crime scene theft of watch), and Case 11 (theft from found wallet), as well as for Case 10 (use of excessive force). While officers in Agency 2 thought that dismissal would result from the four most serious cases, officers in Agency 23 expected that dismissal would follow only one scenario, Case 5 (theft from a crime scene).

The most systematic and dramatic difference between Agencies 2 and 23, however, is evident in their attitudes toward The Code of Silence. In both agencies, few officers said that they or their police colleagues would report any of the least serious types of corrupt behavior (Cases 1, 2, 4, and 8). Officers from Agency 2 reported that they and their colleagues would report the behavior described in the seven other cases. In Agency 23, however, there was no case that the majority of officers indicated they would report. In sum, while The Code is under control in Agency 2, it remains a powerful influence in Agency 23, providing an environment in which corrupt behavior can flourish.

CONCLUSIONS AND IMPLICATIONS

Redefining the problem of police corruption (i.e., the abuse of police authority for gain) as a problem of police integrity—the normative inclination among police to resist temptations to abuse their authority—enables the direct measurement of the major propositions of an organizational/occupational theory of police integrity. The research reported in this Research in Brief demonstrates that police attitudes toward the seriousness of misconduct, the discipline that should and would result, and the

(continued)

Box 2-4 *(continued)*

willingness of officers to tolerate misconduct in silence can be measured. Moreover, the measurements reported in this national sample are relatively easy to collect. At the same time, they demonstrate substantial differences in the environments of integrity in U.S. police agencies.

The ability to measure environments of integrity in police agencies holds great potential for academic studies of police and for practical police administration. For researchers, quantitative cross-cultural, historical, and national comparisons that were previously unthinkable have now become feasible.

Equally important, such measurements have direct implications for practical police administration because each of the propositions of an organizational/occupational theory of integrity implies a specific administrative response. If officers do not know whether certain conduct violates agency policy or what disciplinary threats the agency makes, administrators have a clear responsibility to communicate this information to officers. If officers do not regard certain misconduct as sufficiently serious, if they regard discipline as too severe or too lenient, or if they are willing to tolerate the misconduct of their police peers in silence, administrators have an obvious obligation to find out why. A police administrator can take specific actions to deal with each of these problems.

The survey instrument used in this study was designed to assess only one aspect of police integrity. In all case scenarios but one—the use of excessive force—the misconduct described was motivated by personal gain. In discussing environments of integrity, therefore, this survey makes no observation about abuses of discretion in arrests, order maintenance, discourtesy to citizens, or other police misconduct not usually motivated by temptations of gain. A second generation of this survey will explore those problems.[6]

A FINAL NOTE

This survey does not measure the extent of corruption in any police agency or institution. Rather, it measures the culture of police integrity—the normative inclination of police officers to resist the temptations to abuse the rights and privileges of their

Box 2-4 *(continued)*

office. The survey does not identify either corrupt or honest police officers; nor does it provide any evidence of abusive or dishonest practices—past, present, or future. The survey findings do describe, in a fairly precise way, the characteristics of a police agency's culture that encourage its employees to resist or tolerate certain types of misconduct.

Notes:

1. Herman Goldstein, *Police Corruption: Perspective on Its Nature and Control* (Washington, DC: Police Foundation, 1975); and H. Goldstein, *Policing a Free Society* (Cambridge, MA: Ballinger, 1977). See also Lawrence W. Sherman, *Scandal and Reform* (Berkeley: University of California Press, 1978); Gary Marx, *Surveillance* (Cambridge, MA: Harvard University Press, 1991); Maurice Punch, *Conduct Unbecoming: The Social Construction of Police Deviance and Control* (London: Tavistock, 1986); and Peter K. Manning and Lawrence Redlinger, "The Invitational Edges of Police Corruption," in *Thinking About Police*, edited by Carl Klockars and Stephen Mastrofski (New York: McGraw-Hill, 1993) pp. 398–412.

2. Note that the notions of "greater than zero (positive)" and "less than zero (negative)" are merely shorthand for discipline perceived as too lenient and too harsh, respectively. In other words, because the data are ordinal, positive or negative differences will not be used in any algebraic context. Rather, these differences will be used solely as indicators to classify respondents into three groups—those who perceive discipline to be fair, too lenient, or too harsh.

3. The frequency distribution of responses to the question about officers' own willingness to report a particular offense was analyzed. The five-point scale of offered answers ranged from 1 = "definitely not" to 5 = "definitely yes." A cumulative frequency above 50 percent for 1 and 2 was interpreted to indicate that police officers would not report the offense. A cumulative frequency above 50 percent for 4 and 5, on the other hand, was interpreted to indicate that the police officers would report the offense.

4. See, for example, Maria Haberfeld, Carl Klockars, Sanja Kutnjak Ivkovich, and Milan Pagon, "Disciplinary Consequences of Police Corruption in Croatia, Poland, Slovenia, and the United States," *Police Practice and Research, An International Journal* 1 (2000): 41–72.

5. An alternative summary ranking system could, of course, be based on the full range of 30-point rankings for each of the 11 scenarios. This type of system would create a scale that could range from 330 (for an agency that scored the lowest of the 30 agencies on all 6 questions for all 11 scenarios) to 1,980 (for an agency that scored the highest of all 30 agencies on all 6 questions for all 11 scenarios). Such a scoring system would, however,

(continued)

Box 2-4 *(continued)*

magnify small and primarily meaningless differences in mean scores, creating a false sense of precision. The ranking system developed for and employed in this research intentionally seeks to blunt any false sense of precision by allowing agencies to score, in a sense, only "high," "middle," or "low" on any given question.

6. A summary of the status of progress with this next generation of measures of police integrity can be found on the videotape of the Research in Progress seminar "Measuring Police Integrity," presented by Carl Klockars at the National Institute of Justice in January 1999. Copies are available through the National Criminal Justice Reference Service at 800–851–3420. Please refer to NCJ 174459.

SURVEY DESIGN AND METHODOLOGY

Case scenarios

The survey questionnaire presented officers with 11 hypothetical case scenarios. Displayed in exhibit A, the scenarios cover a range of activities, from those that merely give an appearance of conflict of interest (Case 1) to incidents of bribery (Case 3) and theft (Cases 5 and 11). One scenario (Case 10) described the use of excessive force on a car thief.

Respondents were asked to evaluate each scenario by answering seven questions (see exhibit B). Six of these questions were designed to assess the normative inclination of police to resist temptations to abuse the rights and privileges of their occupation. To measure this dimension of police integrity, the six questions were paired as follows:

Two questions pertained to the seriousness of each case— one addressed the respondent's own view and the other concerned the respondent's perception of the views of other officers.

Two related to severity of discipline—one addressed the discipline the respondent felt the behavior should receive and the other addressed the discipline the officer felt it would receive.

Two concerned willingness to report the misconduct—one addressed the respondent's own willingness to report it, and the other concerned the respondent's perception of other officers' willingness to report it.

Box 2-4 *(continued)*

The remaining question asked respondents whether the behavior described in the scenario was a violation of the agency's official policy.

The incidents described in the scenarios were not only plausible and common forms of police misconduct, but ones that were uncomplicated by details that might introduce ambiguity into either the interpretation of the behavior or the motive of the officer depicted in the scenario. Some scenarios were based on published studies that had employed a case scenario approach. Others drew on the experience of the authors. Respondents were asked to assume that the officer depicted in each scenario had been a police officer for 5 years and had a satisfactory work record with no history of disciplinary problems.

Survey sample. The sample consisted of 3,235 officers from 30 U.S. police agencies. Although these agencies were drawn from across the Nation and the sample was quite large, it was nonetheless a convenience sample, not a representative sample. The majority of the police officers surveyed were employed in patrol or traffic units (63.1 percent). The overwhelming majority of respondents were line officers; only one of five police officers was a supervisor. The mean length of service for the entire sample was 10.3 years.

The sample has some biases, including overrepresentation of particular types of police agencies and particular regions of the country. Because it includes no State police agencies, only one sheriff's agency, and only one county police agency, the sample overrepresents municipal police agencies. The sample also overrepresents police agencies from the Northeast. Although the sample does include agencies from the South, Southeast, and Southwest, it does not include agencies from the West, Northwest, or Midwest.

The sample likely has another bias because not all agencies that were asked to participate in the study accepted the invitation. The reason for an agency's refusal to participate could include a fear of revealing something untoward. Agencies declined to participate despite assurances that their participation in the survey would be kept confidential; that all individual

(continued)

Box 2-4 *(continued)*

respondents would remain anonymous; and that respondents would be asked about only their opinions, not any actual misconduct.

Nevertheless, the sample includes some seriously troubled police agencies. Key contacts in a number of such agencies, including senior officers and high-ranking union officials, exercised sufficient influence to arrange the participation of these agencies in the survey.

A number of studies of police corruption have employed a research strategy that asked police officers to evaluate hypothetical corruption scenarios. These include Janet E. Fishman, *Measuring Police Corruption* (New York: John Jay College of Criminal Justice, 1978); Christine Martin, *Illinois Municipal Officers' Perceptions of Police Ethics* (Chicago: Illinois Criminal Justice Information Authority, 1994); Gail F. Huon, Beryl L. Hesketh, Mark G. Frank, Kevin M. McConkey, and G. M. McGrath, *Perceptions of Ethical Dilemmas* (Payneham, Australia: National Police Research Unit, 1995); and Larry S. Miller and Michael C. Braswell, "Police Perceptions of Ethical Decision-Making: The Ideal vs. the Real," *American Journal of Police* 27 (1992): 27–45.

Exhibit A: Case scenarios

Case 1. A police officer runs his own private business in which he sells and installs security devices, such as alarms, special locks, etc. He does this work during his off-duty hours.

Case 2. A police officer routinely accepts free meals, cigarettes, and other items of small value from merchants on his beat. He does not solicit these gifts and is careful not to abuse the generosity of those who give gifts to him.

Case 3. A police officer stops a motorist for speeding. The officer agrees to accept a personal gift of half of the amount of the fine in exchange for not issuing a citation.

Case 4. A police officer is widely liked in the community, and on holidays local merchants and restaurant and bar owners

Box 2-4 *(continued)*

show their appreciation for his attention by giving him gifts of food and liquor.

Case 5. A police officer discovers a burglary of a jewelry shop. The display cases are smashed, and it is obvious that many items have been taken. While searching the shop, he takes a watch, worth about 2 days' pay for that officer. He reports that the watch had been stolen during the burglary.

Case 6. A police officer has a private arrangement with a local auto body shop to refer the owners of cars damaged in accidents to the shop. In exchange for each referral, he receives payment of 5 percent of the repair bill from the shop owner.

Case 7. A police officer, who happens to be a very good auto mechanic, is scheduled to work during coming holidays. A supervisor offers to give him these days off, if he agrees to tune up his supervisor's personal car. Evaluate the supervisor's behavior.

Case 8. At 2:00 a.m., a police officer, who is on duty, is driving his patrol car on a deserted road. He sees a vehicle that has been driven off the road and is stuck in a ditch. He approaches the vehicle and observes that the driver is not hurt but is obviously intoxicated. He also finds that the driver is a police officer. Instead of reporting this accident and offense, he transports the driver to his home.

Case 9. A police officer finds a bar on his beat that is still serving drinks a half-hour past its legal closing time. Instead of reporting this violation, the police officer agrees to accept a couple of free drinks from the owner.

Case 10. Two police officers on foot patrol surprise a man who is attempting to break into an automobile. The man flees. They chase him for about two blocks before apprehending him by tackling him and wrestling him to the ground. After he is under control, both officers punch him a couple of times in the stomach as punishment for fleeing and resisting.

(continued)

Box 2-4 *(continued)*

Case 11. A police officer finds a wallet in a parking lot. It contains an amount of money equivalent to a full day's pay for that officer. He reports the wallet as lost property but keeps the money for himself.

Exhibit B: Case Scenario Assessment Options

1. How serious do YOU consider this behavior to be?
   —1 (Not at all serious)
   —2
   —3
   —4
   —5 (Very serious)

2. How serious do MOST POLICE OFFICERS IN YOUR AGENCY consider this behavior to be?
   —1 (Not at all serious)
   —2
   —3
   —4
   —5 (Very serious)

3. Would this behavior be regarded as a violation of official policy in your agency?
   —1 (Definitely not)
   —2
   —3
   —4
   —5 (Definitely yes)

4. If an officer in your agency engaged in this behavior and was discovered doing so, what if any discipline do YOU think SHOULD follow?
   —1 None
   —2 Verbal reprimand
   —3 Written reprimand
   —4 Period of suspension without pay
   —5 Demotion in rank
   —6 Dismissal

5. If an officer in your agency engaged in this behavior and was discovered doing so, what if any discipline do YOU think WOULD follow?

Box 2-4 *(continued)*

—1 None
—2 Verbal reprimand
—3 Written reprimand
—4 Period of suspension without pay
—5 Demotion in rank
—6 Dismissal

6. Do you think YOU would report a fellow police officer who engaged in this behavior?
—1 (Definitely not)
—2
—3
—4
—5 (Definitely yes)

7. Do you think MOST POLICE OFFICERS IN YOUR AGENCY would report a fellow police officer who engaged in this behavior?
—1 (Definitely not)
—2
—3
—4
—5 (Definitely yes)

Validity of Survey Responses

The validity of the survey's results hinges on the honesty of police officers when responding to the survey questions. Several steps were taken to enhance the legitimacy of the survey results. First, officers were asked only about their attitudes, not about their actual behavior or the actual behavior of other police officers. They also were assured that their responses would remain confidential, although police respondents are naturally suspicious of such promises.

To further allay officers' fears that their identities might be discovered, they were asked only minimal background questions: their rank, length of service, and assignment and whether they held a supervisory position. They were not asked standard questions about age, race, gender, or ethnicity in an effort to assuage fears that disclosing such information, in combination

(continued)

Box 2-4 *(continued)*

with their rank, assignment, and length of service, would make it possible to identify them.

In addition, at the end of the survey, each police respondent was asked two questions about the validity of the responses. The first was "Do you think most police officers would give their honest opinion in filling out this questionnaire?" The second was "Did you?" In answer to the first question, 84.4 percent of police respondents reported that they thought most officers would answer the questions honestly, and 97.8 percent reported that they themselves had done so. The responses of the 2.2 percent of police officers who reported that they had not answered the questions honestly were discarded when the survey results were analyzed.

The survey questions also were designed to minimize any temptation for officers to manipulate responses to create a favorable impression on the public or on their supervisors. Some officers, for example, might have been inclined to report that certain types of misconduct were more serious than they actually thought them to be. At the same time, however, these officers would be unlikely to report that misconduct should be punished more severely than they thought appropriate because of the possibility that they might one day be subject to such discipline, if administrators believed that they were recommending it.

Furthermore, if any substantial manipulation of answers had occurred, it would have been evident in differences in correlation coefficients among the questions about seriousness, discipline, and willingness to report. In fact, the rank order correlation between all six questions is extraordinarily high. Indeed, one could predict with great accuracy the ranking of a scenario on any one of the six questions by knowing the ranking for any other.

Sources:
Carl B. Klockars, Sanja Kutnjak Ivkovich, William E. Harver, and Maria R. Haberfeld, *The Measurement of Police Integrity* (Washington, DC: National Institute of Justice, 2000).

Carl B. Klockars, Ph.D., is professor in the Department of Sociology and Criminal Justice at the University of Delaware. Sanja Kutnjak Ivkovich, Ph.D., is a doctoral student at Harvard Law School. William E. Harver, Ph.D., is assistant professor of social science in the College of Arts and Sciences.

Box 2-4 *(continued)*

at Widener University. Maria R. Haberfeld, Ph.D., is assistant professor in the Department of Law, Police Science, and Criminal Justice Administration at the John Jay College of Criminal Justice, City University of New York. The study reported in this Research in Brief was supported by the Office of Community Oriented Policing Services and NIJ through NIJ grant number 95-IJ-CX-0058.

RESPONSIBILITIES

Law enforcement cannot be a profession unless its members have a strong sense of obligation to their responsibilities. Officers must accept the fact that their responsibilities extend far beyond the specific orders given by supervisors. All actions reflect dedication to ethical principles that transcends specific assignments. Only a deep, abiding commitment to integrity carries people through the rough times that are inevitable in a police career.

People all have basic desires, and they all have responsibilities as well. They should be aware of their own strengths and weaknesses and know that it is possible to remain honest and succeed in a world that is often riddled with dishonesty. They need to have a healthy self-esteem and believe in themselves. Although stealing and lying will "reward" for a moment, they create "losers" and short-lived success.

Community Leaders and Role Models

Corporations must comply with high standards of self-imposed responsibility, standards based on the understanding that the trust customers have in them cannot be betrayed. This responsibility includes integrity in leadership. The standard for policing must be even higher than that for corporations.

Law enforcement is generally recognized as vital to every community. Officers, of course, have the same duties to their community as all citizens: to pay taxes, vote, participate in community activities, serve on juries, and live as civic-minded members of the local area. To fulfill their duties, police comply with a high standard of self-imposed responsibility.

Officers must accept their responsibility to provide leadership within their communities. They are perceived to be natural role models. When someone has a problem, needs advice, or seeks assistance, they are often sought, even when off duty. This is very similar to the way a clergy member is sought for advice and help—it is a role that cannot be ignored or taken lightly.

Member of Fellowship

True professionals realize they owe a sincere, dedicated, and loyal commitment to their profession. Regardless of title, assignment, or seniority, every sincere person is a member of an everlasting fellowship of integrity.

To promote professionalism is never corny or outdated. In fact, few feelings are more satisfying than giving your best effort for a worthy cause.

Relationship with Citizens

When veteran officers think back to when they were rookies they'll probably recall the main reason they wanted to be an officer was to help others. Law enforcement has been and always will be the profession that people call on most often when they really need help. Even people who would not hesitate to curse at officers scream and shout for their help when in serious trouble. All officers have an obligation to give every citizen the same level of professional help. These moments can determine if officers have what it takes to be true professionals.

It's easy to understand why some officers become hardened and cynical after several years of "working the street"; they can lose sight of the fact that most people are still decent individuals. However, they often meet good people who are going through one of their worst moments: after an emotional car accident; at their home during a rare family fight; or as a victim of theft, burglary, or assault and not in a particularly good mood. Times of tragedy are sometimes the only occasions people meet an officer or deputy.

Most professions have established terms that explain the relationship between the professional and their "client." Relationships of physician/patient, lawyer/client, and teacher/pupil are logical and easily understood. In these situations confidence and trust exist and a bond of respect is directed toward the people providing the assistance and guidance.

Similarly, trust, sincerity, and confidence can be built between citizens and law enforcement agencies. This is the basis for community-oriented policing. Every police department has a responsibility to the citizens it serves, without exceptions. Honesty, integrity, and respect should be the basis of leadership for all leaders.

Most citizens form an opinion of their local law enforcement agency based on one or two isolated incidents with individual officers. Frequently, individuals' respect or lack of respect stems from incidents that occurred years ago in other communities.

TEMPTATIONS

At one time or another during their careers, all officers face situations that test their character. There is no place in law enforcement for weak character—and a few are so weak that they engage in major thefts, drug dealings, or bribery—and one bad officer is one too many.

Common, everyday situations present choices between right and wrong and offer temptations that are strong enough that some officers try to justify doing something that they know is wrong. The following paragraphs provide insight and guidance for surviving such difficult situations.

Gratuities

A gratuity is something given voluntarily in return for or in anticipation of a favor or service. Based on this definition, few officers would agree that it is right to take a gift knowing the giver expects a "professional favor." However, it is sometimes difficult to determine whether the giver expects something in return. Many people who give gratuities state that they want nothing in return but in reality expect special treatment regarding police services.

There is a big difference between receiving a free cup of coffee from a restaurant and accepting a free set of tires from a local car dealer. Some officers recognize the term "open account" as another way of saying "payoff." Officers who tell merchants to put merchandise or services on their accounts rarely have intentions of paying for them—they really should not be cops.

It is difficult to be certain what people are thinking when they give gratuities. The only way to be certain that citizens expect no special treatment or favors in return for police services is to not accept gratuities to begin with. This may not be as easy as it sounds if you work within a department in which officers routinely take gratuities. Do not give in to peer pressure; stand up for what you know is right.

Perjury

Is it ever ethical for an officer to lie? In many instances deception is justified. Common examples include decoy cops, undercover investigations, and surveillance. In these situations deception is justifiable. In other circumstances it is not, as explained in the following paragraphs.

Can police commit crimes or infractions in order to further law enforcement? Yes, such as when officers speed to catch a speeding traffic violator. Unfortunately, though, some officers commit more serious infractions by claiming the end justifies the means. For example, an officer may exaggerate an incident to establish probable cause for an arrest. A detective may distort circumstances of violations so that he'll have a high clearance rate. A motorcycle officer may intentionally change details of traffic citations in order to issue a certain number during the month.

It is not always easy, but we should all have the courage to stand up for what is fair, right, and honest—it takes a lot of guts. The fact is, once cops distort the truth for any self-serving reason, they lose self-respect. Lying becomes easier with time, and soon intentionally forgetting details or exaggerating facts may be part of sworn testimony during depositions or trial. Such cops do not honor their sworn oath or their badge.

Ticket Fixing

The fixing of tickets has been practiced for decades. It generally means doing something that permits a traffic offender to escape lawful process, usually canceling a ticket. Sometimes friends ask officers to fix tickets or motorists offer gratuities to officers to reduce or cancel traffic offenses. At other times officers are requested by someone in the department to fix tickets in order to take care of influential or wealthy citizens who have committed offenses.

It is wrong for anyone to be above the law because of wealth or contacts. Law enforcement has a long way to go to overcome the stigma of ticket fixing.

Blind Loyalty, Code of Silence

At the moment a rookie is sworn in, the bond of fellowship begins. Initially, all veteran officers are role models for rookies. New officers look to them for approval, advice, and guidance, and often friendships form. Camaraderie and esprit de corps are stronger than in most occupations.

As the years go by, the phrase "taking care of your own" assumes a special meaning. Cops on the street watch out for each other. They have to be able to trust each other as partners. Loyalty to each other is crucial, and it would be difficult to survive without it.

Bad cops think other officers will not speak up about their corruption. They do not care about law enforcement or fellow officers—only themselves. We know that there are 700,000 officers in the nation. Only about three hundred are decertified each year, less than half of one percent. Perhaps most professions cannot boast of such low numbers. Your job in protecting yourself and the profession is to inform superiors when officers steal or commit perjury. To keep silent would end your career.

Remember, if you are going to be an officer and good or even great at what you do, have the guts to stand up for what is right. Remain loyal to the principles for which other cops have died. Officers whose weak character allows them to become dishonest and deceitful have no place on the force.

Internal Politics

Disenchantment and a lack of comradeship are common within departments in which people place blame or become defensive when things go wrong. Yet it is virtually impossible to develop a strong, healthy character without passing through and learning from difficult times. Learn from difficult situations, correct whatever caused them to happen, and move on to better times. Remember, those who blame others often are to blame themselves.

To develop and maintain a good public image takes a never-ending effort. No agency can afford the time and effort spent bickering and fighting among its own people—far too many problems exist on the street that must be taken care of.

Defending the Badge

America is starting to undergo a rebirth of concern for ethics and integrity, especially in law enforcement. Wall Street insider trading scandals, Iran-Contra, impeachments, Watergate, sex scandals in the White House, and the arrest of public officials have generated attention to dishonest and unethical practices. Fortunately, even the business world has realized that conscious ethical training has a new tone of morality.

The business community has found that the effort is both worthwhile and efficient. As an example, the 1999 CEO of the Year, Herb Kelleran of Southwest Airlines, says that his leadership philosophy is simple: treat all people with dignity and respect and follow the Golden Rule, and you will be repaid a thousand times over.[9]

The struggle against ethical abuse is ongoing. Keep in mind that a single act of corruption can destroy the reputation of an entire department for decades. In order to gain the respect of those you serve, make a commitment to be an ethical, conscientious cop.

Life isn't always fair. There will be hard times in both your personal and professional lives. It's all part of being human. Accepting disappointment as merely a temporary setback in a long line of accomplishments will allow you to have a much more satisfying, richer life.

No one can control everything that is going to happen on the street, in your community, or in your own department. You can, however, control yourself; for example:

- Make the most of yourself rather than spending time trying to blame or change others.
- Live for the future rather than spending time regretting or living in the past.
- Strive to become the best person you can be rather than developing a habit of criticizing others.
- Discover your own shortcomings and improve yourself rather than becoming a burden by nagging or arguing.
- Allow other individuals to be human and in control of their own destinies.
- Do not judge others.

Pride, loyalty, and high ethical standards are honorable. Likewise, integrity and professionalism ingrained throughout an agency cause the entire organization to develop a healthy, positive tone. Camaraderie between officers will reinforce the conviction that protects the badge and the force from corruption. Law enforcement and every cop in America have respect to earn and a reputation to protect.

Another area in which the police sometimes fall short of their stated principles is in their use of force. A study regarding the use of force by police is presented in Box 2-5.

There do not appear to be any empirically validated research studies which support the assertion that race, ethnicity, gender, or age of police officers are related to misuse of physical or deadly force.[10]

New York State Commission on Criminal Justice and the Use of Force, Report to the Governor

Box 2-5
Excessive Use of Force

This is one of six sections contained within the Research Report titled Use of Force By Police: Overview of National and Local Data By Kenneth Adams, Geoffrey P. Alpert, Roger G. Dunham, Joel H. Garner, Lawrence A. Greenfeld, Mark A. Henriquez, Patrick A. Langan, Christopher D. Maxwell, and Steven K. Smith, National Institute of Justice and Bureau of Justice Statistics, October 1999, Research Report, Jointly published with the Bureau of Justice Statistics.

Acknowledgments
The authors are indebted to many individuals and organizations for their valuable assistance and insights. Special thanks are extended to the law enforcement agencies that cooperated with the researchers whose findings appear in this report. In so doing, the following agencies demonstrated the type of leadership so critical to the advancement of policing practice and policy: Charlotte-Mecklenburg (North Carolina) Police Department, Colorado Springs (Colorado)

(continued)

Box 2-5 (continued)

Police Department, Dallas (Texas) Police Department, Eugene (Oregon) Police Department, Miami-Dade (Florida) Police Department, St. Petersburg (Florida) Police Department, San Diego (California) Police Department, San Diego County (California) Sheriff's Department, Springfield (Oregon) Police Department, and the many departments that have participated in the use-of-force database project of the International Association of Chiefs of Police. Points of view expressed by contributors to this report do not necessarily represent the official positions or policies of the U.S. Department of Justice.

The National Institute of Justice and the Bureau of Justice Statistics are components of the Office of Justice Programs, which also includes the Bureau of Justice Assistance, the Office of Juvenile Justice and Delinquency Prevention, and the Office for Victims of Crime.

Collecting and interpreting information on police use of force is a persistent problem for police managers and researchers. Although such data are critical to both the police and the public, they remain difficult to collect, measure, and interpret objectively. There has been an energetic effort to collect data on all police use-of-force incidents, including excessive force, by various groups and by assorted methods.[1] The problems with data collection on such organizationally sensitive and controversial acts suggest the need for standardizing measurement and providing reliable and valid measures.[2]

This chapter presents information collected from the police departments of the sister cities of Eugene and Springfield, Oregon, and the Miami-Dade Police Department. After a brief description of the sites and a presentation of their use-of-force information, the concept of the "force factor," which is a measure of police force incorporating the officers' actions relative to the suspects' physical resistance, is developed.

Description of the Sites

Eugene and Springfield, Oregon, are located in the Willamette valley, cover 52 square miles, and had a combined population of 178,000 in April 1995, when the data were collected. The two

Box 2-5 *(continued)*

police departments had 204 officers, 110 of whom were assigned to patrol duties. The departments had 150,841 contacts with the public, 7 complaints of excessive force, 31 complaints of discourtesy, and 2 lawsuits during 1995.

The Miami-Dade Police Department (MDPD), located in Dade County, Florida, is responsible for all law enforcement activities in the unincorporated areas of the county. (It was formerly known as the Dade County Sheriff's Department and Metro-Dade Police Department.) In addition, MDPD contracts with many municipal agencies in Dade County to perform specialized services within those agencies' jurisdictions. In 1995, the unincorporated areas of Dade County had a population of approximately 2 million, and the county included 1,840 square miles. The Department had 2,725 sworn officers, 845 of whom were assigned to patrol. There were more than 1 million reported contacts (arrests and nonarrests) during the 3-year study period (fourth quarter 1993 through 1995), of which 133 resulted in complaints of excessive force, 243 in complaints of discourtesy, and 18 in lawsuits.

These police departments differ on important characteristics. There are obvious geographic and size differences that make the findings relevant to a wide audience. Further, differences in the social and ethnic environments of the cities studied provide diverse contexts in which to analyze police use of force. Unfortunately, different data elements were collected from the sites, which make some comparisons problematic.

EUGENE AND SPRINGFIELD POLICE DEPARTMENTS

The Eugene and Springfield dataset was created from items in the Police Officers' Essential Physical Work Report Form, which was completed by department members during April 1995. These data are unique because they include a broad range of police work but were not collected to evaluate force used by the police. This dataset was part of a larger effort to identify physical abilities necessary for police work. Data included all police-public contacts, including those related to forceful encounters. As a result, an unobtrusive measure of police use of force was available.

(continued)

Box 2-5 *(continued)*

The findings from the Eugene and Springfield Police Departments are reported in the following order:

Circumstances surrounding the incidents.
Suspects' characteristics and actions.
Officers' characteristics and actions.

Most of the 562 police actions analyzed were initiated by dispatched calls (57 percent), although 33 percent of the incidents were initiated by the officer who observed a situation and reacted to it.

Circumstances Surrounding the Contacts

The most common type of incident was street violence (25 percent). However, 14 percent of all incidents involved domestic violence, and another 14 percent pertained to resisting an investigation. Thirty-two percent of incidents did not fall into one of the predefined categories. Most of the police action was taken to apprehend or control a person (76 percent).

Suspect Characteristics and Behavior

Suspects ranged in age from 12 years to 86 years. The average age of suspects was between 28 and 29. Eighty-four percent of the suspects were males. Although no ethnic information about suspects was collected on the agency form, there were very few minorities. Fifty-two percent of suspects were calm, reasonable, and cooperative. However, 19 percent were reported as under the influence of drugs or alcohol and 17 percent as emotionally upset or abusive. Eleven percent of suspects appeared mentally unstable and unpredictable, and 2 percent were violent. Most suspects were perceived by officers to be average (55 percent) or below average (20 percent) in physical abilities. The majority of suspects did not resist the officer (61 percent); 18 percent put up only slight resistance. Four percent were characterized as having a high level of resistance, 2 percent as violent, and 1 percent as explosive. The most common type of resistance was to push or pull the officer to resist an arrest or to escape.

Box 2-5 *(continued)*

Officer Characteristics and Behavior

The ages of the officers ranged from 25 to 60, with a mean of 37 years. Length of service as an officer ranged from 9 months to nearly 34 years. Average length of service was 12 years. Eighty-six percent of the officers were males. Most officers were assigned to patrol (91 percent).

CONTROL TACTICS RANKED BY SEVERITY

At least two verbal or physical control tactics were used per attempt to apprehend a suspect. Of the 546 incidents covered by the exhibit,

- All involved at least one tactic (96 percent being verbal);
- 93 percent, two tactics; and
- 87 percent, three.
- There is a fairly large percentage drop for incidents involving use of a fourth tactic (41 percent). Use of a fifth (8 percent of incidents) or sixth (5 percent) tactic was relatively uncommon.

Use of Multiple Tactics and How They Fall on a Use-of-Force Continuum

When an incident involves at least one tactic type, the tactic listed as the first used is almost always the lowest level of force: a verbal command (used in 96 percent of incidents). Three percent of such incidents involved handcuffing as the first tactic used, also at the low end of the continuum of force. Very few of such incidents involved higher levels of force as the first tactic used.

When incidents involved at least two tactic types, the second did not include verbal commands, in contrast to 94 percent of the incidents involving handcuffing the suspect. Searching the suspect occurred in 4 percent of the incidents; few involved force more severe than a search as a second tactic.

For incidents entailing three tactic types, no officers listed verbal commands or handcuffing as the third used. Most listed searching the suspect (95 percent of the incidents); about 4 percent of the incidents involved a wrist or arm lock as the third

(continued)

Box 2-5 *(continued)*

tactic, which is the next level of force on the continuum; and very few incidents were recorded as involving force levels further down the continuum.

The pattern that emerges follows the traditional use-of-force continuum.

- The first tactic used in an incident is nearly always the least severe use of force on the continuum.
- The second tactic used in an incident is nearly always the second-most lenient.
- Officers apparently follow the continuum with very few exceptions, and those exceptions seem to deviate by only a small degree in relation to the whole range.

This same pattern seems to pertain to those incidents involving use of a fourth tactic by officers. None listed the first three levels of force.

- In 82 percent of four-tactic incidents, officers listed use of wrist or arm lock techniques (fourth level on the continuum) as the fourth tactic used.
- In 11 percent of incidents with four tactics, officers listed takedowns, which constitute the next degree of force on the continuum.
- The exception at the fourth-tactic stage is firearm use (4 percent of such incidents).
- Apparently, continuum adherence breaks down more often in incidents when four types of force are necessary. This becomes even more apparent in situations when five or six types of force are used by the officer. In these situations, the use of force is more scattered and distributed along the more severe end of the continuum.

Findings indicate that officers used multiple force tactics most of the time, usually two tactics, three tactics in 87 percent of the incidents, and four in about 40 percent. In these instances, officers also seem to follow a typical continuum of force, with minor deviations that do not vary by more than one or two levels on the continuum. However, in the few instances when more than

Box 2-5 *(continued)*

four force tactics per incident are used, they are scattered over the more extreme end of the force continuum.

Although we can infer a probable order of tactics from the data, a temporal sequence is not clear in all cases. Future research should focus on this sequential ordering of officers' use of multiple force tactics and the concurrent level of suspect resistance. A well-conducted interaction model could contribute to understanding police/suspect interactions in these dangerous situations.

Control Tactics Used With Varying Amounts of Suspect Resistance

The purpose of this analysis was to determine how many officers followed the typical continuum of force for a given level of suspect resistance. The continuum of force reflects an escalation from verbal commands to deadly force. Nearly 97 percent of the incidents involved initial use of a verbal command when the suspect offered no resistance. Deviating from this typical process of verbally directing the suspect increased when suspect resistance was moderate or high (13 percent of all suspects) and violent or explosive (12 percent). Three percent of officers deviated from first handcuffing the suspect during the encounter when there was no or slight resistance by the suspect. Deviating from the typical control process increased to almost 16 percent of officers when suspect resistance was moderate to high. Less than 1 percent (0.4 percent) deviated from searching the suspect when there was no resistance. Slightly more than 4 percent of the officers deviated from this typical process when resistance was slight, 19 percent when resistance was moderate or high, and 13 percent when resistance was violent or explosive.

Highest Level of Force Used

The next analysis involved determining the highest level of officer force used in each incident and comparing that with the level of resistance by the suspect. This analysis provides another way to determine if the level of the force used by an officer was consistent with the level of the suspect's resistance.

According to the data, when there was no resistance by the suspect (327 incidents), most incidents involved officer verbal

(continued)

Box 2-5 *(continued)*

commands (8 percent), handcuffing (65 percent), or wrist/arm locks (27 percent). However, three incidents (1 percent) did involve use of a firearm. The force used by some officers when facing slight resistance was more than the force used by officers who faced no resistance. When the suspects used slight resistance, most incidents involved officer use of verbal commands, handcuffing, or wrist/arm locks (altogether 90 percent). There were a few cases of takedowns (3 percent), one incident in which an officer struck a suspect, and six situations in which an officer used a firearm (6 percent) as the most severe tactic used. When suspects resisted at a moderate or high level, officers used verbal commands, handcuffing, or wrist/arm locks as their highest level of force in 48 percent of incidents.

Finally, when suspect resistance was violent or explosive, all incidents involved force beyond verbal commands and handcuffing. When suspects acted violently, officers reported four incidents in which a wrist or arm lock was the highest level of force used against the suspect (24 percent). The most frequently used type of force was a takedown (29 percent), followed by striking the suspect (18 percent), wrestling the suspect (12 percent), and using a baton (12 percent). One officer reported an incident involving use of a firearm (6 percent). The data seem to suggest that, in terms of the incidents as a whole, officers' use of force reflected a continuum ranging from lower to higher levels.

MIAMI-DADE POLICE DEPARTMENT

The Miami-Dade dataset included 882 official Control-of-Persons Reports from the last quarter of 1993 and all of 1994 and 1995. These data were reported by the officer's supervisor after interviewing the officer, suspect, and available witnesses. The department's computerized information was used to create the dataset.

Findings from the Miami-Dade Police Department are reported in the following order:

Suspects' characteristics and actions.

Arresting officers' characteristics and actions.

Analyses of interaction patterns between officers and suspects.

Analysis of officer and suspect ethnicity.

Box 2-5 *(continued)*

Suspect Characteristics and Behavior

Suspects ranged in age from 12 to 90. The mean age was 28.6 years. Of the 882 suspects, 46 percent were black and 54 percent white. Thirty-five percent of the total number of suspects were Hispanic, most of whom were white. Eighty-nine percent of the suspects were male, and 11 percent were female. Of the 42 percent of suspects who appeared impaired by alcohol or drugs at the time of the incident, 24 percent were reported affected by alcohol and 18 percent were affected by a variety of illegal drugs. A number of suspects were highly agitated or erratic in their behavior during the encounter with the police officer. Officers reported erratic behavior 24 percent of the time. However, 23 percent of the time, suspects were calm when interacting with the officer.

Suspect Resistance and Injury. Because these cases involved some degree of use of force by the officer, it is not surprising that almost all cases involved suspects who showed some degree of resistance (97 percent). The category of resistance most often reported was actively resisting arrest (36 percent), followed by assaulting the officer (25 percent). Twenty-one percent of suspects attempted to escape or flee the scene.

The most common type of suspect injury was a bruise or abrasion (48 percent of those injured). The next most common injuries were lacerations (24 percent) and injuries from gunshots (4 percent). Most suspects resisted by using their hands and arms only (65 percent). An additional 14 percent used their fists against the officer, and 12 percent used their feet or legs. Less than 5 percent used a gun (handgun, rifle, or shotgun). One percent used a vehicle to assault the officer, and another 1 percent used a cutting instrument.

The most common type of force used by the suspect was striking or hitting the police officer (44 percent). In 27 percent of incidents, the suspect pushed or pulled the officer, and in another 20 percent, the suspect grabbed or held the officer. Eight percent of incidents involved verbal threats or threatening movements or behaviors by the suspect.

(continued)

Box 2-5 *(continued)*

**Role of Alcohol or Drug Impairment on the Suspects'
Behavior.** Another important question addressed was
whether the suspect appeared intoxicated by alcohol or
impaired by drugs and how that affected the confrontation. The
370 suspects who were reported intoxicated by alcohol or
impaired by drugs were less likely to be calm and more likely to
appear visibly upset (23 percent and 18 percent, respectively),
and more likely to be erratic in their behavior (24 percent) or
highly agitated (33 percent).

Suspects who were reported impaired were no more or less
likely to resist the officer than sober suspects, but when they did
resist, they resisted in different ways. Impaired suspects were
more likely to resist actively or to directly assault the officer
than non-impaired suspects. In spite of this, suspects who were
reported impaired were no more likely to receive force by the
officer or to be injured during the arrest than were sober suspects. Similarly, suspect impairment by drugs or alcohol was not
related to whether the officer was injured during the incident.

Although the overall significance of the relationship between
impairment and type of suspect resistance was not statistically
significant, there was a fairly large difference in resistance with
a gun. Suspects reported as impaired were more than twice as
likely as sober suspects to use a gun to resist the police.

Officer Characteristics and Behavior

The officers ranged from 21 to 66 years of age, with a mean age
of 34. Most officers were Anglos (54 percent), Hispanics (31 percent), and blacks (14 percent). Eighty-nine percent of the officers
were male, and 11 percent were female. Most officers were
assigned to patrol (92 percent), and 5 percent were sergeants.

Officer Force and Injury. The most common type of force
used by officers was use of hands and arms (77 percent of use-
of-force incidents). In 8 percent of use-of-force incidents, officers
used (discharged) their weapons, and in another 7 percent they
used dogs (K–9s). In a majority of the incidents (64 percent),
officers grabbed or held the suspects. The next most common
use of force was to strike or hit the suspect (10 percent of the
incidents).

Box 2-5 *(continued)*

The most common injury to officers was bruises or abrasions (64 percent of those injured), followed by sprains or strains (15 percent), and lacerations (15 percent). Of injured officers, 2 percent were bitten by the suspect, 2 percent suffered broken or fractured bones, and 1 percent were injured by gunshots. The vast majority of injured officers received no treatment (76 percent).

However, 12 percent were given first aid, and 6 percent were treated by emergency rescue personnel at the scene. Less than 1 percent of officers were treated at a hospital or by their personal physician.

Role of Officer Characteristics. In no department do all officers respond precisely the same to situations, although rules, regulations, and policies of the department should narrow the range of officers' responses to within acceptable and appropriate limits. In the cases examined here, officer characteristics did not make much of a difference in whether force was used or in the level of force used. There were no statistically significant differences in the level of force used by male and female officers. Further, the ethnicity of the officer did not affect the general level of force used or whether force was used. Officer age differences were statistically significant, but the differences may reflect the differences in assignments of younger versus older officers, which was not studied. As the age of the officers increased, the level of force they used decreased.

Interaction Patterns Between Officer and Suspect

This section focuses on the interaction patterns between officer and suspect. In other words, is there a relationship between the suspect's initial behavior and the officer's response? Ninety-two percent of suspects offered some resistance. The categories included "attempted to flee" (31 percent), "actively resisted the officer" (23 percent), "passively resisted" (20 percent), "assaulted the officer" (17 percent), and "resisting to incite others" (1 percent). Although calm suspects were the least likely to actively resist or assault the officer, they were the most likely to attempt to flee, even more so than suspects perceived to have mental deficiencies or problems (as defined by Florida's Baker Act).

(continued)

Box 2-5 *(continued)*

Further, it was the suspects who initially acted in a calm manner who were the most likely to resist an officer with a gun or to assault the officer with a vehicle.

The initial behavior of the suspect did not influence whether the suspect was injured during the arrest, but it did influence the level of force used by the officer. Suspects who were initially calm were the least likely to have force used against them. They were no more likely to have slight force used against them than other suspects. However, they were among the top two groups to be forcibly subdued by the officer using some method other than hands.

An analysis of suspects' initial behavior and officers' injuries resulted in an interesting finding relating to the dangerousness of Baker Act suspects. Suspects who were described as visibly upset or highly agitated inflicted more officer injuries than other suspects (40 percent and 39 percent respectively), and Baker Act suspects inflicted fewer injuries than other suspects (20 percent).

There was a strong relationship between the level of officer force and the chance of officer injury. Increasing levels of officer force, regardless of the level of suspect resistance, corresponded with higher probabilities of officer injury. When no force was used, 2 percent of officers were injured. Minimal force situations resulted in 15 percent of officers being injured, and situations involving officers forcibly subduing suspects with their hands resulted in 69 percent of officers being injured. However, when officers used force other than their hands, injuries were reduced to 15 percent.

Clearly, increasing levels of suspect resistance increase the chance of an injury to the attending officer. No resistance or passive resistance seldom resulted in an officer injury. However, when the suspect attempted to flee or actively resisted arrest, the chance of an officer injury was increased dramatically. The chance of an officer injury increased even further when the suspect incited others or directly assaulted the officer.

Ethnicity of Officers and Suspects

The relationship between the ethnicity of the officer and that of the suspect in force situations is important. Officers used higher levels of force against suspects of their own ethnic group than

Box 2-5 *(continued)*

against suspects of other ethnic groups. For example, Anglo officers used higher levels of force against Anglo suspects than black or Hispanic officers used against Anglo suspects. Black officers used higher levels of force against black suspects than did Anglo or Hispanic officers, and Hispanic officers used more force against Hispanic suspects than did Anglo or black officers. The differences were the least pronounced for Anglo officers and the most pronounced for black officers.

Among other explanations, this could be due to a tendency to deploy officers in areas with a preponderance of citizens of their own ethnicity. However, with the greater diversity of neighborhood ethnicity in recent years, this finding may reflect a proclivity on the part of officers to respond differently to members of various ethnic groups. If this were true, each ethnic group might feel more comfortable using force on suspects from its own group. Another interpretation is an officer's possible concern that race and politics might be dragged into the situation when an officer uses force against a suspect of another ethnic group. As a result, officers may try to avoid such situations.

Data compared officer/offender ethnic matches with the degree of resistance by suspects. Although there does not seem to be a relationship between ethnic matches and whether a suspect offers resistance, there are differences in the levels of resistance. Although based on a small number of cases, the ethnic match resulting in the greatest likelihood of a suspect assaulting the officer occurs when a black officer is arresting an Anglo suspect (46 percent). Contrast this to the likelihood of assault when an Anglo officer is arresting an Anglo suspect (14 percent), or when a black officer is arresting a black suspect (17 percent).

Officer ethnic matches were compared with the level of force used by the officer. Force was used most often when the officer was black and the suspect was Anglo (100 percent) or Hispanic (100 percent). Force was used least often when the officer was Hispanic and the suspect black (93 percent). Force with hands was used most often when the officer was black and the

(continued)

Box 2-5 *(continued)*

suspect was either Anglo (73 percent) or Hispanic (77 percent). Force, other than hands, was used most often when the officer was Anglo and the suspect black (32 percent).

THE FORCE FACTOR

Prior research on use of force by police has focused on the highest level of force used or the highest level reached in an encounter. This analysis differs from previous ones because its focus is on the level of force used by the police relative to the suspect's amount of resistance, which we call the force factor.[3] This section describes the force factor and concludes with comments on its implications as it applies to policy and training.

To calculate the force factor, both the suspects' level of resistance and the officers' level of force must be measured and scaled in the same manner. Even though the force factor is a relative measure, in situations in which the level of police force is greater than the level of resistance, there is no necessary implication that the level of police force was excessive or improper. For example, an officer may justifiably use more force than does a suspect to gain control of a situation. Similarly, it is possible that a suspect's resistance may exceed the level of force used by the officer. A force factor representing such a disparity does not necessarily mean that the officer's level of force was too weak or improper. A weaker police use of force, relative to the suspect's level of force, could represent an incident in which a suspect shoots an officer who was unable to respond. Similarly, it could represent a suspect who attacked an officer but who was controlled with a minimum of police force. In any case, the most interesting cases are those that reflect the greatest differences between force and resistance.

An important application of the force factor is the analysis of police use of force within a police department. Comparisons can be made between units to understand the use of force and the reasons for differences. Other comparisons can be made for various officer characteristics, such as tenure with the department, training, and assignment, to gain insight into variations of use of force found within the department. Findings can help guide training and supervision.

Box 2-5 *(continued)*

Oregon Use-of-Force Data

Using the Oregon data, we measured the level of suspect resistance in four ordinal categories: (1) no resistance, (2) slight resistance, (3) moderate or high resistance, and (4) violent or explosive resistance. The corresponding categories for officer levels of force are (1) no force, (2) slight force, (3) forcibly subdued suspect with hands, and (4) forcibly subdued suspect using methods other than hands. To calculate the force factor, we subtracted the level of resistance (1–4) from the level of police force (1–4), Force minus Resistance = Force Factor. The range of the force factor is from −3 to +3. A zero is interpreted as force commensurate with the level of resistance. For example, no resistance and no force would be 1 minus 1 = 0, or passive resistance and minimal police force would be 2 minus 2 = 0. If the level of force is higher than the level of resistance, the force factor is positive, with one point for each level of incongruence up to a maximum of +3. If the level of force is lower than the level of resistance, then the force factor is negative, one point for each level of discongruence up to a maximum of −3.

The report depicts the Oregon police officers' use of force in relation to suspects' resistance. The distribution of scores resembles a normal (bell-shaped) curve. This distribution of cases indicates that most incidents fall in the middle, with fewer cases at the extremes. In the Oregon data, the distribution is slightly skewed to the positive side, meaning that, on average, more force than resistance was used.

Miami-Dade Use-of-Force Data

In this dataset, the level of civilian resistance from the Control-of-Persons Reports was recoded into four ordinal categories similar to those used to analyze the Oregon data: (1) no resistance, (2) passive resistance, (3) active resistance, and (4) assaulted officer. The corresponding categories for levels of police force are (1) no force, (2) minimal force, (3) forcibly subdued suspect with hands, and (4) forcibly subdued suspect using methods other than hands. The force factor was calculated using the same method explained above. The distribution of scores for the Miami-Dade data is close

(continued)

Box 2-5 *(continued)*

to a normal curve, but slightly skewed to the negative side, indicating, on average, the use of less force than resistance.

Although a comparison between the two sites of Miami-Dade and Eugene/Springfield is compelling, interpreting any differences could be problematic because each dataset represents a different selection of incidents as discussed above.

CONCLUSIONS AND IMPLICATIONS FOR POLICY AND TRAINING

Police use-of-force policies set the tone for how legitimate force can be used against civilians in a particular jurisdiction. Whether departmental policies have an impact in the area of nonlethal force is an empirical question that has yet to be answered. However, research on policies regarding the discharge of firearms and pursuit driving indicates that policies, training, and accountability systems make a significant difference in the number of firearm discharges and pursuits in which officers and agencies are involved.[4] Assuming that use-of-force incidents follow the same trend, a relationship should exist between the use of force by police and the policies that govern such behavior. Policies that govern use of force should focus on four main objectives: maximizing the safety of officers, minimizing injuries to civilians, protecting the rights of those against whom force is used, and providing officers with the tools needed to make arrests effectively and restore order. The major objective of the policies and training is to reduce or minimize injuries.

The Oregon and Miami-Dade data paint somewhat different pictures of the injuries suffered by officers during use-of-force incidents. Of 803 incidents analyzed for injuries from Miami-Dade, 308 (38 percent) resulted in a reported officer injury. The vast majority of reported injuries (79 percent) were minor and consisted of bruises, strains, or soreness. Nevertheless, 45 officers were lacerated, 6 were bitten, 5 suffered a broken bone or fracture, 1 received a puncture wound, 1 received internal injuries, and 3 were shot.

The report depicts the chances of officer injury (not including simple soreness) according to some of the more common ways in which Miami-Dade officers reported using force. These figures suggest that Miami-Dade officers are significantly at

Box 2-5 *(continued)*

risk for injury any time they use force, particularly when they strike a suspect with their fists or use their hands and arms to control a suspect. Because most use-of-force incidents (80 percent) involve the use of hands, arms, or fists, Miami-Dade officers are most at risk for injury when using precisely the type of force that they report using most frequently.

Overall, Oregon data show far fewer injuries to officers during incidents involving the use of force. Of 504 reported incidents where force was used, 9 (1.8 percent) resulted in an injury to an officer. Officers in Springfield and Eugene are most at risk for injury when wrestling (21.1 percent), striking (12.5 percent), or taking a suspect to the ground (3.8 percent). In none of the eight incidents when a police baton or pepper spray was used did an officer suffer an injury.

The chances of suspect injury are significant no matter what type of force is used by the police. A suspect is more likely to suffer injury if struck with a fist than with a PR-24 police baton. This may be due to the training that police receive in how to use the baton in a manner that minimizes the risk of injury. In any event, the chances of a suspect being injured are greatest when the officer uses his fists, hands, arms, feet, or legs during the encounter.

The force factor analysis of the Miami-Dade data yields two important findings with respect to injuries. First, the data indicate that officers are more likely to be injured when using less force relative to the resistance of the suspect. In other words, if an officer does not escalate the amount of force used in response to an increasingly violent suspect, the officer is more likely to be injured. Second, the data show that injuries to suspects increase only minimally as the amount of force used by the police increases relative to the amount of resistance. Although suspects are more likely to receive injuries when police use more force relative to resistance, this increased likelihood of injury is small. Furthermore, even in cases where a suspect was injured, the force factor mean was still negative (-0.114), indicating that, overall, officers use force that is less than the resistance offered by suspects. These findings can be an important source of information for formulating policies and training that help reduce the possibility of injuries.

(continued)

Box 2-5 *(continued)*

In addition to the policy implications above, the findings from this research point to several training issues that need to be addressed by police agencies. These issues include:

- Better training is needed in the use of weaponless (empty hand) control tactics. Because the vast majority of use-of-force incidents are low level in nature, police officers will continue to rely on their hands, arms, and feet to control most resistive suspects. Currently, these common types of encounters result in a disproportionate number of injuries to officers and suspects. If officers were better trained and prepared to deal with these types of encounters, it seems likely that the number and severity of injuries arising from them would decrease.
- A use-of-force continuum that matches suspect resistance with officer response levels, combined with a robust training program that reinforces what level of force is appropriate in a given encounter, should help reduce officer and suspect injuries.
- Significantly more training is needed in the proper use of chemical agents. The Oregon data indicate that pepper spray was used in 2 of 547 use-of-force encounters. Similarly, pepper spray was used 4 times in 803 encounters by the Miami-Dade police. The Miami-Dade figures are undoubtedly low because the police department does not issue chemical agents to patrol officers but does permit use of chemical agents in specialized tactical operations. The Oregon officers appear to be using pepper spray infrequently. More training on the use and potential abuse of chemical agents may help reduce the number of officer and suspect injuries.
- If the PR-24 baton is to be retained, officers need regular retraining and practice in how to use it effectively. In Dade County, every reported instance when the PR-24 side-handled baton was used involved a strike. To those who advocate its use, the advantage of the PR-24 is its ability to be used as a defensive and control-type weapon. When employed properly, the PR-24 can be used to trap and hold the hands and arms of suspects to bring them under control. Apparently, the PR-24 is not being used to its full capacity.

Box 2-5 *(continued)*

This is not surprising because the use of a PR-24 is a diminishing skill that takes a great deal of practice to retain one's ability to use it to full advantage. If officers cannot remain proficient in its proper use, then police agencies should reevaluate whether to continue to issue the PR-24 or whether another impact weapon may be more appropriate.

- Officers need more and better training in how to avoid or defuse violent encounters before they arise. If future policies require officers to take reasonable measures to avoid the use of force, then officers must be properly trained in conflict avoidance and crisis management techniques. How successful an officer is at avoiding violence is a function, at least in part, of how well trained the officer is in defusing emotionally charged situations.

DIRECTIONS FOR FUTURE RESEARCH

In examining the use-of-force landscape and in discussing the findings of this research, at least four important areas remain unexplored. First, we know very little about the effectiveness of various types of nonlethal force used by police. What is needed is a comprehensive evaluation of the effectiveness of all types of police force commonly used in street-level encounters.

Second, research is needed that identifies in detail the sequential order of how violent encounters unfold. As noted above, there is a great need to develop an interactive model that can better explain the active and reactive aspects of these encounters. Although anecdotal evidence is abundant, there is little empirical research on what factors immediately trigger the use of force by and against police, how force is actually used by suspects against police, and how officers respond.

Third, little reliable research exists that identifies the extent of police use of excessive force. Although we can say with relative conviction that police use of force occurs on an infrequent basis, we cannot conclude with nearly the same certainty how many of those incidents involve excessive force.

Finally, there is a need to explore measurement issues and uses of the force factor. Studying police use of force without

(continued)

Box 2-5 *(continued)*

taking into account levels of suspect resistance should be avoided. Research results that do not include the relative measure of force fail to impart a thorough understanding of the police-public encounter. Creating force factor scores for individual officers, assignments, units, and departments can be an important step in understanding and controlling police use of force.

Of course, measuring excessive force is highly problematic; indeed, even defining excessive force is difficult and definitions may vary considerably depending on the situation.[5] In spite of this difficulty, if we consider the importance to the Nation of knowing how often its police officers abuse their authority, comprehensive research on excessive force must continue to receive a high priority.

Notes:

1. Lawrence A. Greenfeld, Patrick A. Langan, and Steven K. Smith, "Police Use of Force: Collection of National Data," Washington, DC: U.S. Department of Justice, Bureau of Justice Statistics and National Institute of Justice, 1997, and Tom McEwen, "National Data Collection on Police Use of Force, Bureau of Justice Statistics," Washington, DC: U.S. Department of Justice, Bureau of Justice Statistics and National Institute of Justice, 1996, NCJ 160113.

2. Geoffrey Alpert and William Smith, "How Reasonable Is the Reasonable Man? Police and Excessive Force," *Journal of Criminal Law and Criminology,* Volume 85, Issue 2 Fall, 1994 481–501.

3. Geoffrey Alpert and Roger Dunham, "The Force Factor: Measuring Police Use of Force Relative to Suspect Resistance," Washington, DC: Police Executive Research Forum, 1997.

4. Geoffrey Alpert, "Police Pursuit: Policies and Training, Research in Brief," Washington, DC: U.S. Department of Justice, National Institute of Justice, pages 12–13, 1997.

5. Geoffrey Alpert and William Smith, "How Reasonable Is the Reasonable Man? Police and Excessive Force," *Journal of Criminal Law and Criminology,* Volume 85, Issue 2 Fall, 1994, 85 81–501.

Source: Geoffrey P. Alpert and Roger G. Dunham, *The Force Factor: Measuring and Assessing Police Use of Force and Suspect Resistance,* National Institute of Justice and Bureau of Justice Statistics, October 1999.

Geoffrey P. Alpert, Ph.D., is Professor of Criminology, College of Criminal Justice, University of South Carolina. Roger G. Dunham, Ph.D., is Professor, Department of Sociology and Criminology, University of Miami.

QUESTIONS FOR DISCUSSION

1. What is the most important lesson to be learned from the Miami Police Department case study on page 45? Can political influence within law enforcement be stopped?

2. The National Law Enforcement Officer Disciplinary Research Project documented and analyzed officers who were "decertified" for misconduct from 1990 through 1995. What facts derived from this research were most surprising to you? How can these findings be used to prevent corruption?

3. Greed- or theft-related offenses are the most common form of corruption for which officers are decertified or arrested. Some officers try to rationalize stealing because they do not receive a high salary. How logical and justified is this argument?

4. During a nationwide research study, most officers indicated that they would report another officer who had committed serious offenses such as stealing from a found wallet, committing a burglary, or accepting a bribe. On the other hand, they stated they would not tell about a fellow officer who committed less serious offenses such as accepting free meals or off-duty driving while intoxicated. Would you report another officer for relatively minor infractions?

5. A gratuity is something given voluntarily in return for or in anticipation of a favor or service. Based on this definition, few officers would agree it is right to take a gift knowing the giver expects a "professional favor." However, it is sometimes difficult to determine whether the giver expects something in return. Many people who give gratuities state that they want nothing in return but in reality expect special treatment regarding police services. What is your opinion about officers accepting gratuities? What should a written departmental policy on gratuities state?

ENDNOTES

1. John Dorschner, "The Dark Side of the Force," *The Miami Herald Sunday Magazine*, March 8, 1987, pp. 1–22.
2. Ibid.
3. Ibid.
4. Dan Christensen, *Miami Daily Business Review*, April 11, 2003.

5. Lawrence J. Dempsey, "The Knapp Commission and You," *The Police Chief*, International Association of Chiefs of Police, Gaithersburg, MD, November 1972, p. 21.

6. Ibid., p. 24.

7. Ibid., p. 25.

8. Bill Burger, Michael Cosgrove, and Neal Trautman, Ethics Training in Law Enforcement, International Association of Chiefs of Police, Ad Hoc Ethics Training Subcommittee, Subcommittee Report and Recommendations, International Association of Chiefs of Police, Gaithersburg, MD, 1996.

9. ABC News, *20/20*, June 13, 1997.

10. New York State Commission on Criminal Justice and the Use of Force, Report to the Governor, Vol. 1, New York: New York State Commission on Criminal Justice and the Use of Force, May 1987: 301.

chapter 3

CHARACTER
OF GREAT COPS

The best cops I have known were the ones that didn't change much when they entered the profession. They knew who they were and what they were about long before they put on the badge. In a line of work where someone will question or criticize nearly everything you do, having a firmly anchored self-image is essential. I also look at what sorts of things the person did before they decided to be cops. Did they choose to serve their country in the armed forces? Did they get involved in the community by doing volunteer work? The person that appears to have awakened one morning and decided that they want a career of public service, with no prior inclination to that end, may have other, more self-serving, reasons for wanting to be a police officer.

Tim M. Dees
Law Enforcement Trainer and Author
Board Member, American Society for Law Enforcement Trainers

OFFICER QUALIFICATIONS: OFFICIAL DESCRIPTION

The following is how the U.S. Bureau of Labor describes the qualifications necessary to be hired and advance within law enforcement. It conveys an accurate yet sterile and incomplete description. Absent, and virtually impossible to explain, is the need for an officer to withstand and persevere through the emotional roller coaster ride every police career brings. Here is the official job description:

> Civil service regulations govern the appointment of police and detectives in practically all States, large municipalities, and special police agencies, as well as in many

smaller ones. Candidates must be U.S. citizens, usually at least 20 years of age, and must meet rigorous physical and personal qualifications. In the Federal Government, candidates must be at least 21 years of age but less than 37 years of age at the time of appointment. Physical examinations for entrance into law enforcement often include tests of vision, hearing, strength, and agility. Eligibility for appointment usually depends on performance in competitive written examinations and previous education and experience. In larger departments, where the majority of law enforcement jobs are found, applicants usually must have at least a high school education. Federal and State agencies typically require a college degree. Candidates should enjoy working with people and meeting the public.

Because personal characteristics such as honesty, sound judgment, integrity, and a sense of responsibility are especially important in law enforcement, candidates are interviewed by senior officers, and their character traits and backgrounds are investigated. In some agencies, candidates are interviewed by a psychiatrist or a psychologist, or given a personality test. Most applicants are subjected to lie detector examinations or drug testing. Some agencies subject sworn personnel to random drug testing as a condition of continuing employment.

Before their first assignments, officers usually go through a period of training. In State and large local departments, recruits get training in their agency's police academy, often for 12 to 14 weeks. In small agencies, recruits often attend a regional or State academy. Training includes classroom instruction in constitutional law and civil rights, State laws and local ordinances, and accident investigation. Recruits also receive training and supervised experience in patrol, traffic control, use of firearms, self-defense, first aid, and emergency response. Police departments in some large cities hire high school graduates who are still in their teens as police cadets or trainees. They do clerical work and attend classes, usually for 1 to 2 years, at which point they reach the minimum age requirement and may be appointed to the regular force.

Police officers usually become eligible for promotion after a probationary period ranging from 6 months to 3 years. In a large department, promotion may enable an officer to become a detective or specialize in one type of police work, such as working with juveniles. Promotions to corporal, sergeant, lieutenant, and captain usually are made according to a candidate's position on a promotion list, as determined by scores on a written examination and on-the-job performance.

The FBI has the largest number of special agents. To be considered for appointment as an FBI agent, an applicant either must be a graduate of an accredited law school or a college graduate with a major in accounting, fluency in a foreign language, or 3 years of related full-time work experience. All new agents undergo 16 weeks of training at the FBI Academy on the U.S. Marine Corps base in Quantico, Virginia.

Applicants for special agent jobs with the U.S. Department of Treasury's Secret Service and the Bureau of Alcohol, Tobacco, and Firearms must have a bachelor's degree or a minimum of 3 years' related work experience. Prospective special agents undergo 10 weeks of initial criminal investigation training at the Federal Law Enforcement Training Center in Glynco, Georgia, and another 17 weeks of specialized training with their particular agencies.

Applicants for special agent jobs with the U.S. Drug Enforcement Administration (DEA) must have a college degree and either 1 year of experience conducting criminal investigations, 1 year of graduate school, or have achieved at least a 2.95 grade point average while in college. DEA special agents undergo 14 weeks of specialized training at the FBI Academy in Quantico, Virginia.

U.S. Border Patrol agents must be U.S. citizens, younger than 37 years of age at the time of appointment, possess a valid driver's license, and pass a three-part examination on reasoning and language skills. A bachelor's degree or previous work experience that demonstrates the ability to handle stressful situations, make decisions, and take charge is required for a position as a Border Patrol agent. Applicants may qualify through a combination of education and work experience.

Postal inspectors must have a bachelor's degree and one year of related work experience. It is desirable that they have one of several professional certifications, such as that of certified public accountant. They also must pass a background suitability investigation, meet certain health requirements, undergo a drug screening test, possess a valid State driver's license, and be a U.S. citizen between 21 and 36 years of age when hired.

Law enforcement agencies are encouraging applicants to take postsecondary school training in law enforcement-related subjects. Many entry-level applicants for police jobs have completed some formal postsecondary education and a significant number are college graduates. Many junior colleges, colleges, and universities offer programs in law enforcement or administration of justice. Other courses helpful in preparing for a career in law enforcement include accounting, finance, electrical engineering, computer science, and foreign languages. Physical education and sports are helpful in developing the competitiveness, stamina, and agility needed for many law enforcement positions. Knowledge of a foreign language is an asset in many Federal agencies and urban departments.[1]

OFFICER QUALIFICATIONS: THE REAL-LIFE REQUIREMENTS

The primary reason people apply to be cops is to help others. Cops face and accept frustrations and adversities so that others may be safe. Veteran officers know that years of working the street will probably make these same officers somewhat callous. However, underneath the exterior hard shell beats a heart that is still caring and dedicated, though no longer idealistic.

Why would officers leave their families each day to spend eight hours dealing with grief, frustration, and crisis? Why would they want to earn a living dealing with sleazy people, those who have been brutally victimized, or people who have enjoyed being brutal? It takes strong characteristics to rebound from this daily emotional stress. Great cops possess several characteristics: tenacity, sensitivity, maturity, intelligence, physical strength, and more.

Great cops might be born with the right characteristics. They also may have been raised in a way that instills in them the character needed to withstand the frustrations and temptations they face as officers. Great cops can also be just ordinary people who rise above the temptations and frustrations in order to face the responsibilities of a noble, worthy cause.

Individuals applying to become officers learn that the process is rigid. Applicants must complete several hiring procedures: written entrance exam, oral interviews, physical fitness test, written psychological exam, oral exam, and a medical exam with drug screening. Few other jobs require applicants to endure such scrutiny.

Professional law enforcement agencies have a thorough hiring process to determine who is suitable to become officers. Although the employment examinations are intended to ensure that hiring standards are met, they cannot judge individuals' integrity or their quality.

Many of the things that make great cops are not measured by preemployment processing. Interviews and assessment centers are the best means to identify the qualities of courage, desire, enthusiasm, integrity, caring, and comradeship—all part of "the right stuff." Intuition, as well as background investigations, can be the best way to evaluate these qualities in the final analysis.

Enthusiasm

Some people seem to possess a trait that brings out the best in both themselves and others: enthusiasm. It can move people through hard times and generate the initiative, drive, and excitement needed to overcome adversity. Few great achievements or successes can be accomplished without enthusiasm.

At times, years of verbal abuse and frustration can create a degree of cynicism and pessimism within officers. Without realizing it, they may become negative and critical of virtually everything. However, no team functions at its optimum level if its members think negatively. Without initiative and enthusiasm, few great achievements can occur. Fortunately, enthusiasm is contagious and it costs nothing. Its rewards, though, are great.

Courage

Courage means putting your fears aside and getting the job done, which is what officers across the nation do daily. Usually they receive little or no publicity but feel that their actions are part of the job.

Most dictionaries define courage as the ability to meet danger or difficulty with unwavering determination and bravery. Many people often envision courage with shoot-outs, fights, or some form of valor or violence. For officers in America, this vision of courage certainly is real. Senior officers can recall when bravery was necessary.

Sometimes aspiring officers feel attracted to the excitement of working the street. They can, however, generate their own crises by overreacting during emotion-filled situations, thereby becoming part of the problem instead of the solution. Some were hailed as courageous but died needlessly, creating their own deadly circumstances because of overzealousness. Others were insecure and thought they had to prove themselves.

Never confuse courage with panic, the John Wayne syndrome, or simply the inability to remain calm, often referred to as "tombstone courage." This tendency is usually seen in inexperienced or immature officers, so experience can provide the necessary wisdom. Law enforcement has an obligation to be courageous if a situation demands it, but actions should always be balanced with intelligence and discretion.

Most acts of courage are thought to be heroic, but it takes courage to carry out many of the tasks on a tour of duty. Most, if not all, veterans have been afraid on the street at one time or another. There is nothing wrong with controlled fear, as long as it can keep you alert and alive. In fact, in some situations fear is beneficial, as long as you are able to control it.

Imagine patrolling a high-crime area as a single-officer unit. It is 0200 hours on a midnight shift as you enter the parking lot of a bar where there are frequent fights, knifings, and shootings. Your city's ordinance prohibits having open alcohol containers outside bars or liquor stores. However, while driving slowly through the parking lot, you discover four or five local adults and two are drinking beer.

Although the drinking adults know that their actions are against the law, they also know that some officers look the other way rather than confront them. Some citizens think that glares and stares intimidate officers, but officers who submit to this type of intimidation make it difficult for both themselves and fellow officers to uphold the law.

Discretion is always appropriate, but it takes guts to confront several lawbreakers. Officers must make confrontations wisely.

Single-officer units should request another officer for assistance and backup. Once the backup arrives, the confrontation can begin. If another officer is not available, the single-unit officer should "check out" with the dispatcher before confronting the suspects. Use survival tactics, such as proper stance, voice commands, positioning, and use of light.

It is uncommon that cops need to react heroically. When it is necessary, best effort is essential, as are common sense and the use of skills developed through officer training. Use discretion, yet still enforce the law; it is foolish to instigate or escalate confrontation. Instead, react with wisdom, skills learned through training, and strong physical ability.

Positive Outlook

Cynicism in any profession is detrimental to both a career and a personal life. It destroys a healthy and positive attitude. Most people get out of life what their perspectives allow. In other words, if they expect the best and work hard to achieve it, they usually will do so. On the other hand, if they are negative and suspicious, the self-fulfilling prophecy will come true. When things go wrong, it helps to view them as temporary setbacks in a long line of accomplishments.

Police sometimes deal with the worst side of humanity. Some officers, as in any profession, become hardened without realizing it. Others may be constant complainers. They may be critical of or dislike their organization, fellow officers, citizens, or themselves. Their personal life is usually equally depressing.

Some cops claim that officers should be cynical because good street cops are suspicious by nature. You can still be positive and optimistic and be a great cop. Attitude is vital, and a positive one helps people—and officers—deal with life and its problems better and more wisely. Negative, unhealthy attitudes cloud proper judgment.

Leading authorities on performance and leadership agree: the formula for personal success is 85 percent attitude and 15 percent skill. Setbacks and bad times are sure to happen to all of us. It is best to move on enthusiastically when they happen, rather than spending energy and time worrying, complaining, or criticizing. Negative, apathetic people lead dull, uneventful lives. Those who are successful, happy, and satisfied with their lives tend to be enthusiastic. Positive thinking is an acquired trait. People aren't born with an optimistic attitude; they have to acquire it. Enjoy the simple moments of life: laughing, caring, smiling, loving, and sharing. Above all, persevere with positive thinking and reasoning.

Discipline

Law enforcement is a tough, demanding profession. Almost every aspect of it requires discipline. For example, it takes discipline to stay in good physical condition, know the facts of a case before testifying, conduct aggressive patrol on midnight shift, deal with the frustration of the judicial system, or ignore the sarcasm of citizens.

Discipline means hard work, but it offers many satisfying rewards. Disciplined individuals are more satisfied with themselves. They understand and accept self-control and effort because they benefit from the healthy self-image and promising future that result from them.

Self-esteem is essential to personal satisfaction. It also helps you feel good about your job and work. If you lack discipline, make a sincere commitment to improve. Do not procrastinate; as you begin to accomplish more, accomplishments will abound and discipline will become habit-forming.

Caring Attitude

Most people respect the police and even admire them. This silent majority understands how tough law enforcement is and respects officers for doing their best. The truth is, though, most citizens do not understand cops or the job that they do. It is sometimes difficult for them to get to know officers, but educating them may change their attitudes.

Although it is hard for someone with no police experience to understand, every veteran cop knows that a lot of officers feel most comfortable when they socialize only with other cops. However, this is not a healthy situation.

Cops have a tendency to be reserved in nature, even among other officers. This may be because as the years pass, they develop callousness as a defense against the continual suffering, pain, and frustration they witness. However, beneath that hard exterior usually beats the heart of someone who really cares.

Officers must remain sensitive toward others and avoid self-centeredness in their hectic, stressful lives. They must remember that, despite the crises and despair they face on the street or behind the desk, they have an honorable purpose and profession.

If they should ever stop caring for those they serve, they would need to seek assistance. It would be helpful also to reevaluate their motives, their beliefs, and the important aspects of the job. Sincerity is extremely important to good cops, and caring comes from appreciating what's really important. Robert Hastings summarized it best in his essay "The Station."

THE STATION

Tucked away in our subconscious is an idyllic vision. We see ourselves on a long trip that spans the continent. We are traveling by train. Out the windows we drink in the passing scene of cars on nearby highways, of children waving at a crossing, of cattle grazing on a distant hillside, of smoke pouring from a power plant, of row upon row of corn and wheat, of flatlands and valleys, of mountains and rolling hillsides, of city skylines and village halls.

But uppermost in our minds is the final destination. On a certain day at a certain hour we will pull into the station. Bands will be playing and flags waving. Once we get there so many wonderful dreams will come true and the pieces of our lives will fit together like a completed jigsaw puzzle. How restlessly we pace the aisles, damning the minutes for loitering—waiting, waiting, waiting for the station. "When we reach the station, that will be it!" we cry. "When I'm 18 . . ." "When I buy a new 450 SL Mercedes Benz . . . !" "When I put the last kid through college . . ." "When I get married . . ." "When I have paid off the mortgage . . ." "When I get a promotion . . ." "When I reach the age of retirement, I shall live happily ever after!" Sooner or later we must realize there is no station, no one place to arrive at once and for all. The true joy of life is the trip. The station is only a dream. It constantly outdistances us.

"Relish the moment" is a good motto, especially when coupled with Psalm 118:24: "This is the day which the Lord hath made; we will rejoice and be glad in it." It isn't the burdens of today that drive men mad. It is the regrets over yesterday and the fear of tomorrow. Regret and fear are twin thieves, who rob us of today. So stop pacing the aisles and counting the miles. Instead, climb more mountains, eat more ice cream, go barefoot more often, swim more rivers, watch more sunsets, laugh more, cry less. Life must be lived as we go along. The station will come soon enough.[2]

Self-Control

In crises officers can never lose self-control. When others are shouting, screaming, and panicking, the cops are responsible for maintaining the calmness and logic necessary to handle situations. Panic is a luxury they cannot afford. Therefore, individuals who have trouble controlling their emotions should choose another profession.

Staying calm is easier said than done. Some are more adept at it than others, but there is no magic formula for controlling anger and maintaining calmness. Officers should remember to be professional, or their careers may be short-lived if emotion overrules logic. They may raise their voices, clench their fists, tense their muscles, and make their bodies rigid. They are being rough on their bodies and probably making fools of themselves.

To prevent people from "getting under your skin," do not let them upset you in the first place. Again, this is easier said than done. If it begins, keep your hands from clenching and lower your voice. If you can, bring your voice down to a whisper, because it will be difficult for people to argue with you when you speak softly. Control your emotions—deliberately and conscientiously. After the crisis, if you are frustrated, talk about it with someone who knows how to listen or manage emotions well.

The days are gone when cops felt they had to be superhuman. Do not suppress your emotions following an incident, because they will build up inside you. Use your agency's counselors or support groups, or talk to a fellow officer, a friend, or your spouse.

Cops see and feel frustration and futility, and it is not unusual for them to need help in maintaining sound mental health. A cop should have the ability to adapt to different situations by losing the feelings of hopelessness and unfamiliarity. If you need assistance and your agency does not have a counseling program, argue for one. More than likely you will have fellow officers who must understand the consequences of suppressing emotions over an extended period of time and also need counseling to work through them.

TRAITS OF GREAT OFFICERS

- The ability to accept people the way they are and then deal with them in their own frame of reference.
- The ability to think independently and make decisions based on facts, law, and what you know to be true and right.
- Physical fitness, primarily for personal well-being and stress reduction. It also helps in job performance.
- The drive to do your best and want to make a difference in some way, even if only a few people can be helped.
- Flexibility, which allows you to get the job done and still deal with politics. It also allows you to adjust to different jobs, different supervisors, and different working conditions.

WISDOM

Wisdom, which can be defined as a high degree of knowledge, is something every officer needs. Officers are called on to be a minister in times of grief, a tireless documenter of facts, an individual who can make split-second legal decisions, and a diplomat who can talk with a transient one moment and a politician the next. They must know about numerous state statutes, local ordinances, departmental rules and regulations, and standard operating procedures. Further, a cop's wisdom should be balanced with empathy for the unfortunate and unyielding firmness for the intimidating.

Paul Harvey, the highly respected commentator, has always been a friend of law enforcement. He summarized officers' duty and wisdom one day during a broadcast:

> He, of all men, is at once the most needed and the most unwanted. He is a strangely nameless creature who is "sir" to his face and "bum" behind his back. He must be such a diplomat that he can settle differences between individuals so that each would think he won. But if the policeman is neat, he is conceited; if he is careless, he is a bum. If he is pleasant, he is a flirt; if he is not, he's a grouch. He must be first to an accident, he must be able

to start breathing, stop bleeding, tie splints, and above all, ensure the victim goes home without a limp or expect to be sued.

The police officer must be able to whip someone twice his size and half his age without damaging his uniform and without being brutal. If you hit him, he's a coward. If he hits you, he is a bully. A police officer must know everything and not tell. He must know where all the sin is and not partake. The police must, from a single human hair, be able to describe the crime, the weapon, and the criminal and tell you where the criminal is hiding. But if he catches the criminal, he is lucky, and if he doesn't, he is a dunce. If he gets promoted, he has political pull; if he doesn't, he is a dullard.

The policeman must chase bum leads to a dead end, conduct a stakeout ten nights to tag one witness who saw it happen but refuses to remember. He runs through files and writes reports until his head aches to build a case against some villain who will get dealt out by a shameless attorney or judge who isn't honorable.[3]

In part, wisdom is nothing more than common sense. It is the ability to be logical and practical, although it takes more than common sense to be wise. It requires a lot of knowledge and tenacity to learn state statutes, city ordinances, and departmental regulations. With few exceptions, knowledge is acquired only through hard work and dedication.

Every street officer deals with people who are upset. Officers must be prepared for the unexpected and always think "survival" in their minds. They cannot interpret citizens' anger as a personal offense. Great cops can distinguish between someone venting their frustration and an individual committing a crime and using verbal abuse. The individual must be arrested without anger and excessive force.

Do not take things personally; just treat others as you would like to be treated. Remember, maybe they are good people who are just frustrated, angry, and need someone to listen. How you listen and respond may determine if someone gets hurt or if the situation is defused and resolved. Be logical and understanding, and let them tell their side of the situation. Psychologists confirm that it is very therapeutic to allow someone to vent anger, so you are doing everyone involved a great service.

This is not always easy; sometimes it requires an enormous amount of control and patience. The following story illustrates the virtue of patience.

One day a young boy was walking by himself through the woods. Curious and adventurous, he had to stop and look at anything and everything. He suddenly discovered a cocoon on the branch of a tree.

As fate would have it, a butterfly was making a hole, preparing to break out of the cocoon. The boy's impatience caused him to help the butterfly out of the hole, and the miracle of life took place before his eyes: the case broke open and the butterfly slowly emerged.

To the young boy's horror, he realized the butterfly's wings were still folded back and unable to open. The butterfly wrenched with all of its strength but was unable to unfold them. So, the boy, feeling helpless and frustrated, unfolded the butterfly's wings. After a few moments, the beautiful butterfly died in the boy's hands. The boy was filled with guilt and realized too late that the butterfly's wings should have unfolded naturally. One of nature's most beautiful things had died in the palm of his hands after a brief yet desperate struggle, and the young boy's impatience had caused its tragic death. Nature had been interrupted, and the boy's lack of control had taught him a horrible but important lesson.

It was a long and tiring walk out of the woods for the boy; the tiny butterfly weighed heavily on his conscience. He had learned a lesson that he would never forget—that patience and control are crucial. For cops, the lack of patience and control—and wisdom—can end in human tragedy.[4]

One of the most difficult lessons to learn is also one of the most valuable when handling people who have lost their temper: controlling your own emotions is absolutely vital. Some officers become defensive and feel the need to "strike back" or take revenge; the answer to this temptation is to not allow yourself to become angry. It cannot even be an option; it's an essential commitment. Controlling your emotions will allow you to work more effectively and professionally and make sound decisions.

HARD WORK AND DEDICATION

While there are exceptions, most worthwhile things in life come with a price. That price usually is hard work and dedication. Herschel Walker, one of football's greatest athletes, summed up his philosophy on life when he said, "The Lord places many challenges ahead of us, and the only way to meet them is head-on." Herschel was probably saying there is no free ride in life. Hard work and determination become a way of life for those who accomplish the most. In doing so, they feel good about themselves, and their self-esteem and self-worth flourish.

Police work has been described as 95 percent boredom and 5 percent pure hell. For most agencies that is an accurate description. Even the mundane, boring times can involve hard work. When calls are backed up and an agency is shorthanded, a shift can be challenging, to say the least.

Whether or not you are a street cop, you are probably over-worked and understaffed. Detectives sometimes do paperwork most of the day; having time to go out on the street can be a luxury. With 50 to 70 cases per month, an investigator may sometimes only interview witnesses or victims and write reports. Other divisions and units are just as overworked.

Hard-working officers find that police work has many rewards. They generally enjoy working, facing challenges, and achieving personal goals and have a zest for life. Their days are filled with hard work, yet they like it that way because achievers thrive on challenges and accomplishments. Usually, too, they are optimistic about the future. Therefore, it is easy to see that hard-working, dedicated optimists will make outstanding cops. On the other hand, people who are somewhat lazy or lack initiative would rather get out of work than face it head-on. These people generally are not happy with other aspects of their life and tend to complain, be pessimistic, and feel dissatisfied with everything.

SUPPORT, TRAINING, AND DEVELOPMENT

Emotional trauma and frustration can jeopardize officers' mental health. As a result, marital or personal problems can be magnified as pressure continues to build within the individuals. Although law enforcement has typically not been good at taking care of its officers, many of them would benefit from professional counseling at some point during their career. It could result in more effective, productive work and happier, healthier people. Communities owe their law enforcement forces this assistance and support.

Agencies, in addition to professional counseling services, should provide adequate training for their officers. Historically, many have offered inappropriate or little training. The last decade has seen vast improvements, but some departments still fail to train personnel properly.

Commitment to train must begin at the top, with the chief, sheriff, director, or superintendent, although this level does not always appreciate the value of and need for continual, effective training.

Individuals assigned the responsibility of training may not have been taught the most effective way to develop and deliver it. To do so, a thorough needs assessment and job-task analysis are essential, as are the development of realistic learning goals, objectives, lesson plans, and pre- and posttests. Effective training will help boost morale, enhance necessary skills, and save officers' lives.

Every organization should realize that its greatest resource is its employees. Still, many American corporations and acclaimed management textbooks note that most organizations fail to provide sufficient employee development. In other words, they do not make the most of what employees have to offer. The skills, abilities, and potential of employees should be discovered, developed, and used.

Human resource programs can simply determine employees' skills and abilities, record them in a computer database for easy reference, and then determine ways to use them to everyone's advantage. Not only will this offer tremendous benefit to an organization, but also employees will feel a new sense of self-worth by knowing that their administration appreciates their talents and abilities.

POLICE CHARACTER: SCHOLARLY RESEARCH

The book *Forces of Deviance: Understanding the Dark Side of Policing* is an excellent source for gaining an understanding of how the characters of police officers develop. Written by professors Victor E. Kappeler, Richard D. Sluder, and Geoffrey P. Alpert, the text provides valuable insight into both academic theories and real-life case studies. Here is a brief segment from a chapter that reviews how officer character and agency cultures are cultivated:

There have been several efforts to explain the unique character of the police. The psychological paradigm suggests that persons with certain personality characteristics are drawn to police work. Often referred to as the predispositional model, this view suggests, for example, that those with authoritarian personalities are attracted to policing. Authoritarian types are likely to be conservative, aggressive, cynical, and rigid. These personality characteristics, according to the psychological perspective, are reflected in the unique character of the police.

The sociological paradigm rejects the notion that police character is solely the product of personality characteristics of those persons employed in policing. Instead, this paradigm proposes that police character is formed, molded and shaped by the police working environment. Important socialization experiences occur in the police academy, during on-the-job training, and in police work groups. These experiences, according to the sociological paradigm, are responsible for forging a unique police character.

The anthropological paradigm provides the most holistic explanation for the development of police character. This view holds that the police are members of a unique occupational subculture. This subculture, moreover, imbues officers with both a unique worldview and a working personality. The working personality instructs officers that while fellow police (i.e. "insiders") are trustworthy, they should be skeptical and ever vigilant of non-police (i.e. "outsiders"). Police training reinforces the insider/outsider distinction by constantly emphasizing the potential for danger in police work. The emphasis on police power and authority further isolates police from others in society, as does the paramilitary model used in policing. Police isolation is also fostered when police are indoctrinated with the idea that they are the "thin blue line" that separates anarchy from order.[5]

There are notable differences among law enforcement agencies in terms of location, type of employing agency, and terms of employment, with the widest variations occurring in agency personnel numbers. In some agencies, the "thin blue line" is thin indeed. A survey of police agencies is presented in Box 3-1.

Box 3-1

Profiles of Agencies: Census of Federal, State, and Local Law Enforcement Agencies

STATE AND LOCAL SWORN PERSONNEL

Sixty percent of full-time State and local sworn employees were assigned to patrol duty on a regular basis. About one in seven sworn personnel were assigned to investigative duties (15%). Approximately one in nine primarily performed duties related to jail (6%) or court (5%) operations. Duties of other State and local law enforcement officers, not broken down here, included administration, training, and technical support.

Size of Agencies

As of June 2000, of the 17,784 State and local law enforcement agencies operating full-time, 1,032, or 6%, employed 100 or more full-time sworn personnel. This included 77 agencies with 1,000 or more officers. The majority of agencies employed fewer than 10 full-time officers (52%), and nearly a third, about 5,600 in all, employed fewer than 5 (31%). These smaller agencies included 1,907, 11% of agencies overall, with just 1 full-time officer and 231, 1% of all agencies, with only part-time officers.

Although State and local agencies with 100 or more full-time sworn officers accounted for just 6% of all agencies, they employed 63% of all State and local full-time sworn personnel. The 77 agencies with 1,000 or more officers accounted for 220,512, or 31.1%, of all full-time sworn personnel. The 77 largest agencies rarely used part-time sworn officers, accounting for just 0.3% of all such personnel nationwide. Nearly half (47%) of part-time sworn personnel were employed by agencies with fewer than 10 full-time officers, and more than two-thirds (69%) worked for agencies with fewer than 25 full-time officers.

(continued)

Box 3-1 *(continued)*

State-by-State Comparisons

- Texas (1,800) had the most full-time State and local law enforcement agencies. The total included 623 county constable offices.
- Pennsylvania (1,166) had the next highest number of agencies, followed by
- Illinois (886) and Ohio (845). California had the most full-time State and local law enforcement employees, about 116,000. Other States with 50,000 or more employees included New York (94,863), Texas (80,535), Florida (68,165), and Illinois (52,769).

States with fewer than 2,000 employees included Vermont (1,459) and North Dakota (1,755). Nationwide, there were 362 full-time State and local law enforcement personnel per 100,000 residents. The District of Columbia (859), Louisiana (527), and New York (500) had the most. West Virginia (229), Kentucky (237), and Vermont (240) had the least.

California (73,662) had the most full-time sworn personnel employed by State and local agencies, followed closely by New York (72,853). Next were Texas (51,478), Illinois (39,847), and Florida (39,452). Vermont (1,034) had the fewest officers.

After the District of Columbia (693), the ratio of full-time sworn personnel per 100,000 residents was highest in Louisiana (415). The next highest ratios were in New York (384), New Jersey (345), and Illinois (321). The lowest ratios were in Vermont (170) and West Virginia (174). Nationwide, the ratio was 252 per 100,000. The per capita ratio of uniformed officers whose regular duties included responding to calls for service was highest in the District of Columbia (357 per 100,000 residents), New York (240), and Wyoming (200). It was lowest in Oregon (104) and Washington (108). The overall ratio for the Nation was 151 per 100,000.[5]

FEDERAL LAW ENFORCEMENT OFFICERS, 2002

As of June 2002, Federal agencies employed more than 93,000 full-time personnel authorized to make arrests and carry firearms in the 50 States and the District of Columbia, according

Box 3-1 *(continued)*

to a survey conducted by the Bureau of Justice Statistics (BJS). Compared with June 2000, employment of such personnel increased by about 6%. From June 2000 to June 2002, the number of Federal law enforcement officers increased 19% at ATF, 11% at Customs, and 8% at INS, U.S. Department of Justice, Office of Justice Programs

Major Employers of Federal Officers

Department of Justice Agencies In June 2002 the largest employer of Federal officers with arrest and firearm authority in the United States was the Immigration and Naturalization Service (INS), with 19,101 (INS functions were moved to the Department of Homeland Security in 2003.) About half (9,830) of INS officers worked for the U.S. Border Patrol. Border Patrol duties included the detection and prevention of smuggling and illegal entry of aliens into the United States, with primary responsibility between the ports of entry. Border Patrol officers worked along, and in the vicinity of, the 8,000 miles of U.S. boundaries.

The INS employed 4,529 immigration inspectors with arrest and firearm authority at ports of entry. These officers are included in the noncriminal investigation and inspection category. INS also employed 2,139 criminal investigators and immigration agents responsible for investigating crimes under INS jurisdiction and 2,603 officers with detention and deportation duties.

The Federal Bureau of Prisons (BOP), the second largest employer of Federal officers, employed 14,305 correctional officers maintaining the security of BOP institutions and the 139,000 inmates in custody. Their duties include supervising inmates, searching for contraband, and responding to emergencies and disturbances. The FBI had 11,248 full-time personnel with arrest and firearm authority. Nearly all were FBI special agents, responsible for criminal investigation and enforcement. The FBI investigates more than 200 categories of Federal crimes including bank fraud, embezzlement, kidnapping, and civil rights violations.

It also has concurrent jurisdiction with the Drug Enforcement Administration (DEA) over drug offenses under

(continued)

Box 3-1 *(continued)*

the Controlled Substances Act. The DEA had 4,020 employees with arrest and firearm authority as of June 2002. These special agents investigate major narcotics violators, enforce regulations governing the manufacture and dispensing of controlled substances, and perform other functions to prevent and control drug trafficking.

The U.S. Marshals Service employed 2,646 officers with arrest and firearm authority. The Marshals Service receives all persons arrested by Federal agencies and is responsible for their custody and transportation until sentencing. With BOP assistance, it transfers sentenced Federal inmates between facilities.

The Marshals Service also has jurisdiction over Federal fugitive matters concerning escaped prisoners, probation and parole violators, persons under DEA warrants, and defendants released on bond. The agency makes more than half of all Federal fugitive arrests. Other Marshals Service responsibilities include managing the Federal Witness Security and Federal Asset Seizure and Forfeiture Programs, and security for Federal judicial facilities and personnel.

Treasury Department Agencies The U.S. Customs Service employed 11,634 officers with arrest and firearm authority, the most of any agency in the Department of the Treasury. This included 8,167 inspectors and 3,467 criminal investigators. Customs Service officers interdict and seize contraband, process persons, vehicles, and items at more than 300 ports of entry, and administer certain navigational laws. The Customs Service has an extensive air, land, and marine interdiction force as well as an investigations component supported by its own intelligence branch. Customs investigates violations of more than 400 laws related to customs, drugs, export control, and revenue fraud. Like the INS, the Customs Service became part of the Department of Homeland Security in 2003.

The next largest employer, the U.S. Secret Service, had 4,256 personnel authorized to make arrests and carry firearms. About two-thirds were special agents with investigation and enforcement duties primarily related to counterfeiting, financial crimes, computer fraud, and threats against dignitaries. Most other Secret Service officers were in the Uniformed Division.

Box 3-1 *(continued)*

These officers provide protection for the White House complex and other Presidential offices, the Main Treasury Building and Annex, the President and Vice President and their immediate families, and foreign diplomatic missions. In 2003 the Secret Service was moved to the Department of Homeland Security.

The Internal Revenue Service (IRS) employed 2,855 special agents with arrest and firearm authority within its Criminal Investigation Division, the law enforcement arm of the IRS charged with enforcing the Nation's tax laws.

The Bureau of Alcohol, Tobacco and Firearms (ATF) employed 2,335 full-time officers with arrest and firearm authority. ATF enforces Federal laws related to alcohol, tobacco, firearms, explosives, and arson. In 2003 ATF became a Justice Department agency.

Other Agencies with 500 or More Officers As of June 2002, the Federal Corrections and Supervision Division of the Administrative Office of the U.S. Courts employed approximately 4,500 probation officers, all of whom have arrest authority. A total of 4,090 were employed in districts where the court authorizes officers to carry firearms while on duty.

About three-fifths of the 3,135 officers in the U.S. Postal Inspection Service were postal inspectors, responsible for criminal investigations covering more than 200 Federal statutes related to the postal system. The others were postal police officers who provide security for postal facilities, employees, and assets, and who escort high-value mail shipments.

The National Park Service employed 2,139 full-time personnel with arrest and firearm authority in June 2002. This included 1,549 park rangers commissioned as law enforcement officers. Additional rangers serving seasonally were also commissioned officers but were considered part-time and excluded from the BJS survey. The Park Service total also includes 590 U.S. park police officers. These officers work mostly in the Washington, D.C., area, but are authorized to provide police services for the entire National Park System.

The Veteran's Health Administration (VHA) employed 1,605 officers with arrest and firearm authority as of June 2002.

(continued)

Box 3-1 *(continued)*

This was nearly 5 times as many as in 2000 as the VHA continued its program to expand firearm authority to its entire force.
The VHA employs about 2,400 police officers with arrest authority at its 173 medical centers.

Source: Bureau of Justice Statistics, U.S. Department of Justice, Census of
State and Local Law Enforcement Agencies, 2002, U.S. Government Printing
Office, October, 2002.

QUESTIONS FOR DISCUSSION

1. Considering both the official and real-life qualifications for
   being an exceptional officer, what do you feel are the most
   important qualifications? Rank the following list from 1 (the
   most important qualification) to 10 (the least important).

   __ Education
   __ Courage
   — Age
   — Physical Ability
   — Enthusiasm
   — Caring
   — Discipline
   — Self-control
   — Wisdom
   — Dedication

2. According to the predispositional model, people with authoritarian personalities are attracted to policing. Authoritarian
   types are likely to be conservative, aggressive, cynical, and
   rigid. Do you agree or disagree? Why?

3. Of the 17,784 state and local law enforcement agencies operating full-time, only 1,032, or 6%, employed 100 or more full-time
   sworn personnel. Does the size of a typical police or sheriff's
   department surprise you? Do you think there should be
   more personnel? If so, how would you justify the hiring of
   additional personnel?

4. This chapter contains profiles and comparisons of the four types of law enforcement agencies: city, county, state and federal. Which type of agency do you believe presents the greatest challenges to an officer's character? Which type of assignment would present the most dilemmas and temptations?

5. List three difficult situations that many new officers face during their first year as an officer. Describe how you will deal with and overcome each situation.

ENDNOTES

1. U.S. Bureau of Labor, Training, Other Qualifications and Advancement Section, Bureau of Labor Statistics, http://www.bls.gov/oes/home.htm (accessed August 2003).

2. Copyright © 2000–2003 by the Christian Ethics Today Foundation. Robert J. Hastings, "The Station," Issue 014, Vol. 4, No. 1, February 1996. www.Christian EthicsToday.com.

3. Paul Harvey. What Are Policemen Made Of? By Paul Harvey, http://www.sover.net/~tmartin/Paul.htm.

4. Patience Stories: An Indian Legend, http://www.story-lovers.com/listsbutterflys.

5. Victor E. Kappeler, Richard D. Sluder, and Geoffrey P. Alpert The Police and Society Touchstone Readings, Chapter 15 Summary, Breeding Deviant Conformity, Police Ideology and Culture, www.policestudies.eku.edu/KAPPELER/pandshome.htm.

chapter *4*

COPS AND THE JUDICIAL SYSTEM

A great cop is an individual committed to service with the courage to do what is right—and understands that our laws were developed to act as tools to solve problems, not to be used as clubs to abuse communities.

Louis M. Dekmar, Chief
La Grange Police Department
La Grange, GA

The dignity of crime victims is often ignored by the criminal justice system, as repeat offenders are set free over and over again. It seems that the system is filled with stagnation, injustice, and inequity.

The frustration that is felt by citizens with the justice process is not new, nor is it a burden known only to America. Injustice occurs in all nations, but some nations deal with judicial concerns more effectively than others.

Most cops feel that the American criminal justice system has its good points. Yet they, too, face frustrations with it. Sometimes criminals are released before officers have completed the related arrest reports. Plea bargaining, early paroles, and a seemingly endless appeal system are more than irritating. Legal technicalities, liberal judges, and a process that appears to forget victims frustrate and complicate the efforts of the police.

Officers play one of the most crucial roles in the judicial system, so they must understand how the system works. Unfortunately, many officers pass through their career and never watch a felony trial in its entirety. Some are never exposed to the problems and complexities of other phases within the system. This lack of understanding can lead to further agitation, and it certainly perpetuates more problems. Similarly, when officers have no working knowledge of legal terms and their meanings, they can contribute to disastrous results to their cases and damage their credibility. (A legal glossary is provided near the end of the chapter to help you become familiar with important vocabulary.)

THE LAW

The criminal justice system is America's means of social control. It is intended to protect society by apprehending, convicting, and rehabilitating offenders of criminal law. Learning more about the process is interesting, revealing, and of course, frustrating. Officers should know how their actions affect other parts of the system.

Millions of people are crime victims each year, and crime directly influences the quality of American life. The criminal justice system, therefore, is held accountable for controlling it. Since crime is directly dependent on and affected by a variety of social ills, the challenge is monumental.

The justice system is enormously complex, but it is still only one part of the process of law. To appreciate the process, we must understand how American criminal law developed. Laws are the formal means of control within a society. They afford society protection and safeguard against physical harm and infringement of personal rights. Life would be reduced to survival of the fittest without laws.

Laws are one form of social control. Other means include tradition, cultural habits, moral standards, peer pressure, and ever-changing fads; people will conform for any of these reasons. In one respect, laws are much different than other means because negative consequences have been established for violating them. The justice system regulates the nature, method, and extent of the consequences.

Primitive societies depend on social customs, tradition, and rules for social regulation. Rules are similar to laws but lack the judicial complexity associated with laws. The judicial process and its associated subsystems set laws apart from rules. As an example, rules may be enforced by family members or private organizations. Laws, however, are enforced by government and its political divisions.

American law is derived from English law. As such, it is also known as Anglo-American criminal justice. Once again, the difference between it and other methods of social control is its complicated decision-making procedures.

More than two hundred years ago America's leaders met to discuss, debate, and develop an everlasting guideline for our country. This document, the Constitution of the United States, guarantees the freedom and rights of all Americans. Police officers dedicate their lives in order to uphold the vision our forefathers encompassed.

Law and its enforcement serve many purposes. Some of the practical benefits include

- Settling disputes,
- Deterring crime,
- Punishing criminal activity,
- Preserving order, and
- Assigning authority among governmental and social agencies.[1]

Throughout the years, patrol officers—the front line of defense—have faced an enormous responsibility: to protect citizens while ensuring their guaranteed rights. To protect the communities officers are sworn to serve is not always easy. America is a violent society; each year millions of Americans are victims of crime. The Constitution can guarantee regulation of commerce, taxation of citizens, the interrelationship of federal and state governments, and the rights of those accused of crimes, but it can only attempt to govern human behavior.

The causes of society's ills are complex and multifaceted. The police have fought hard and long to combat crime, usually going far beyond what could be expected, especially given the hardships and tragedies they must face. Law enforcement officers are sworn to uphold and enforce the Constitution and all the rights and liberties it guarantees. Thousands of officers have given their lives in the daily struggle for protection and justice—the ultimate sacrifice so that others may live with liberty, justice, law, and order.

Objectives and Purposes

Achieving the key objectives of the criminal justice system is crucial to maintaining the standard of life that Americans have come to both expect and demand. These aspirations also serve as the primary purpose of criminal law in the United States. They include protecting citizens from being harmed, preventing crimes, punishing individuals who commit crimes, and rehabilitating criminals. Virtually everyone agrees that there are many aspects of the judicial system that are ineffective. Conversely, it is difficult to find a system of criminal justice that works better.

Historical Perspectives

From its initial efforts at colonization, America has felt a commitment to protect the individual rights of citizens from the abuse or misuse of government. This is partially due to the fact that the United States was founded as a result of Britain's abuse of early colonists. The original Constitution of 1788 and the Bill of Rights resulted from our commitment to protect against abuse.

Delegates from 12 of the original 13 states (all except Rhode Island) met on September 17, 1787. Their purpose was to propose a new Constitution to the Continental Congress and have it ratified by the states. The origins of the Constitution (and its first ten amendments added four years later) date back to ancient Greece and Rome, and several hundred years of English history helped to further refine attitudes and perspectives. Though the courage and insight of these delegates are obvious, there was considerable debate and disagreement. Several delegates strongly disagreed; in fact, Rhode Island refused to attend or sign the document.

The first ten amendments were proposed by Congress on September 25, 1789. These are now referred to as the Bill of Rights. Ratification of the Bill of Rights was not completed until December 15, 1791. Since this date, it has represented America in its commitment to the importance of citizens' rights and limitations toward government. The Bill of Rights (Box 4-1) protects the liberties that each of us cherish. Box 4-2 highlights the development of law in early America.

Types of Laws

Police officers must understand criminal law. Most officers deal with statutory laws, especially those that have been enacted by state legislatures. Criminal laws are punitive in nature, and violations result in punishment.

Box 4-1

The Preamble to the Bill of Rights

Congress of the United States begun and held at the City of New-York, on Wednesday the fourth of March, one thousand seven hundred and eighty nine.

THE Conventions of a number of the States, having at the time of their adopting the Constitution, expressed a desire, in order to prevent misconstruction or abuse of its powers, that further declaratory and restrictive clauses should be added: And as extending the ground of public confidence in the Government, will best ensure the beneficent ends of its institution.

RESOLVED by the Senate and House of Representatives of the United States of America, in Congress assembled, two thirds of both Houses concurring, that the following Articles be proposed to the Legislatures of the several States, as amendments to the Constitution of the United States, all, or any of which Articles, when ratified by three fourths of the said Legislatures, to be valid to all intents and purposes, as part of the said Constitution; viz.

ARTICLES in addition to, and Amendment of the Constitution of the United States of America, proposed by Congress, and ratified by the Legislatures of the several States, pursuant to the fifth Article of the original Constitution.

CONSTITUTIONAL AMENDMENTS 1–10: THE BILL OF RIGHTS

Note: The following text is a transcription of the first ten amendments to the Constitution in their original form. These amendments were ratified December 15, 1791, and form what is known as the Bill of Rights.

Amendment I

Congress shall make no law respecting an establishment of religion, or prohibiting the free exercise thereof; or abridging the freedom of speech, or of the press; or the right of the people peaceably to assemble, and to petition the Government for a redress of grievances.

Box 4-1 *(continued)*

Amendment II

A well regulated Militia, being necessary to the security of a free State, the right of the people to keep and bear Arms, shall not be infringed.

Amendment III

No Soldier shall, in time of peace be quartered in any house, without the consent of the Owner, nor in time of war, but in a manner to be prescribed by law.

Amendment IV

The right of the people to be secure in their persons, houses, papers, and effects, against unreasonable searches and seizures, shall not be violated, and no Warrants shall issue, but upon probable cause, supported by Oath or affirmation, and particularly describing the place to be searched, and the persons or things to be seized.

Amendment V

No person shall be held to answer for a capital, or otherwise infamous crime, unless on a presentment or indictment of a Grand Jury, except in cases arising in the land or naval forces, or in the Militia, when in actual service in time of War or public danger; nor shall any person be subject for the same offence to be twice put in jeopardy of life or limb; nor shall be compelled in any criminal case to be a witness against himself, nor be deprived of life, liberty, or property, without due process of law; nor shall private property be taken for public use, without just compensation.

Amendment VI

In all criminal prosecutions, the accused shall enjoy the right to a speedy and public trial, by an impartial jury of the State and district wherein the crime shall have been committed, which district shall have been previously ascertained by law, and to be informed of the nature and cause of the accusation; to be confronted with the witnesses against him; to have compulsory process for obtaining witnesses in his favor, and to have the Assistance of Counsel for his defense.

(continued)

Box 4-1 *(continued)*

Amendment VII

In suits at common law, where the value in controversy shall exceed twenty dollars, the right of trial by jury shall be preserved, and no fact tried by a jury, shall be otherwise reexamined in any Court of the United States, than according to the rules of the common law.

Amendment VIII

Excessive bail shall not be required, nor excessive fines imposed, nor cruel and unusual punishments inflicted.

Amendment IX

The enumeration in the Constitution, of certain rights, shall not be construed to deny or disparage others retained by the people.

Amendment X

The powers not delegated to the United States by the Constitution, nor prohibited by it to the States, are reserved to the States respectively, or to the people.

Source: The National Archives and Records Administration, 8601 Adelphi Road, College Park, MD

Box 4-2

Groundbreaking Survey of Criminal Justice Agencies

The following is a segment of a research report written by George L. Kelling, titled "Broken Windows" and Police Discretion. The research and its report were funded by the National Institute of Justice in October, 1999. The findings highlighted here were pioneering in that it exposed for the first time, the reality of how discretion is used in American criminal justice.

"In 1953, Supreme Court Justice Robert H. Jackson, believing criminal justice to be in a state of crisis, called for a major

Box 4-2 *(continued)*

national study of criminal justice agencies by the American Bar Association (ABA). At first administered by the ABA and funded by the Ford Foundation, the survey also became the first project of the ABF, the ABA's newly created research arm. As first conceived, the study was designed to apply methodologies used in previous local surveys: official data would be analyzed to learn the extent to which agencies adhered to prescribed standards.

Under the leadership of Remington and Lloyd Ohlin (Emeritus Touroff-Glueck Professor of Criminal Justice at Harvard Law School), however, the survey went in a different direction. In some respects, the new direction was an outgrowth of a serendipitous mix of the University of Wisconsin Law School's "law in action" tradition as embodied by Remington and the Chicago School of Sociology's tradition of field observation as represented by Ohlin, a Ph.D. from the University of Chicago.

Ohlin notes that Remington, the first staff director of the study, "decided from the outset that the ABF survey would be different from earlier studies, much less concerned with official summary statistics and more concerned with the analysis of the criminal justice system in daily operation."[2] In other words, the survey would study law as it operated rather than law as it was found in the books and, as a consequence, would rely heavily on observational data of low-level decision-making. Field staff filled out the checklists devised by the experts to be true to the original proposal, but only for that purpose.[3] Remington and Ohlin's decision to reshape the survey transformed it into one of the most important social/legal research studies of the 20th century.

Initially, three sites were selected for the study: Kansas, Michigan, and Wisconsin. Additional sites were to be added later. After the survey began in 1956, however, researchers, confronted by the enormity of the study and the data set, decided to limit their study to the original three sites.

STUDY FINDINGS

The study focused on the line personnel in criminal justice agencies—police, prosecutors, judges, and corrections

(continued)

Box 4-2 *(continued)*

officers—conducting their routine work. Conventional thinking was turned on its head:

- Discretion was found to be used at all levels of criminal justice organizations. The idea that police, for example, made arrest decisions simply on the basis of whether or not a law had been violated—as a generation of police leaders had led the public to believe—was simply an inaccurate portrayal of how police worked.
- Low-level decision-making by line personnel in light of practical and real-life considerations was found to be a significant contributor to the crime control and problem-solving capacity of criminal justice agencies. This was true not only for police but for prosecutorial and other decision-making personnel as well.
- Criminal law was used to solve many social problems, not just serious crimes.
- Behaviors designated as unlawful in criminal codes, such as assault, were found to be extraordinarily diverse in nature and included everything from private debt settlement and spousal abuse to attacking strangers.
- The policies of each criminal justice agency were found to have an impact on other criminal justice agencies.[4]

Eliminating police discretion completely, even in the decision not to arrest, has always been a minority view. Goldstein's view has been most intensely debated as it pertains to domestic violence—a problem largely invisible to the public prior to the ABF report. Prosecutorial discretion in the handling of domestic violence was also highlighted by early ABF reports.[5] Since then, discussion, debate, and policy regarding police and prosecutorial handling of domestic violence have changed directions several times. A review of research on the impact of criminal justice responses to domestic violence testifies, more than anything, to the complexity of the problem and the need for preventive problem-solving approaches.[6]"

Civil laws are noncriminal. They concern matters such as civil disputes, contracts, property litigation, personal grievances, or other disagreements that do not violate a criminal law. Officers must be able to distinguish between situations over which they have authority to take action and those which are civil. They should be careful not to give legal advice in civil situations; rather, they should advise citizens to consult with attorneys.

Protecting citizens' rights while maintaining law and order is difficult. Laws and criminal procedures were developed to maintain the delicate balance that the pursuit of justice requires. The more legal safeguards are implemented to protect individual rights, the more difficult it is to maintain law and order. On the other hand, if legal regulation is decreased, the protection of citizens becomes easier, but individual liberty is jeopardized.

Limitations

Laws are affected by many social factors; their development and enforcement are subject to influence and have limitations. Understanding the limitations of laws allows us to deal with them more effectively.

Laws are subject to interpretation. Written laws must be interpreted to be enforced; therefore, some inequality exists. Officers apply their interpretation of statutes to particular situations to decide if an offense has been committed and whether there is sufficient evidence for an arrest. Prosecutors interpret the laws and apply them to cases. Judges interpret "case law" and compare it to circumstances of cases. The appeal process revolves around comparing specific circumstances to the interpretation of law. Legal interpretation is influenced by changes in social attitudes and customs, and there is a natural evolution in interpretation itself.

Enforcement of laws requires facts. Our system of justice demands that the prosecution and defense determine and present facts through testimony. The finding of truth is sometimes hampered by witnesses who lie and by the suppression of important evidence that cannot be presented to the jury for particular reasons. Apathy, fear, or unavoidable circumstances occasionally prevent the determining of fact. In the pursuit of representing their "side" of a case, attorneys may even exaggerate or mislead jurors. Presenting facts in the furtherance of justice can become complicated and difficult.

Law itself cannot control crime. Making a particular act illegal does not prevent it from occurring. Laws offer protection from unacceptable behavior, yet there will always be individuals who, for an assortment of reasons, commit the acts regardless of legislation. Laws are limited to merely forbidding actions and specifying consequences. Someone somewhere will refuse to conform.

Creation and enforcement of laws are subject to unjust influence. The judicial process is subject to human weaknesses and frailties because it depends on individuals who work within it. Legislators may be unfairly influenced during the legislation process. Police officers, attorneys, and judges sometimes yield to favoritism or corruption. These and other influences limit the ability to enforce the laws.

Laws change slowly. Everyone has heard the phrase "There ought to be a law." Making that wish come true is very time-consuming. Sometimes the need for a law exists, but it goes unheeded until legislators act. In other instances unfair or outdated laws remain in effect beyond their realistic usefulness. The evolution of law is a never-ending process. By its very nature, legislation will lag behind changes in society's or a community's attitudes.[7] As changes in laws and their interpretation occur, they are merely a reflection of how society has changed.

Government Branches and the Law

It is important to understand how the basic rights afforded to us by the Constitution and the Bill of Rights are applied in everyday life. Officers should understand how laws are enforced in order to appreciate the significance of criminal procedure.

The three branches of government are judicial, executive, and legislative. Each is required by the Constitution to protect individual rights. The judicial branch is charged with the greatest role; it has the duty to declare what is law and then interpret it. The courts must decide when laws conflict with the Constitution and should be declared invalid.

Congress is responsible for enacting legislation that guarantees constitutional rights and applies them to specific situations. Like the courts, Congress is charged with an awesome responsibility. Once laws are passed by Congress, the executive branch is responsible for implementing them. This branch creates procedures and regulations pertaining to the administration of law.

Other forms of regulations, such as city or county ordinances, exist, although federal and state laws affect Americans to the greatest degree. The power of the federal government is limited only by the Constitution. Federal agencies use their authority for matters such as relationships with foreign governments, disputes among states, and situations of national concern. States, however, concern themselves with matters within their domain.[8]

Every cop in America should understand the United States Constitution. The failure to understand it, especially the Bill of Rights, can increase the probability of violating it. The Bill of Rights is the first ten amendments to the Constitution. They have an enormous influence on officers' actions, their role in society, and the mission of law enforcement. The amendments were written as safeguards to individual liberty. Violating the amendments most likely means violating the rights and privileges of a defendant. In doing so, particular evidence or an entire offense may be dismissed.

AMERICAN CRIMINAL JUSTICE

Few see crime as the police do. Officers see and deal with the victims and their despair and face the hostility of criminals. They are the individuals people turn to in times of turmoil and confusion; frequently no other individuals can help.

A street officer's job can include times that are challenging or boring, events filled with terror, and moments that are rewarding. Throughout all these moments society expects officers to act the way cops do in television programs or in the movies. Society wants a happy ending. Happy endings may be easy to write, but they are not always reality.

Fortunately, at the core of the American justice system is a real effort to protect citizens while it helps officers defuse the confrontations, violence, and tragedies. Officers are often referred to by citizens as the thin line between society and the violence that is heard and read about daily. The police are essential to society and everyday life. Without them the justice system of our nation would soon begin to crumble.

Our system of criminal justice has three distinct components: law enforcement, courts, and corrections. Each has separate responsibilities, yet they are interwoven and dependent on each other. The effectiveness of each phase directly influences other areas of the system. Within every subunit or major component, an organized, complex sequence of procedures occurs. The process is intended to ensure that individuals' rights are protected. No citizen may be punished without being afforded due process of legal protection.

While the protection of rights is important, the criminal justice system must also safeguard citizens. The apprehension, prosecution, and punishment of criminals is a primary concern. The American justice system intentionally sacrifices part of its effectiveness in order to prevent the infringement of innocent people's liberties. Sometimes it seems that too much effectiveness is sacrificed at the expense of crime victims. Officers, therefore, must understand the system thoroughly and learn how to function within its limitations, still upholding the protection of citizens' rights with honesty, ethics, and honor. Cops have a serious job to do, and great cops take their jobs seriously. They have to; crime in America shows little sign of abating, as the statistics in Box 4-3 attest.

Box 4-3

FBI Uniform Crime Index Press Release: The Crime Index 2002

According to preliminary data released by the Federal Bureau of Investigation's Uniform Crime Reporting Program today, the number of Crime Index offenses reported to law enforcement during the first 6 months of 2002 increased 1.3 percent when compared to figures reported for the same period of 2001. The Crime Index, which is viewed by many as an indicator of the Nation's crime experience, is comprised of violent crime offenses and property crime offenses. The Modified Crime Index includes arson as a property crime.

Overall, violent crime, which includes murder and non-negligent manslaughter, forcible rape, robbery, and aggravated assault, decreased 1.7 percent when comparing data reported for the 6-month periods. Property crime, which includes burglary, larceny-theft, and motor vehicle theft, increased 1.7 percent. Arson offenses, tabulated separately from the Crime Index, decreased 2.6 percent for the first 6 months of 2002 when compared to data from that same period of 2001.

The violent crime offenses of murder and forcible rape both showed increases in 2002 when compared to 2001 numbers, with

Box 4-3 *(continued)*

murder increasing 2.3 percent and forcible rape, 1.8 percent. However, robbery showed a decrease of 0.4 percent, and aggravated assault declined 2.8 percent.

All of the property crimes increased in the six-month period. Burglary and motor vehicle theft each rose 4.2 percent, and larceny-theft, 0.5 percent.

Among the city population groups, cities with populations of 10,000 to 24,999 and those with populations under 10,000 inhabitants had decreases—0.4 percent and 1.9 percent, respectively—in the number of Crime Index offenses reported. Increases in Crime Index offense volumes ranged from 0.2 percent for cities with 1 million or more inhabitants to 3.1 percent for cities with populations of 50,000 to 99,999.

The number of reported Crime Index offenses in suburban counties rose 3.6 percent; in rural counties, the number of offenses decreased 1.9 percent.

By region, the West showed a 5.9-percent increase in Crime Index offenses, and the South reported an increase of 0.6 percent. Decreases in the volume of Crime Index offenses were noted in the Northeast, 2.1 percent, and in the Midwest, 1.4 percent.

Source: Federal Bureau of Investigation, FBI National Press Office, Washington DC, December 16, 2002

THE CRIMINAL JUSTICE PROCESS

Officers know that a substantial number of crimes are undetected and unreported. This number varies according to the type of crime. During the initial stage of the judicial process the police play a crucial role, due to their enormous power of discretion. City ordinances and state statutes offer guidelines that officers use to enforce the laws. All officers are responsible for interpreting the law and applying it to their evaluation of particular situations.

As years pass, rookie cops learn the value and wisdom of discretion. Officers are the ones who decide whether to begin the criminal justice process. If officers choose not to make an arrest, nothing happens. When probable cause exists, though, strong extenuating circumstances must justify the decision not to arrest.

Other judicial employees working in the courts or corrections must follow through on officers' decisions to arrest; they are responsible for responding to the alleged acts.

Once officers investigate the report of a crime, they determine whether there is probable cause to suspect that a particular individual committed the offense. If so, an arrest is justified; if not, a report is forwarded that triggers further investigation or documentation. Following an arrest, the alleged offender must have an initial appearance. The initial appearance is a hearing before a judge during which the offender is officially informed of the charges, bail is set, and the offender is officially advised of his or her rights. If charges against the offender are not dismissed within a specified time, a preliminary hearing is scheduled, in which evidence against the defendant is examined by a judge. Charges may be reduced, or if sufficient evidence exists for further prosecution, the case is forwarded for continued action.

> *A great cop is a person who understands the nature of policing in a free society. That person should be able to* empathize *with persons who are victims of crime, be compassionate with those less fortunate, and treat all people, even those accused or convicted of criminal activity, with evenhanded temperance.*
>
> J. Dale Mann
> Executive Director Georgia Public Safety Academy

PROSECUTION

The initial appearance and the preliminary hearing are facets of prosecution. The prosecution is sometimes referred to as the prosecutor, district attorney, or DA. In other areas it is known as the state attorney. Prosecution is vital to the police and justice. Some prosecuting attorneys have excellent reputations, while others bear the brunt of criticism.

Prosecutors have virtually total control over the processing of cases. As an example, there seldom is a problem establishing a prima facie (valid, sufficient at first impression) case during preliminary hearings. Defendants often waive their rights to preliminary hearings because prosecutors have so much influence over the pretrial process. Prosecutors decide whether to drop or continue a case. In some cities, as many as two-thirds of all cases are reduced. The prosecutor must make and justify such decisions.[9]

One of the challenges of the judicial system is correcting the tendency of the various subunits to not understand or not appreciate the problems of other divisions within the system. For example, the police are often unsympathetic toward the problems of the prosecution or the courts and vice versa. A frequent complaint from officers is that prosecutors do not prepare their cases well enough for trial. Many officers can recall instances when it was obvious that a prosecutor was unfamiliar with the facts of a case. One reason for this is that most prosecutors are overworked. This is true in many law enforcement–related offices, but attorneys daily are assigned more cases than they can prosecute adequately. They simply do not have time to prepare or prosecute all cases appropriately. In fact, they often miss depositions or pretrial hearings because they cannot be in more than one place at the same time. For example, after a trial ends, prosecutors attend a hearing with a judge and defense attorneys to determine which trial is next. Many times the new trial will begin the same day, leaving little time for preparation.

Every cop needs to understand the significance of prosecutors' workloads, but that is unlikely to ever change. In addition to being overworked, most prosecutors are underpaid and up against the expertise of more experienced defense attorneys. Officers need to appreciate the overwhelming caseload of prosecutors and accept it as a fact of life. Most prosecutors are sincere, dedicated attorneys. They are frustrated with the system, too, but do their best under strained and exasperating conditions.

Among the most productive things officers can do are to understand that the police and prosecution are on the same team and to do their best to assist them, not to end their job as soon as the arrest is made. Officers are professionally and ethically obligated to assist in the prosecution of cases; officers must prepare thorough investigations; write concise, thorough reports; prepare for depositions; and deliver professional testimony in order to help convict defendants. Box 4-4 presents a picture of law enforcement from the prosecutor's side.

COURTS

The American system of criminal justice was conceived long ago by our forefathers. Their vision was to provide a means of equal protection for all citizens through a due process of law. In their minds it was equally important to provide physical protection to society from individuals who would harm others. Unfortunately, according to citizen opinion studies, most Americans have little confidence in

Box 4-4

American Prosecutors

In 2001:

1. Half the prosecutors' offices Nationwide employed 9 or fewer people and had a budget of $318,000 or less.
2. The 2,341 State court prosecutors' offices employed over 79,000 attorneys, investigators, and support staff; a 39% increase from 1992 and 13% from 1996.
3. Over three-quarters of the Nation's chief prosecutors occupied full-time positions compared to about half in 1990. Sixty-five percent of all offices had at least one full-time assistant attorney.
4. Forty-one percent of the prosecutors' offices had a staff person who had been threatened or assaulted compared to 49% in 1996.
5. Over two-thirds of all offices reported the use of DNA evidence during plea negotiations or felony trials compared to about half of the offices in 1996.
6. Approximately 69% of all offices indicated having proceeded against an estimated 32,000 juveniles in criminal court.
7. Four out of ten offices prosecuted computer-related crimes (felony or misdemeanor) under their State's computer statutes.
8. About 23% of prosecutors' offices assigned prosecutors to handle community-related activities.

STATE COURT PROSECUTORS IN LARGE DISTRICTS 2001

1. Over 14,000 assistant prosecutors and supervisory attorneys who litigated cases were employed by prosecutors' offices in large districts.
2. Large district offices had combined total budgets of $2.9 billion for prosecutorial functions in 2001. The median office budget was $14 million.
3. Annually, prosecutors' offices in large districts closed over 1 million felony cases, with a median conviction rate of 85%.

Box 4-4 *(continued)*

4. 65% of prosecutors' offices in large districts reported a threat or assault against an assistant prosecutor, 41% the chief prosecutor, and 22% a staff investigator.

5. During the previous 12 months, prosecutors' offices in large districts proceeded against almost 11,000 juvenile cases.

STATE COURT PROSECUTORS IN SMALL DISTRICTS

1. Full-time offices serving districts with a population under 250,000 had combined budgets of over $1 billion in 2001.

2. Almost two-thirds of full-time offices serving districts with a population under 250,000 used DNA evidence in plea negotiations and half of full time offices used it during felony trials.

3. Nine out of ten full-time prosecutors' offices serving districts with a population under 250,000 handled domestic violence and child abuse cases.

Source: Bureau of Justice Statistics, U.S. Department of Justice, *American Prosecutors: 2001* (Washington, DC: U.S. Government Printing Office, 2002).

the courts to properly convict and sentence criminals. This perceived ineptness of the judicial system has degraded the American lifestyle.

Some people feel as though they cannot be comfortable and free from harm in their own neighborhoods. Contrary to popular belief, the courts are doing their best. Like other facets of the judicial system, the courts are overwhelmed with cases. There are not enough judges, courtrooms, bailiffs, clerical staff, or public defenders.

Each state has the authority to legislate specific state statutes and develop rules of criminal procedure. This authority is influenced by political climate; therefore, it varies in effectiveness and efficiency. All judicial circuits conform to the Constitution and are influenced by prior-case law. In addition, proceedings vary according to the type of court system. The rules of discovery are substantially different in federal court than they are in state court. Further, procedures differ in misdemeanor and felony systems. As experienced officers know, there is also a substantial difference between adult and juvenile courts (a higher concern is placed on the welfare of each juvenile).

Lastly, the preponderance of evidence in civil court is vastly different from that in criminal court. Criminal courts strive to ensure that due process of law is observed. Defendants have the opportunity to confront witnesses and be formally notified of charges against them, and they have the right to an impartial jury, to legal counsel, and to present evidence on their own behalf. Due process is a constitutional right. Though it complicates, slows, and at times is a frustration to swift justice, it is absolutely essential to prevent injustice.

Efforts to protect the innocent have generated more limitations on prosecutors. Criminal cases must be proven beyond a reasonable doubt. Through the years, case law has interpreted the Constitution. In doing so, continued restrictions have been placed on the prosecution. Every officer recognizes names and phrases such as *Miranda*, *Mapp*, the exclusionary rule, and fruits of the poisoned tree. Some view such guidelines with disdain or believe these restrictive regulations do nothing but create injustice.

No officer should let frustration with the system cause bad feelings toward prosecutors. Remember, the American system of criminal justice has been developing for more than two centuries. During that time, hundreds of thousands of people have devoted their lives to uphold procedures that are intended to safeguard all citizens.[10] Obviously, it is far from perfect. Many countries do not restrict their police and prosecution to the same extent that America does. On the other hand, many of them send more innocent people to prison. The best that officers can do is commit themselves to know the law, understand the system, and always do their best to live by the law enforcement code. Box 4-5 gives statistics regarding some of those who are processed through our court system.

Box 4-5

Criminal Case Processing Statistics

FELONY DEFENDANTS

1. An estimated 56,606 felony cases were filed in the State courts of the Nation's 75 largest counties during May 1998.
2. About a fourth of these felony defendants were charged with a violent offense, usually assault (12.2%) or robbery (6.1%). Those charged with murder (0.7%) or rape (1.3%) accounted for a small percentage of defendants overall.

Box 4-5 *(continued)*

3. About three-fourths of defendants were charged with a nonviolent felony. The most frequently charged nonviolent offenses were drug trafficking (17.7%), other drug offenses (19.4%), theft (9.9%), and burglary (7.5%).

4. About 3 in 8 defendants had an active criminal justice status at the time of the current charged offense, including 16% who were on probation, 14% on pretrial release, and 5% on parole.

5. Fifty-two percent of all defendants were convicted of a felony, and 15% were convicted of a misdemeanor.

6. The highest felony conviction rates were for defendants charged with a murder (68%), drug trafficking (66%), burglary (58%), a weapons offense (57%), or a driving related offense (56%).

7. The lowest felony conviction rate was found among assault defendants (34%).

8. Ninety-six percent of convictions occurring within 1 year of arrest were obtained through a guilty plea. About 3 in 4 guilty pleas were to a felony.

9. Murder defendants (28%) were the most likely to have their case adjudicated by trial. Seventy-seven percent of all trials resulted in a guilty verdict.

10. Overall, 68% of the defendants whose most serious conviction charge was a felony were sentenced to incarceration. Nearly all of the remaining convicted defendants received a probation sentence.

JUVENILE DEFENDANTS IN CRIMINAL COURTS

Under certain circumstances, juvenile defendants (as defined by State law) can be considered adults and tried in criminal courts. A BJS study conducted in 40 of the Nation's largest urban counties found:

1. An estimated 7,100 juvenile defendants were charged with felonies in adult criminal court in 1998.

2. In criminal courts in these 40 counties, juveniles (64%) were more likely than adults (24%) to be charged with a violent felony.

(continued)

Box 4-5 *(continued)*

3. These juvenile defendants were generally treated as serious offenders, as 52% did not receive pretrial release, 63% were convicted of a felony, and 43% of those convicted received a prison sentence.
4. States have expanded the mechanisms by which juveniles can be charged in criminal courts. In 1998, statutory exclusion was the most common method (42%) used to charge juvenile defendants compared to the more traditional use of juvenile waiver (24%).
5. About two thirds (66%) of the juvenile felony defendants in the 40 large counties were convicted, either of a felony or a misdemeanor. Of those convicted, 64% were sentenced to jail or prison as the most serious penalty. The average prison sentence received was 90 months.
6. In 1998, in the 40 counties, 62% of the juvenile felony defendants were black, 20% were white, 16% were Hispanic, and almost 2% were another race.

In Juvenile Courts

A BJS study in the Nation's 75 largest counties from 1990, 1992 and 1994 found:

1. An estimated 24% of the 370,000 sampled defendants were referred for violent offenses, 46% for property offenses, about 18% for public order offenses, and 13% for drug-related offenses.
2. More than half (55%) of the juvenile defendants formally processed in juvenile courts in the Nation's 75 largest counties were adjudicated delinquent.
3. Among juvenile defendants adjudicated delinquent, 40% 1received a disposition of residential placement and 50% received formal probation.

Source: Bureau of Justice Statistics, U.S. Department of Justice, *Criminal Case Processing Statistics* (Washington, DC: U.S. Government Printing Office), 2002.

It takes a special kind of person to be a police officer. They must remain alert during hours of monotonous patrol yet react quickly when need be; switch instantly from a state of near somnambulism to an adrenaline-filled struggle for survival; learn their patrol area so well they can recognize what's out of the ordinary.

It takes initiative, effective judgment, and imagination in coping with complex situations—family disturbances, potential suicide, robbery in progress, gory accident, or natural disaster. Officers must be able to size up a situation instantly and react properly, perhaps with a life or death decision.

Officers need the initiative to perform their functions when their supervisor is miles away, yet they must be able to be part of a strike force team under the direct command of a superior. They must take charge in chaotic situations yet avoid alienating those involved. They must be able to identify, single out, and placate an agitator trying to precipitate a riot.

They must have curiosity tempered with tact, be skillful in questioning a traumatized victim or a suspected perpetrator. They must be brave enough to face an armed criminal, yet tender enough to help a woman deliver a baby. They must maintain a balanced perspective in the face of constant exposure to the worst side of human nature, yet be objective in dealing with special interest groups. And if that isn't enough, officers must be adept in a variety of psychomotor skills: operating a vehicle in normal and emergency situations; firing weapons accurately in adverse conditions; and strength in applying techniques to defend themselves while apprehending a suspect with a minimum of force.

Then, when it's all over, they must be able to explain what happened— in writing, to someone who wasn't there, in such a way there's no opportunity for misunderstanding—and to document their actions so they can relate their reasons years later.

Bill Clede
Retired Police Officer and Trainer
Member, American Society of Law Enforcement Trainers
Charter Member, International Association of Law Enforcement Firearms Instructors
Former Technical Editor, *Law and Order* Magazine
Author of Four Books for Police

CRIME AND JUSTICE

Most law enforcement agencies across the nation complete the Uniform Crime Report (UCR) each year. Statistics for individual communities, states, and the nation are compiled, published, and distributed. UCR statistics document the overall crime rate, individual offense categories, and other areas of concern. When crime rates increase, agencies claim that more officers and equipment are needed and the statistics are used as justification. When crime rates decrease, chief administrators praise their agencies for their excellent work and citizens are commended for their community involvement.

Regardless of the number of laws, the crime rate has always been too high. Legislation evolves slowly, reflecting the evolution of society. Legislation responds to a public outcry to control behavior. During the '20s and '30s, robberies, crimes against persons, and Prohibition-related offenses were prevalent. After World War II, a new breed of criminals and crime developed. Today assorted frauds, thefts, and computer-related offenses occur. Future overall crime rates will decrease but be more violent due to drug-related attacks.

Criminologists, sociologists, and those within the criminal justice system generally agree that to substantially diminish crime for the long term would be an overwhelming task. Nonetheless, there has been a gradual decrease in many crime rates during recent years, mainly due to the baby boom generation's aging out of most of the crime-prone age group.

Law enforcement cannot stop crime. To a degree, crime prevention units, neighborhood watch associations, antirobbery divisions, and decoy operations make a difference, though they sometimes seem futile. No matter how hard you work or how good a job you do, there will be an endless stream of criminals. Still, doing one's personal best is one of life's great accomplishments. The lives of great officers have been ruined because they could not accept the fact that they could not change everything that is bad or evil.

To eliminate crime, America must eliminate unemployment, racism, inadequate education, poverty, dysfunctional family life, drug abuse, juvenile delinquency, problems of the mentally ill and elderly, greed, discrimination, and inequality. In other words, we have little possibility of preventing virtually all crime, unless citizens are willing to give up their constitutional rights. Officers, therefore, will continue to struggle with law enforcement, and true leaders will never lose sight of what our nation would be like without it.

COURT DECISIONS

The best that officers can do to improve the justice system is to work from within it. This is an honorable goal; for all of its problems, the American justice system currently is one of the best judicial systems in the world. Let us examine frustrations associated with some court decisions in our system.

Unfair court decisions frustrate officers because they appear to restrain the police. For example, crucial evidence may be declared inadmissible; confessions may be dismissed; and rapists, murderers, and robbers may go free.

Amendments to the Constitution were originally created for protection of citizens. The Fifth Amendment, for example, regards self-incrimination: "No person . . . shall be compelled in any criminal case to be a witness against himself . . ." The intent of this Amendment was fairness; most people agree that it would be wrong for anyone to be coerced into testifying against himself or herself.

The Fourteenth Amendment states, "No state shall . . . deprive any person of life, liberty, or property, without due process of law. . . ." Once again, no one can argue with this amendment; it makes sense. Decade after decade, the courts struck what they believed was a balance between the right of society to be protected and the rights of the accused. The system emphasized the totality of circumstances surrounding particular situations.

During the 1960s, however, the courts began to substantially adjust their reasoning. One example is the *Miranda* decision, which occurred in 1966. Supreme Court Justice Earl Warren explained the majority reasoning as he wrote "police interrogations were so inherently coercive" that courts should consider to first advise them of their rights.

Other respected legal authorities disagree with the reasoning behind Supreme Court decisions such as *Miranda*. Professor Emeritus Fred Imbau of the Northwestern University School of Law states the impact of the *Miranda* decision has been devastating to police effectiveness.[11] Others claim that the monumental Supreme Court decisions of the 1960s simply went too far and ignored the rights of victims and favored the accused.

These court decisions created untiring, unprecedented controversy. Public outcry and frustration often rose very high. As years passed, the turmoil gradually began to lessen. The 1970s and 1980s found citizen attitude more accepting, even though numerous victim advocate organizations were created. During the late 1980s, several court decisions started to move more in favor of the victim. The future political and social climate will determine just how far these decisions will go.

CIVIL SUITS AGAINST LAW ENFORCEMENT

Most cops have an enormous amount of sincerity and would never intentionally violate legal rights or deprive someone of their liberties. America is not plagued with widespread police abuse.

Supreme Court decisions of the 1960s regulated actions of the police strictly. Patrol officers had begun to be the focus of civil suits prior to the 1970s. The threat of civil litigation against law enforcement prevailed in the 1980s and 1990s. The frequency of litigation increased in the 1980s. Case law 42 USC 1983 was passed as a federal law intended to prevent officers from violating defendant's rights and abusing the Constitution "under the color of state law." It expanded civil liability to all levels of a law enforcement agency's hierarchy. Some officers who found themselves the focus of civil suits avoided liability by proving they acted "in good faith." Unfortunately, this often caused further media attacks to fall on their agency. Sometimes superior officers were sued for lack of training and/or supervision.

The ability of law enforcement to withstand the wave of litigation took a serious blow in 1978, when the Supreme Court held that cities violating constitutional rights under local custom, policy, or practice could be held liable under 42 USC 1983. Anyone bringing claims against the police could now challenge a city's customs, policies, or traditions. Before long, another ruling held that municipalities could no longer claim the good faith defense to constitutional violations.[12]

From the officers' point of view, the storm of civil litigation against them seems unjust. After all, most cops are on the street doing the best that they can. They are not lawyers who have months to examine a situation and then act accordingly. On the streets, they must often make split-second decisions under stressful conditions.

While it may be unfair to closely examine each move and then sue someone or their agency for every penny possible, it is everyone's right to file suit. Civil litigation against the police is unlikely to change. Always remember that professionalism will defend you. Surprisingly, there have been substantial positive effects resulting from the increase of civil litigation against the police. Law enforcement is held more accountable for its actions.

The benefit of testifying in criminal court is that every action is examined, which causes officers to reassess their actions. If mistakes were made, they will learn from them. When officers and their departments are sued, it likewise forces everyone to examine themselves, their policies, their methods of operation, and the effectiveness of training. A positive effect of litigation against the police is that it has caused law enforcement to become more professional. This has affected sheriffs, chiefs, and county and city administrators.

In February 1989 the Supreme Court ruled that cities can be held liable for some injuries if the concerned police officers' training was inadequate. The *City of Canton* v. *Harris* ruling expanded the civil liability of local governments. If a failure to train amounts to a "deliberate indifference" to constitutional rights and is responsible for the damages that have occurred, the agency and government can be held accountable.

Good police work can usually prevent and refute false accusations. This requires working the street effectively and being equally conscientious about all actions. Write good reports; never do anything to lose your most prized possession, your integrity; revise departmental procedures when needed; and document effective training. When officers are guilty, they must be responsible for their own actions. When allegations of misconduct and abuse are true, litigation does us all a favor, because officers who engage in such behavior should not be on the force.

PLEA BARGAINING

Most criminal convictions are obtained through plea bargaining. Each year thousands of criminals receive reduced sentences, probation, withholding of adjudication, or adjudication of a lesser charge. Often plea bargaining enrages victims, witnesses, or entire communities. Some officers vent their frustration over cases of plea bargaining by becoming enraged or acting out—actions they will regret later. Others, though unhappy, accept the fact.

At times, plea bargaining is an exasperating but necessary element of the criminal justice system. In a few isolated instances negotiations between the prosecutor, defense, and judge result in a mockery of justice.

The frustration, anger, and outrage felt about plea bargaining is the result of not understanding or refusing to accept the realities of the American judicial process. Without plea bargaining, many criminals would go unpunished and others would receive much lighter sentences. There simply are not enough resources to process the caseload, and the system and those within it are already over-worked, backlogged, and overstressed. Imagine what it would be like if all the cases that ended through plea bargaining were suddenly scheduled for trials. For some of the reasons why our courts and jails are so clogged, see Box 4-6. For a snapshot of the prison and jail populations, see Box 4-7.

Box 4-6

Corrections

PRISON AND JAIL INMATES AT MIDYEAR 2002

Presents data on prison and jail inmates, collected from National Prisoner Statistics counts and the Annual Survey of Jails in 2002. This report provides, for each State and the Federal system, the number of inmates and the overall incarceration rate per 100,000 residents. It offers trends since 1995 and percentage changes in prison populations since midyear and the end of 2001. The midyear report presents the number of prison inmates held in private facilities and the number of prisoners under 18 years of age held by State correctional authorities. It includes total numbers for prison and jail inmates by gender, race, and Hispanic origin as well as counts of jail inmates by juvenile status, conviction status, and confinement status. The report also provides findings on rated capacity of local jails, percent of capacity occupied, and capacity added.

Highlights include the following:

1. In the year ending June 30, 2002, the number of inmates in custody in local jails rose by 34,235; in State prison by 12,440; and in Federal prison by 8,042.
2. At midyear 2002, a total of 3,055 State prisoners were under age 18. Adult jails held a total of 7,248 persons under age 18.
3. At midyear 2002, there were 113 female inmates per 100,000 women in the United States, compared to 1,309 male inmates per 100,000 men.

Source: Bureau of Justice Statistics, U.S. Department of Justice, Prison and Jail Inmates at Midyear 2002, U.S. Government, Printing Office, May 2003.

Box 4-7

Prison and Jail Populations

FACTS FROM THE BUREAU OF JUSTICE STATISTICS

Lifetime Likelihood of Going to State or Federal Prison

If recent incarceration rates remain unchanged, an estimated 1 of every 20 persons (5.1%) will serve time in a prison during their lifetime.

1. Lifetime chances of a person going to prison are higher for men (9%) than for women (1.1%); blacks (16.2%) and Hispanics (9.4%) than for whites (2.5%)
2. Based on current rates of first incarceration, an estimated 28% of black males will enter State or Federal prison during their lifetime, compared to 16% of Hispanic males and 4.4% of white males.

Characteristics of State Prison Inmates

1. Women were 6.6% of the State prison inmates in 2001, up from 6% in 1995.
2. Sixty-four percent of prison inmates belonged to racial or ethnic minorities in 2001.
3. An estimated 57% of inmates were under age 35 in 2001.
4. About 4% of State prison inmates were not U.S. citizens at yearend 2001.
5. About 6% of State prison inmates were held in private facilities at yearend 2001.
6. Altogether, an estimated 57% of inmates had a high school diploma or its equivalent.

Among the State prison inmates in 2000:

1. Nearly half were sentenced for a violent crime (49%)
2. A fifth were sentenced for a property crime (20%)
3. About a fifth were sentenced for a drug crime (21%)

(continued)

Box 4-7 *(continued)*

Characteristics of Jail Inmates

1. Women were 10% of the local jail inmates in 1996, unchanged from 1989.
2. Forty-eight percent of jailed women reported having been physically or sexually abused prior to admission; 27% had been raped.
3. Sixty-three percent of jail inmates belonged to racial or ethnic minorities in 1996, up slightly from 61% in 1989.
4. Twenty-four percent of jail inmates were between the ages of 35 and 44 in 1996, up from 17% in 1989.
5. Over a third of all inmates reported some physical or mental disability.
6. About 8% of local jail inmates were not U.S. citizens.
7. Altogether, 54% of inmates had a high school diploma or its equivalent.
8. Thirty-six percent of all inmates were not employed during the month before they were arrested for their current offense—20% were looking for work; 16% were not looking.

Among the local jail inmates in 1996:

1. A fourth were held for a violent crime.
2. A fourth were held for a property crime.
3. About a fifth were held for a drug crime.
4. More than 7 of every 10 jail inmates had prior sentences to probation or incarceration.
5. A quarter of the jail inmates said they had been treated at some time for a mental or emotional problem.

Comparing Federal and State Prison Inmates

In 1997, Federal inmates were more likely than State inmates to be:

1. Women (7% vs. 6%)
2. Hispanic (27% vs. 17%)
3. Age 45 or older (24% vs. 13%)

Box 4-7 *(continued)*

4. With some college education (18% vs. 11%)
5. Noncitizens (18% vs. 5%)

In 2000:

1. An estimated 57% of Federal inmates and 21% of State inmates were serving a sentence for a drug offense; about 10% of Federal inmates and 49% of State inmates were in prison for a violent offense.
2. Violent offenders accounted for 53% of the growth in State prisons from 1990 to 2000; drug offenders accounted for 59% of the growth in Federal prisons.

Recidivism

1. Of the 272,111 persons released from prisons in 15 States in 1994, an estimated 67.5% were rearrested for a felony or serious misdemeanor within 3 years, 46.9% were reconvicted, and 25.4% were sentenced to prison for a new crime.
2. The 272,111 offenders discharged in 1994 accounted for nearly 4,877,000 arrest charges over their recorded careers.
3. Within 3 years of release, 2.5% of released rapists were rearrested for another rape, and 1.2% of those who had served time for homicide were arrested for a new homicide.

Sex Offenders

1. On a given day in 1994 there were approximately 234,000 offenders convicted of rape or sexual assault under the care, custody, or control of corrections agencies; nearly 60% of these sex offenders are under conditional supervision in the community.
2. The median age of the victims of imprisoned sexual assaulters was less than 13 years old; the median age of rape victims was about 22 years.

(continued)

Box 4-7 *(continued)*

3. An estimated 24% of those serving time for rape and 19% of those serving time for sexual assault had been on probation or parole at the time of the offense for which they were in State prison in 1991.

Child Victimizers

1. Offenders who had victimized a child were on average 5 years older than the violent offenders who had committed their crimes against adults. Nearly 25% of child victimizers were age 40 or older, but about 10% of the inmates with adult victims fell in that age range.

Inmate Victimizers

1. About 4 in 10 inmates serving time in jail for inmate violence had a criminal justice status—on probation or parole or under a restraining order—at the time of the violent attack on an inmate.

2. About 1 in 4 convicted violent offenders confined in local jails had committed their crime against an inmate; about 7% of State prisoners serving time for violence had an inmate victim.

3. About half of all offenders convicted of inmate violence and confined in a local jail or a State prison had been drinking at the time of the offense. Jail inmates who had been drinking prior to the inmate violence consumed an average amount of ethanol equivalent to 10 beers.

4. About 8 in 10 inmates serving time in State prison for inmate violence had injured or killed their victim.

Use of Alcohol by Convicted Offenders

1. Among the 5.3 million convicted offenders under the jurisdiction of corrections agencies in 1996, nearly 2 million, or about 36%, were estimated to have been drinking at the time of the offense. The vast majority, about 1.5 million, of these alcohol-involved offenders were sentenced to supervision in the community: 1.3 million on probation and more than 200,000 on parole.

Box 4-7 *(continued)*

2. Alcohol use at the time of the offense was commonly found among those convicted of public-order crimes, a type of offense most highly represented among those on probation and in jail. Among violent offenders, 41% of probationers, 41% of those in local jails, 38% of those in State prisons, and 20% of those in Federal prisons were estimated to have been drinking when they committed the crime.

Women Offenders

1. In 1998 there were an estimated 3.2 million arrests of women, accounting for 22% of all arrests that year.
2. Based on self-reports of victims of violence, women account for 14% of violent offenders, an annual average of about 2.1 million violent female offenders.
3. Women accounted for about 16% of all felons convicted in State courts in 1996: 8% of convicted violent felons, 23% of property felons, and 17% of drug felons.
4. In 1998 more than 950,000 women were under correctional supervision, about 1% of the U.S. female population.

Reentry Trends in the United States

Inmates returning to the community after serving time in prison

1. At least 95% of all State prisoners will be released from prison at some point; nearly 80% will be released to parole supervision.
2. At yearend 2001, 1,406,031 prisoners were under the jurisdiction of State or Federal correctional authorities.
3. In 2000, about 571,000 State prison inmates were released to the community after serving time in prison.
4. Nearly 33% of State prison releases in 1999 were drug offenders, 25% were violent offenders and 31% were property offenders.

(continued)

Box 4-7 *(continued)*

5. 653,134 adults were under State parole supervision at yearend 2001.

6. By the end of 2000, 16 States had abolished discretionary release from prison by a parole board for all offenders.

Among State parole discharges in 1999, 42% successfully completed their term of supervision; relatively unchanged since 1990.

Source: Bureau of Justice Statistics, U.S. Department of Justice, Facts for the Bureau of Justice Statistics (Washington, DC: U.S. Government Printing Office, 2003).

DEFENSE ATTORNEYS

Few things are more infuriating to dedicated cops than to have their testimonies and cases torn apart and distorted before juries. It is also frustrating for a jury to hear the truth twisted and distorted. Sometimes it seems as though justice is lost in the shuffle, as a few defense attorneys appear more concerned with winning and collecting fees from their clients. Some even intentionally withhold evidence or unethically coach witnesses. Fortunately, rules of criminal procedure and courtroom limitations usually prevent defense attorneys from such behavior.

Officers should never lose sight of what truth and justice mean. Few things are more precious and valuable than living with honor and dignity. As with any profession, there will be a few unethical attorneys among the many good ones. If attorneys try to mislead or distort your testimony, stay calm, collected, and factual. Your honesty, professionalism, and sincerity will be apparent, and so will their deceitfulness.

LEGAL GLOSSARY

It is almost impossible to work effectively within the justice system without understanding frequently used terms. Understanding the vocabulary will help prevent disastrous results for your cases.

Know the proper spelling as well to avoid damage to your credibility. Study the following terms to help you build a practical, effective legal vocabulary.

Abrogate To repeal, cancel, or annul.

Abscond To leave a jurisdiction of the courts to avoid legal process.

Accessory Any person who has knowledge that an individual has committed a felony or has been charged with a felony and aids that person with the intent that the individual avoid arrest, trial, or conviction. An accessory must have knowledge that the individual has committed, been charged with, or been convicted of the felony.

Accused The defendant in a criminal case.

Acquittal The formal finding of innocence of an individual charged with an offense.

Adjudicate To make a final determination.

Adversary An opposing party in an action.

Affidavit A sworn written declaration or factual statement given before an individual having authority to administer oaths.

Amend To correct an error.

Appeal The process of obtaining a review and retrial by a superior court.

Arraignment A legal procedure by which a defendant is informed by the court of the charges against him or her, is advised of his or her legal rights, and determines his or her plea.

Bench Warrant A process issued by a court for the arrest of an individual. It is usually issued by a judge when an individual fails to appear for court.

Beyond a Reasonable Doubt A phrase intended to satisfy the judgment of a jury that a defendant committed the concerned crime. It is typically used as a portion of a statement such as "proved beyond a reasonable doubt."

Capias A term that refers to several types of documents that require an officer to take the defendant into custody.

Certiorari A document issued by a superior court to a lower court requesting that the record of a case be sent to it for review.

Change of Venue The moving of a trial begun in one jurisdiction to another jurisdiction for trial.

Circumstantial Evidence The circumstances surrounding and conditions from which the existence of the main fact may be logically and reasonable inferred.

Coercion The act of compelling by force or threat.

Concurrent At the same time, as in "The defendant received two sentences that will be served concurrently."

Consecutive Served one after the other, as in "The defendant received consecutive sentences."

Conveyance A written paper on which property or title to property is transferred from one individual to another; also a type of vehicle.

Corpus Delicti Basic facts required to prove the commission of a crime.

Corroboration Additional evidence that supports the testimony of a witness.

Count Used to specify more than one part of an indictment or information, each charging a separate offense. Frequently used synonymously with "charge."

Criminal Intent The intent to commit a crime.

Curtilage An enclosed space that immediately surrounds a dwelling.

Deliberate To determine the guilt or innocence of a defendant by weighing the evidence.

Deposition A statement obtained through questioning, usually transcribed, signed, and sworn to.

Direct Evidence Evidence of proof that tends to show the existence of a fact without considering any other fact.

Duces Tecum Latin, meaning "bring with you." Generally appears on a subpoena requiring someone to appear and bring certain items with them.

Duress Forcing someone to do something against their will.

Entrapment The act by the police of inducing an individual to commit a crime.

Evidence The means through which an allegation is established or disproved. Proof that is usually presented at trial for the purpose of establishing belief.

Exclusionary Rule A rule that prevents evidence seized illegally from being admitted in a trial.

Ex Parte Done for or by only one party; on behalf of only one party.

Fruits of a Crime Material objects obtained through the commission of a crime and which may constitute the subject of a crime.

Gross Negligence The obvious failure to exercise the extent of care required by particular circumstances.

Habeas Corpus Documents that command someone to produce a detained individual before court.

Hearsay Evidence not from the personal knowledge of a witness, but from what has been heard from others.

Impeachment A technique of indicating a witness is not believable. Also, a criminal proceeding intended to remove a public officer from office.

Indictment The formal charge of crime issued by a grand jury after hearing evidence surrounding the offense.

Information An accusation of a criminal offense against an individual, issued without an indictment.

Infraction A minor offense, primarily a traffic offense.

Injunction A document that prohibits the performing of a particular action.

Inquest A legal inquiry by a medical examiner or court into a sudden or unusual death.

Judgment The official order or sentence of a court in an official proceeding.

Leading Question A question that is influential or suggestive when asked of a witness.

Magistrate A lower court judge.

Mens Rea Guilty knowledge, a wrongful purpose, or criminal intent.

Misdemeanor An offense that is not a felony; a minor offense.

Modus Operandi The method of operation used by an offender.

Preponderance of the Evidence Evidence that, when compared to evidence in opposition, produces a more convincing truth.

Prima Facie   Evidence that is sufficient to establish a fact when first considered.

Probable Cause   A statement of facts that would lead a reasonable person to believe the accused individual committed the offense.

Res Gestae   Things done during an entire event; actions or statements immediately after an incident that are considered part of the incident.

Respondent   The defendant during an appeal process.

Sequester   To isolate the jury of a legal proceeding; also, to separate witnesses from other witnesses to prevent them from hearing testimony.

Subpoena   A document that commands appearance of a witness.

Subpoena *Duces Tecum*   A document commanding an individual to produce documents for a court proceeding.

Utter   To publish or circulate.

Venue   The location where a fact is alleged to have occurred; the location where a court with jurisdiction may hear a legal proceeding.

Writ   A judicial instrument used by a court to command an action by an individual.

QUESTIONS FOR DISCUSSION

1. The dignity of crime victims is often ignored by the criminal justice system, as repeat offenders are set free over and over again. It seems that the system is filled with stagnation, injustice, and inequity. How much does this fact trouble you? What do agencies do to help officers who become bitter and frustrated about it?

2. Our system of justice demands that the prosecution and defense determine and present facts through testimony. The finding of truth is sometimes hampered by witnesses who lie and by important evidence that cannot be presented to the jury for particular reasons. What circumstances would justify an officer committing perjury during a trial? How often do you think officers intentionally lie during court proceedings?

3. Which of the first ten amendments to the Constitution (Bill of Rights) is the most important to you? Why?

4. The American justice system intentionally sacrifices part of its effectiveness in order to prevent the infringement of innocent people's liberties. Sometimes it seems that too much effectiveness is sacrificed at the expense of crime victims. Officers, therefore, must understand the system thoroughly and learn how to function within its limitations, still upholding the protection of citizens' rights with honesty, ethics, and honor. Some cynical officers would say the preceding statement is a bunch of bull_ _ _ _ and that sometimes justice only comes from stretching the facts to put a bad guy in prison where he belongs or knocking the teeth out of the abusive husband who has just done the same to his wife. What will you say and do if you work with such an officer someday?

5. To eliminate crime, America must eliminate unemployment, racism, inadequate education, poverty, greed, dysfunctional family life, drug abuse, juvenile delinquency, problems of the mentally ill and elderly, and discrimination and inequality. Are these issues what community-oriented policing and problem-oriented policing can or should be addressing? If so, how well do you believe it is working?

ENDNOTES

1. Hazel B. Kerper, *Introduction to the Criminal Justice System* (St. Paul, MN: West Publishing, 1972), pp. 7–14.

2. Ohlin, Lloyd E., "Surveying Discretion by Criminal Justice Decision Makers," in Discretion in Criminal Justice: The Tension Between Individualization and Uniformity, ed. Lloyd E. Ohlin and Frank J. Remington, Albany, NY: State University of New York Press, 1993: 6.

3. Personal conversations with Herman Goldstein.

4. The findings were first used in Kelling, George L., "Toward New Images of Policing: Herman Goldstein's Problem-Oriented Policing," Law & Social Inquiry 17 (3) (Summer 1992): 545.

5. Miller, Frank, Prosecution: The Decision to Charge a Suspect with a Crime, ed. Frank J. Remington, Boston: Little, Brown and Company, 1970.

6. For a summary of the thinking in the area of domestic violence and an example of an individual author's evolution in thinking, see Parnas, Raymond I., "Criminal Justice Responses to Domestic Violence Issues," in Discretion in Criminal Justice: The Tension Between Individualization

and Uniformity, ed. Lloyd E. Ohlin and Frank J. Remington, Albany, NY: State University of New York Press, 1993: 175-210.

7. Ibid., pp. 22–24.

8. John N. Ferdico, *Criminal Procedure* (New York: West Publishing, 1989), pp. 4–6.

9. The President's Commission on Law Enforcement and Administration of Justice, *The Challenge of Crime in a Free Society* (Washington, DC: U.S. Government Printing Office, 1967).

10. The President's Commission on Law Enforcement and Administration of Justice, *The Challenge of Crime in a Free Society* (Washington, DC: U.S. Government Printing Office, 1967).

11. Eugene H. Methvin, "The Case of Common Sense vs. Miranda," *Reader's Digest*, August 1987, pp. 98–99.

12. Candace McCoy, "Lawsuits Against the Police: Do They Really Deter?" Nov.-Dec., 1983. Reprinted: Criminal Justice Annual Editions: 1985 (Connecticut: Duxbury Press), pp. 57–58.

chapter 5

SURVIVING THE STREET

Being a good law enforcement officer is not an event, but a process. Each day you will be challenged on many different fronts, but never compromise yourself. You see, character is really what matters most. At the end of your career you will reflect back on many things, but all will be viewed through the lens of your character. Take care of yourself and take care of those around you.

Kevin Thom
Director, Division of Criminal Investigation
Office of Attorney General
State of South Dakota

Cops are good people. Some develop a cynical, tough exterior as a defense against the crime on the street. "The Blue Wall" comprises people who risk their welfare for the protection of others, for no other reason than it is just the right thing to do.

RISKY BUSINESS

If you were to ask someone applying to an agency why he or she wanted to be an officer, 95 percent of the time the answer would be "to help others." Their feelings may change as the years pass because of the frustration from working the street and the injustices of the justice system. It takes a special blend of sincerity and courage to intentionally put yourself in the middle of violent or tragic situations daily. Imagine exposing yourself to brutality, violence, and hatred in order to resolve situations so that others will not be injured. It is an act that requires an equal amount of courage and nobility to survive. Every moment of every day an officer somewhere in the nation is at risk. It may be when a cop is in an alley at 0430 hours, walking up to a vehicle, separating a husband and wife during a disturbance, or arresting someone for assault. Officers do not do this for medals or other recognition; they do it simply because it is their job. Box 5-1 points out just some of the dangers officers face.

Box 5-1

Police Work and Danger

1. Police/law enforcement officers run a high risk of being attacked, wounded or even killed by criminals, hoodlums and other people whose behavior disagrees with the law and the society's norms. They may also suffer from "friendly fire."
2. Many police/law enforcement officers are involved in work-related accidents—vehicle crashes, falls during chase, rescue and similar operations, etc.
3. Police/law enforcement officers usually live under constant apprehension of physical danger, work long and irregular hours, and are exposed to unpleasant sides of life. This often results in psychological stress, family and personality problems.
4. Police/law enforcement officers may develop health problems as a result of spending much time outdoors, including under the sun or in bad weather.

Accidents

1. Accidents are most likely during emergency response of the policeman/law enforcement officer and may occur especially while doing first aid work, patrol car driving and riot control.
2. Slips, trips, and falls while ascending and descending from roofs or while chasing suspects in a crime.
3. Wounds caused by knife or other object (metal rod, baseball bat, etc.), as a result of being attacked by persons contacted

Box 5-1 *(continued)*

in the course of duty (suspects, offenders, their sympathizers, etc.).

4. Wounds caused by random or careless shooting by others (incl. "friendly fire").
5. Self-inflicted wounds caused during firearms cleaning, loading, etc.
6. Car or motorcycle accidents while chasing fleeing vehicles, or while driving fast in response to emergency calls.
7. Unavoidable physical contact with people who have contagious diseases (especially HIV) is a serious health hazard.

Physical Hazards

1. Exposure to ambient environmental factors (low or high air temperatures, rain, wind, snow, sun) resulting in acute (common cold, heat stroke, dehydration, etc.) or chronic (rheumatism, etc.) diseases.
2. Exposure to high noise levels from the emergency horn or on the firing range.

Chemical Hazards

1. Exposure to lead while directing traffic, working on the firing range, or doing fingerprinting work.
2. Exposure to excessive levels of carbon monoxide while directing traffic.

Biological Hazards

1. Risk of contracting a contagious disease (HIV, infectious hepatitis, rabies, etc.) as a result of needle stick injury, human or animal bite, or close contact with infected/ill people (esp. members of high-risk groups).
2. Infection caused by insects or rodents while entering polluted or abandoned places (esp. cellars, basements, etc.) for the purpose of inspection, search, observation, etc.

(continued)

Box 5-1 *(continued)*

Ergonomic, Psychosocial, and Organizational Factors

1. Long periods of time spent inside vehicles may in the course of time result in musculoskeletal disorders (esp. low-back pains).
2. Cumulative trauma disorders of lower extremities (e.g., flatfoot) as a result of long-time, extensive foot patrolling assignments.
3. Post-traumatic stress disorder (PTSD), most likely if the incident witnessed by the policeman has resulted in serious injury or death to any of those involved.
4. Exposure to various psychological stressors (stress-related disorders may be manifested as behavioral problems, marital or family problems, or sometimes as alcohol or substance abuse).
5. Personal and/or family problems caused by shift work, irregular work hours (incl. at night), constant state of alertness (incl. when off duty), relations with peers and superiors within an hierarchical system typical of police and law-enforcement forces, and similar psychosocial factors.
6. Fear of being prosecuted afterward for actions which seemed to be clearly indicated as necessary during an event, but later not considered as such (particularly by others) when the moments of peak stress were past.
7. The paperwork duties, as opposed to active law enforcement, are often experienced as a major stressor.

Preventative Measures

1. When on duty, wear the personal protective equipment provided for the job at hand, e.g., bulletproof clothing.
2. Wear appropriate hearing protection on the firing range.
3. In rescue operations or when dealing with drug addicts, take precautions to avoid contact with body fluids; in particular do not expose cuts or other open skin wounds to body fluids, to avoid contamination with agents causing diseases such as AIDS, hepatitis, etc., gloves.

> **Box 5-1** *(continued)*
>
> 4. Learn relaxation exercises and perform them during long waiting periods.
> 5. Seek psychological or vocational advice if experiencing work-related stresses or burnout.
> 6. Select a shift work schedule that would have the least harmful effect on the employee's health, family and personal life—consult employees and specialists in shift scheduling.
>
> *Source:* International Occupational Safety and Health Information Centre (CIS), *International Hazard Datasheets on Occupation Police/Law Enforcement Officer* (Geneva, Switzerland: CIS), http://www.ilocis.org/default.html. Copyright © 1998 International Labour Organization. Accessed 4-14-2004.

Circumstances of Officer Murders

About twice a week in America, a cop dies while performing official duties. Roughly 80 officers are murdered each year. About 20 more die in the line of duty by other means. As they take their last breath, a little bit of America departs with them. The question is, did they have to die? Is there anything they could have done to survive? In most cases, there were techniques that could have increased their chances of survival. To learn these techniques, every cop should know the answers to the questions when, where, how, why, and by whom. Information on officers killed during 2000 is presented in Box 5-2.

Anticipating Danger

One of the most beneficial and effective ways officers can safeguard themselves on the street is to develop the ability to anticipate danger. This should not be confused with being scared, being timid, or overreacting. A great deal of mental preparation and control are required to ensure that you will not overreact. Most officers resort to the way they have been trained. If you have not been well trained, however, no one can tell what you will do!

Box 5-2
Law Enforcement Officers Killed During 2000

METHODOLOGY

Section contains statistics on felonious and accidental deaths of duly sworn local, state, and federal law enforcement officers meeting the following criteria: they are working in an official capacity, they have full arrest powers, they wear a badge (ordinarily), they carry a firearm (ordinarily), and they are paid from governmental funds set aside specifically for payment of sworn law enforcement representatives.

The Uniform Crime Reporting (UCR) Program receives data on officers' deaths from several sources. First, local and state law enforcement agencies participating in the UCR Program notify the national Program of duty-related deaths. Contributors submit preliminary data about any officer killed in the line of duty within their jurisdictions.

In addition, FBI field divisions and legal attache offices also report such incidents occurring in the United States and its territories, as well as those in which a United States law enforcement officer dies while assigned to duties in another country. Finally, the Bureau of Justice Assistance, administrator of the Public Safety Officers' Benefits Program, maintains contact throughout the year, supplying the national UCR Program with information regarding officers whose survivors have received benefits. This threefold reporting procedure ensures the validity and completeness of the data.

Once the national Program receives notification of a line-of-duty death, the staff send inquiries through FBI field divisions to the victim officer's employing agency to obtain additional details concerning the circumstances surrounding the incident. Additionally, the national staff furnishes the agency with information concerning two federal programs that provide benefits to survivors of federal and nonfederal law enforcement officers killed in the line of duty. The national Program staff also obtained pertinent criminal history data concerning the individuals identified in connection with felonious killings from the FBI's Interstate Identification Index.

Box 5-2 *(continued)*

Overview

During 2000:

1. A total of 51 law enforcement officers fell victim to murder while performing their official duties.
2. City police departments employed 27 of the fallen officers.
3. County police and sheriffs' offices, 21 victims; and state agencies, 3 officers.
4. Law enforcement agencies in 21 states and Puerto Rico lost officers through line-of-duty felonious killings.
5. Fifty separate incidents, one of which occurred 43 years ago and another which occurred 23 years ago, claimed the lives of the 51 officers.
6. Arrests or circumstances of exceptional means cleared 49 of these incidents.
7. The number of officers slain in 2000 increased 21.4 percent from the 42 officer fatalities of 1999.
8. Five- and 10-year trends show the number of officers slain in 2000 was 16.4 percent lower than in 1996 and 28.2 percent lower than in 1991.

Victims

1. The data reported to the national Program about victim officers show that the average age of the 51 officers slain during 2000 was 38.
2. Five fallen officers were under the age of 25, and 11 were between 25 and 30 years of age.
3. Eighteen victims were aged 31 through 40, and 17 were over 40 years of age.
4. Fifty of the officers who lost their lives in 2000 were male, and 1 was female.
5. Thirty-nine of the officers slain were white, and 11 officers were black. Race was not reported for one victim. On the average, victim officers in 2000 had 9 years of law enforcement experience.

(continued)

Box 5-2 *(continued)*

6. Twenty victim officers had served the law enforcement community more than 10 years, and 11 fallen officers had between 5 and 10 years of service.
7. Additionally, 17 victims had 1 through 4 years of service, and 3 officers had less than 1 year of service.

Circumstances Surrounding Deaths

1. The data collected on the circumstances surrounding officers' deaths reveal that 13 officers were slain while conducting traffic pursuits/stops, 12 were killed during arrest situations, 10 were killed in ambush situations, and 8 were murdered upon responding to disturbance calls.
2. Six officers were killed while investigating suspicious persons or circumstances, and 2 were slain while handling or transporting prisoners.
3. Of the 12 officers slain during arrest situations in 2000, 2 officers were killed by burglary suspects, 2 by robbery suspects, 3 by suspects during drug-related situations, and 5 by assailants suspected of other crimes.

Types of Assignment

1. In 2000, the data reported to the national Program show that 39 of the 51 victims were assigned to vehicle patrol.
2. Of those officers killed while on vehicle patrol, 31 were assigned to one-officer vehicles and 8 to two-officer vehicles.
3. Seven of the 51 victims were performing detective duties or were on special assignment, and 5 officers were off duty but acting in an official capacity as law enforcement officers when they were killed.
4. From 1991 through 2000, most of the victim officers, 63.5 percent, were conducting vehicle patrols at the time of the felonious incidents that led to their death.
5. In addition, 14.6 percent of the total victim officers were acting in an official capacity though off duty at the time of their fatal incidents.

Box 5-2 *(continued)*

6. Data collected regarding the officers' assignments also reveal that during the 10-year period, 49.6 percent of the vehicle patrol officers were alone and unassisted when they were killed, 41.7 percent of the foot patrol officers were alone and unassisted, and 30.2 percent of the victim officers on other types of assignments were alone and unassisted.

Alleged Assailants

1. The data collected by the national UCR Program on alleged assailants reveal that a total of 65 suspects were identified in conjunction with the 50 separate incidents in which an officer was feloniously killed.
2. Two offenders remain unidentified. Of the 65 identified suspects, 37 were under the age of 31.
3. By gender, 63 were male and 2 were female. Race data, which were not reported for 2 suspects, indicate that 47 of the identified suspects were white, and 16 were black.
4. The criminal histories of the 65 identified suspects show that 52 had previous arrests; 20 of those arrests were for crimes of violence and 9 specifically for assaulting an officer or resisting arrest.
5. Thirty of the identified suspects had prior convictions, and 20 had been apprehended for weapons violations.
6. At the time of the killings, 12 of the identified suspects were on probation or parole.
7. In 2000, law enforcement agencies arrested 51 of the 65 identified suspects in conjunction with officers' felonious deaths.
8. Victim officers justifiably killed 3 of their assailants, and persons other than the victim officers justifiably killed 6 suspects.
9. Five subjects committed suicide after slaying an officer.
10. The time period for disposition data for known assailants lags 2 years behind current year's data in this publication due to sometimes lengthy court proceedings.

(continued)

Box 5-2 *(continued)*

11. For the 10-year period 1989 through 1998, the dispositions of the 910 persons identified in connection with officers' murders show that 720 suspects were arrested and charged, 178 died prior to their arrest, and 12 assailants remain fugitives.

12. Further, of the 178 deceased assailants, 109 were justifiably killed, 63 committed suicide, 4 died under other circumstances, and 2 were murdered while at large.

13. The adjudication process determined that 500 of the 720 persons arrested and charged between 1989 and 1998 were guilty of murder.

14. Of the 500 offenders found guilty of murder, 107 were sentenced to death, 236 received life imprisonment, 155 were given prison terms ranging from 18 months through 396 years, and 2 were placed on probation.

15. Further, of these 720 arrestees, another 70 were found guilty of a lesser offense that was related to murder, and 39 were found guilty of a crime other than murder.

16. Fifty-six arrestees were acquitted or had charges against them dismissed or nolle prossed, 24 have cases that remain pending or their dispositions are unknown at present, 16 have been committed to psychiatric institutions, and 10 died in custody before a final disposition was determined.

17. Sentences remain indeterminate for 5 of the persons charged.

Weapons data reported to the national program reveal the following information.

Weapons

1. Assailants used firearms in 47 of the 51 officer killings in 2000, including the victim officer's service weapon in one instance.

2. Of these firearms used, 33 were handguns, 10 were rifles, and 4 were shotguns.

3. The most common handgun cartridge type used against officers was the 9 mm, which accounted for 8 of the handguns used in the officers' deaths.

Box 5-2 *(continued)*

4. In addition to those killed by firearms, 3 officers were intentionally struck by vehicles, and 1 was slain with a knife.

5. From 1991 through 2000, 601 or 93.3 percent of the 644 officers slain in the line of duty were killed by firearms, including 70.2 percent by handguns, 17.7 percent by rifles, and 5.4 percent by shotguns.

6. Other weapons, i.e., knives or cutting instruments, blunt objects, etc., were used in 6.7 percent of officer deaths.

7. Furthermore, during this 10-year period, 51 officers were slain with their own weapons, and 142 victim officers fired their service weapons.

8. In addition, the weapons of 104 officers were stolen.

9. Among the 601 officers who died of gunshot wounds from 1991 to 2000, 50.4 percent were within 5 feet of their assailant at the time of the fatal attack.

10. The data collected about location of the fatal wounds show that 48.4 percent of the firearm fatalities were a result of wounds to the head.

11. Upper torso wounds claimed the lives of 45.6 percent of the victim officers, and wounds below the waist took the lives of 6.0 percent.

Body Armor

1. The data collected over the past 10 years show that 293 officers wearing body armor died from gunshot wounds—168 suffered gunshot wounds to the head, 109 to the upper torso, and 16 below the waist.

2. Of 109 victim officers who died of upper torso gunshot wounds despite their body armor, 46 officers were killed as the result of bullets entering between the side panels or the armholes of the vests.

3. Additionally, of these 109 officers, wounds above the vest area claimed the lives of 35 officers, and penetration by bullets that went through their vests caused the deaths of 20 officers.

(continued)

Box 5-2 *(continued)*

4. Eight officers died as a result of wounds in the abdominal or lower back area not protected by their vests.

5. During the years 1991–2000, 12 officers wearing body armor were killed by weapons other than firearms.

6. Seven were intentionally struck by vehicles, 2 were beaten or strangled, 2 were stabbed, and 1 was struck on the head with a blunt object.

Places

1. By region, the data show that 32 of the 51 officer fatalities in 2000 occurred in the South.

2. Thirteen officers were killed in the Midwest, and 4 officers were killed in the West.

3. No officer fatalities occurred in the Northeast. Two officers were slain in Puerto Rico.

4. In the past 10 years, the South reported 281 officer fatalities; the West, 122; the Midwest, 118; and the Northeast, 70.

5. Fifty-three law enforcement officers were killed in U.S. Territories.

Times

1. During the past decade, the data contributed by law enforcement agencies show that 59.1 percent of the felonious incidents resulting in officers' deaths occurred from 6:01 p.m. to 6 a.m.

2. The greatest number of officers were slain during the 6-hour period from 8:01 p.m. to 2 a.m., and the fewest were killed during the 4-hour period from 4:01 a.m. to 8 a.m.

3. From 1991 to 2000, more officers were slain on a Monday than on any other day of the week.

4. The fewest number of fatalities occurred on a Tuesday.

5. The monthly data for the same time frame show January and April as the months with the highest number of officer fatalities with 63 and 69, respectively.

6. The fewest officers, 42, were murdered in November.

Box 5-2 *(continued)*

Accidental Deaths

1. According to reported data, 84 officers lost their lives in 2000 due to accidents while serving in their official capacity.
2. Automobile, motorcycle, and aircraft accidents claimed 55 law enforcement officers' lives, making vehicle accidents the greatest cause of accidental deaths.
3. Fourteen officers were accidentally struck by vehicles.
4. Three officers were accidental shooting victims, and 12 were killed in other types of accidents.

Source: Federal Bureau of Investigation, "Law Enforcement Officers Killed 2000," *Uniform Crime Reports*, U.S. Department of Justice, Washington, DC, 2002.

To anticipate danger, take full advantage of all your physical senses and be prepared for the unexpected. Like most aspects of police work, survival on the street is a matter of attitude. Stay alert, be aware of your surroundings, and develop effective intuition. Anticipating danger is a practice that must be your constant partner. The following examples of techniques and strategies can help make the best survival tactics become a way of life.

- Always think and plan ahead as you respond to a call.
- Know where you are at all times.
- Anticipate the unexpected at all times and in all places.
- Learn how to verbally defuse potentially violent situations.
- Use all your physical senses to their maximum.
- Always have a plan of action in case you are assaulted.
- Be constantly alert to any signs of danger.
- Do not patrol the same way every day.
- Never lose sight of a suspect's hands.
- Always keep your gun hand free and stand so that it is away from all civilians.
- Never become too comfortable on the street.

Psychological Changes and Reactions in Crises

Wherever you happen to be at this moment, whomever you happen to be with, imagine someone bursting into the room and shooting in your direction. Before you would have time to react, your body would undergo enormous physiological changes so startling that they would substantially alter your ability to react.

Nature provided us with incredible physical abilities. The immediate physiological changes in times of crisis are intended to help us survive. Within a fraction of a moment, blood vessels constrict throughout the body. In times of severe trauma, the constricted vessels assist in reducing blood flow. Contracted blood vessels cause a chain reaction of additional changes. Because blood carries oxygen to the brain, constricted vessels prevent sufficient oxygen from traveling to it. Therefore, the brain signals the heart to beat harder and stronger so it will receive more oxygen. All of us can relate to the feeling of a quickened heartbeat during high-anxiety situations.

The brain also signals the lungs to breathe deeper and faster. This forces oxygen into the bloodstream. Some officers recall witnessing people fainting on receiving death notices. This is caused by constricted blood vessels suddenly preventing sufficient oxygen from reaching the brain.

Additional changes also occur during crises. A sudden rush of adrenaline provides the body with unusual strength and power. Anyone who has been in an extreme crisis may have experienced "tunnel vision," a phenomenon allowing one to see only what is directly in front. Despite screaming, shouting, or gunfire nearby, the individual probably will not hear anything. Even though the person is running or struggling with every ounce of strength, it can seem like everything is moving in slow motion. Even the pupils dilate to allow better night vision. The body is remarkable, especially when it is kept well-conditioned.

Officers who have been in shootouts agree they experienced all or many of these sensations. Yet the most important physical change has not been mentioned. The lack of oxygen from less blood flow causes a decreased ability to think clearly, which is so important to survival. Most officers do not even know it occurs, and yet it happens every time a high-stress circumstance arises.

Not being able to think clearly and quickly in a crisis is obviously unwanted, especially in that moment requiring a split-second decision. Yet, your mind may go numb at precisely that moment. Afterward, as the months pass and the judge, jury, media, and defense attorneys scrutinize every fraction of a second, no one but you will appreciate the difficulty of that brief moment.

If you have ever started to give a speech or respond to questions only to face the sensation that your mind has gone blank, the sensation is due to the stress of being called on to speak in front of other people. As a result, oxygen flow to your brain is quickly reduced and you cannot think very well. This happens in life-and-death situations. The difference is that instead of not being able to recall something, your mind and body will probably experience total numbing. Senses will be distorted and a feeling of being in slow motion will encompass you.

To combat the physiological phenomena that strip officers of their mental abilities when they are needed the most, understand, appreciate, and expect that it will probably happen. While responding to a call, take advantage of every second. Plan ahead; use each moment to plan what you will do when you arrive at the scene. Once you arrive at the scene and the crisis is in motion, you will not be able to think as well. Think about what you are going to do, so that you will not have to live with the consequences.

To better prepare for these physiological phenomena, you must complete sound training. Good training will also help you through the rough times—at those times it is important that your natural reaction is to respond as you have been trained to.

Good Cops and Bad Cops

For the purposes of this discussion, the terms "good cops" and "bad cops" have nothing to do with corruption but instead refer to their quality of work. It has everything to do with pride and honor. Good cops care about their jobs and those they are sworn to protect. Bad cops, on the other hand, write sloppy, inadequate reports and never do anything by their own initiative. They complain about everything and just do not care much about anybody or their jobs anymore.

To demonstrate in a practical sense how crucial it is to have a survival state of mind, let us look at how bad cops think when responding to a call. Then we will compare that to the thoughts of a good cop in the same situation. The difference is obvious.

Our example involves a family disturbance call, although the same principle can be applied to any situation. The bad cop hears the dispatcher advise, "Be in route to a family disturbance at 000 Bahama Road." The officer acknowledges the call, drives to the house, handles the call, and later advises the dispatcher that he or she is back in service. The officer has responded to hundreds of such disturbances, and they have become routine. The officer feels that he or she can handle anything that comes along, and there is no reason for concern.

The good cop handles the same call differently. After receiving the dispatch, he or she may ask probing questions. Was the disturbance in progress? Were the parties armed? If so, with what types of weapons? These are the essential facts to know. This officer is planning ahead, thinking survival the moment the call is received. A great street cop takes advantage of the time spent driving to the scene by gathering as much information as possible. It pays off if there is a split-second decision to be made after arrival.

If the dispatcher advises that the disturbance is "hot," the officer would ask for the location to be pinpointed. As an example, knowing that the address is three houses west of a certain cross street on the north side of the road would allow the officer to arrive much faster than if he or she had to drive slowly enough to check for house numbers. In addition, if it were dark, he or she would be able to find the house quickly, even with the vehicle lights off.

Good cops do not just drive to the scene of a crime. They are professionals, and every moment is seized and utilized to plan. If they have backup, the officers coordinate the routes and time of their arrival at the scene. The probability of apprehending a fleeing suspect is increased dramatically as a result of arriving at the same time as the backup.

While continuing to drive to the scene of a hot call, good officers think about everything that may help after arrival. They prepare by trying to remember or discover anything about the people who live at the scene. Are they known to be violent? What types of weapons will they probably have? What does the inside of the house look like, and what is the layout of the rooms? What do other officers know about the suspects? Have the suspects had other recent problems?

Once the officer arrives at the scene, he or she parks away from the house to decrease the risk of assault while getting out of the car. He or she parks so the vehicle is between himself or herself and the house. Before getting out, the officer pauses to look at the house, windows, doors, and the surrounding area. Instead of casually walking toward the house, he or she concentrates on the windows and doors, looking for anyone or anything suspicious. If someone appears, the officer focuses on the person's hands. Great cops know that the best survival technique is anticipating danger.

While nearing the house, the officer looks for trees, vehicles, or other objects to use for cover. A great cop follows these procedures because he is a professional. Just as there is a difference in the quality of physicians, mechanics, attorneys, or accountants, some officers are extremely good at what they do. This scenario is an example of how they think. Attitude is everything!

When walking to the house, the officer is careful not to pass directly in front of doors or windows and listens for sounds or voices. Also, the officer studies door hinges to determine whether doors will open toward the inside or outside; this helps to avoid the possibility of them being suddenly slammed into him or her. The officer also knows to stand off to one side to avoid being shot. If any doors open, the officer studies them as they begin to open and watches for signs of an attack through the cracks of the doors.

As the example has shown, two officers can respond to the same call in dramatically different ways. The mental aspect of staying alive on the street is very private. No other person except for officers and their partners, who work beside each other every day, knows these thoughts. Officers who are conscientious will gradually develop reputations as good cops.

Officers who cannot develop a survival state of mind need help in developing one from a trainer or supervisor. The street is no place to be lackadaisical and careless. If a cop will not maintain a survival attitude for himself or fellow officers, surely it should be done for his or her family. If you have children, think about your kids growing up without you. If you do not have children, then think about your family and friends carrying on their lives without you. Then decide what kind of cop you are going to be.

Things that go wrong in life are predictable, and predictable is preventable.

Gordon Graham, Captain
California Highway Patrol
National Lecturer, Police Leadership

DANGEROUS MYTHS

Statistics give us the data we need for effective survival training and awareness, but they cannot replace the wisdom gained through many long years of working the street. All too often misconceptions are born from apathy and indifference. When it is left unchallenged, ignorance can lead to tragic and unnecessary deaths.

The following myths can get you killed! Inexperienced officers or those who are apathetic and careless usually believe them. Be sure to confront officers who feel these statements are true—you may be saving their lives.

- It is not necessary to handcuff children, women, or the elderly.
- All the hype about wearing a vest, especially during the day, is ludicrous. Nothing has ever happened to me, and it never will.
- After you have responded to the same burglary or robbery alarm several times, do not take it seriously.
- Cleaning a firearm is a waste of time. No one ever inspects it, and a dirty firearm is as safe and useful as a clean one.
- Officers who inspect their shotgun at the beginning of their tour of duty are either rookies or insecure.
- Asserting your authority physically and taking names is what good police work is all about.
- Being loyal and dedicated is stupid. You have got to look out for "number one" if you want to get anywhere.
- If the department wants anything from me, it better expect to pay me for it.
- Juveniles today are less dangerous then those of past decades.
- No good street cop is ever afraid of the street. Mental conditioning is nothing more than a way for trainers to make extra money.
- No suspect will ever get away from me in a vehicle pursuit.
- You do not have to worry about getting stabbed if you have your vest on; a knife cannot go through it.
- Real cops do not need a backup.
- Robbery alarms are always false.

- You do not need more than one officer to search a building or make an arrest.
- Checking out a situation before you stop a vehicle or walk up to a suspect means that you cannot handle the job.

MENTAL PREPAREDNESS

In the world of athletics, the best of the best know the value of mental preparedness. Athletes and other professionals train themselves to envision success and achievement. Some individuals refer to it as positive self-imaging, or mental preparedness.

As in the world of athletics, the real winners in life are competent and poised for success. They see themselves accomplishing their goals, and subconscious thoughts of failure do not exist. These winners have convinced themselves that they can accomplish anything if they work hard enough and keep the right attitude.

Law enforcement personnel can train themselves to use the same insight. A positive mental process can be applied to any police circumstance. Even before going on duty, pause to contemplate and reaffirm your survival mind-set. Like a world-class athlete, the professional police officer knows how to prepare for the task ahead. Tell yourself, "I will anticipate danger. I will stay alert. I will not overreact. I will survive."

When responding to a call, mental preparedness is crucial. Even routine calls must be handled as though they are not routine. Expect the unexpected. Think. Have a plan for any situation.

WORKING THE STREET

No rookie can understand how to work the street right after graduation from the academy. Many academies prepare officers, but there are many things that cannot be learned in the classroom. The practical, realistic strategies and techniques that follow usually are learned only through years of experience.

Control with Voice Commands

Voice commands, used effectively, are the "unsung hero" of working the street. Lack of training in the proper use of voice commands can result in tragedy. Most cops who have not had the value of voice commands explained or demonstrated use them faithfully after learning their benefits.

Imagine responding to a call of unknown trouble at a convenience store. When you arrive near the rear of the store, you pause to look at the surrounding area then quietly exit your car. You draw your revolver and cautiously walk along the side of the building toward a tree for cover. You are about to have a dispatcher phone the inside of the store when an armed perpetrator suddenly runs around the corner of the building. The perpetrator appears surprised to see you as you assume a combat stance, raise your handgun, and shout as loudly as you can in a mean, ugly tone, "POLICE! STOP!"

Your expression matches your voice and convinces the perpetrator in a split second that you mean business. If your voice command is an ear-splitting scream, its power will startle the perpetrator. Try this technique in a training class with an instructor. Present the same scenario and role-play (without guns) the part of the officer who shouts. Every person in front of you will jump if your voice is powerful enough.

In the perpetrator scenario, your voice command has accomplished two important things. First, it has intimidated the perpetrator into not testing you. Second, if the perpetrator starts to fire, he or she will be shooting while off balance, and the chances of shooting you are greatly lessened. If an officer in the same situation uses a weak and timid voice command, the perpetrator is more likely to shoot. The officer fails to control the perpetrator, who, in turn, size up the officer. The likelihood of being tested will usually increase when an officer's voice and body language do not convey that he or she is someone who is taking charge of the situation. It is obvious to the perpetrator that he or she can get something through violence or threats. After all, he or she has probably lived with or used intimidation extensively.

The use of aggressive voice commands also alerts everyone in the immediate area of danger. Innocent bystanders will quickly scatter as you are verbally stunning the perpetrator. Additionally, the use of voice commands does not interfere with drawing and/or firing your firearm.

"POLICE! STOP!" is a command recommended by some authorities because it is brief, direct, and instills quick reaction. Some officers, especially rookies, like to use a long string of words mixed with profanity. This may be suitable for movies or television programs, but in real life it is unprofessional, hurts your credibility in court, wastes time, and requires preplanning.

Most situations do not require aggressive voice commands. In fact, the majority of police encounters can be controlled or defused with speech that de-escalates potentially emotional situations. In situations such as traffic stops, family disturbances, or neighborhood quarrels, words that control rather than incite flared tempers are best. Keep in mind that you do not need to take a lot of verbal abuse. Rather, the art of "verbal communication" is a useful skill not easily acquired, but worth the effort.

Telegraphing

The word *telegraph* means to make known by signs or gestures, to communicate, or to make aware. In law enforcement, to telegraph means doing things or making movements that let a suspect know where you are, such as on the other side of a wall or about to come around a corner. It is usually done thoughtlessly by putting the barrel of a handgun beyond your position of cover and concealment or looking around an object with a brimmed cap or hat protruding several inches. For cops, not telegraphing is a vital survival tactic that can save their lives.

Street cops will inevitably face situations where the potential for sudden attack literally lurks around a corner. They may or may not have reason to believe that a suspect is concealed or waiting to attack. Proper training will allow them to respond without overreacting and reduce their risk.

Think of what a scared perpetrator with a 9mm will do when spotting the barrel of your gun or the brim of your cap coming around a corner. There is a good chance that he or she will try to shoot—at your head. When you telegraph your presence, the suspect has just enough time to sight you and shoot a weapon. It does not matter if he is in a hallway, behind a tree, or under a truck— the probability of your death has increased dramatically. It is wise to practice stillness with an experienced, knowledgeable survival trainer in order to appreciate the dangers of telegraphing (but do so without firearms).

Building Searches

Building searches usually take place at night. Although the events that led to conducting the search may be typical, the search should never be considered routine. Open doors in buildings may mean they were left innocently unlocked, or just the opposite may be true, and an armed perpetrator may be hiding inside. Officers assigned to search the premises of buildings should do so as if a perpetrator is inside. They should anticipate danger.

Seasoned officers sometimes do not take building searches seriously. All too often they do little more than walk through the rooms and hallways. To make matters worse, rookie officers can be influenced by lackadaisical or arrogant veterans, even though the academy and FTO program taught them properly.

A serious mistake takes place even before the door is opened—searching without backup. Some officers, even though assistance is available, insist on searching alone. Unless it is impossible to get any assistance, wait for backup. Searching a building alone shows an indifference to staying alive.

While still outside any door, stand off to the side. The officer nearest the doorknob should open the door. With guns drawn, quickly move inside to each side of the doorway. Pause to listen and let your eyes adjust to the change in light. If you are wearing a cap or hat, turn the bill to the back of your head, if agency policies permit.

When entering a building, looking around a corner, or going into a room, do not look, but peek. Glance only long enough to comprehend what you see, not long enough to give someone a chance to shoot you in the head. It takes a fraction of a second to comprehend what is on the other side of a doorway. If you are not sure what is there, peek again at a different height.

Your first peek should never be at eye level. A perpetrator preparing to shoot you usually aims around five feet high because that is the height at which she or he expects your head to appear. It takes little effort to squat and peek around a corner at three feet. If you need a second glance, stand up so that you are at a different height. If you see an armed subject, get behind cover and request assistance—do not be foolhardy.

Use Light Effectively for Safety

Light can help you stay alive, and it can be the cause of your death. Understanding what helps you stay safe in terms of light is nothing more than common sense. We just discussed pausing inside a darkened room to allow your eyes to adjust. This is a simple, effective, and logical survival technique, and there are many more.

It is a common but dangerous practice to silhouette yourself in a darkened area. You should use quick flashes of a flashlight rather than leave it on continuously. Hold a flashlight far enough in front of you so that backlight does not illuminate you or your uniform. Do not carry your flashlight in your gun hand.

The proper use of flashlights is obviously crucial to street survival. As an example, since you will have another officer with you during a building search, you should be positioned on opposite sides of a doorway before entering a darkened room. Crouch down, turn the flashlight on, and then roll it across the floor to your partner. The light will illuminate half of the room as it rolls to your fellow officer. When your partner rolls it back to you, it will light the other part of the room. Avoid rolling the flashlight into the middle of the room because it may shine back on you.

When peeking around a corner in darkness, squat and hold your flashlight high above your head. Synchronize flashing the light at the same time you peek around the corner.

Use a flashlight that has a push-button switch in addition to the permanent light switch. A push button will reduce the chance of keeping the light on too long. It also prevents the possibility of illuminating yourself if it is dropped during an assault. Remember, your gun should be the only thing carried in your gun hand.

Light can be a devastating enemy if it makes you visible. On the other hand, it can be an asset that works for you. You must decide whether it will be an ally or an enemy. For example, a nighttime traffic stop is much safer when you aim the headlights and spotlight inside and slightly to the left of the vehicle. You will be able to see the occupants better, and if any of them should turn around, they will be blinded by the light. In addition, it is wise to order the driver, via your loudspeaker, to turn on the inside dome light.

Position Yourself Safely

Officers walk up to potential suspects all the time, which can be risky. As you walk up to someone, use all of your senses. Never lose sight of the suspect's hands, and watch the suspect's eyes, which can tell you much more than just where he or she is looking. Sense the suspect's overall demeanor; the value of an officer's extra senses, or intuition, should never be underestimated. Is the suspect overly nervous or about to run? Do you sense that there is something wrong? Although intuition is difficult to explain in court or to newspaper reporters, it can keep you alive—do not ignore it.

When approaching a subject, walk to his or her right front. Stand at a 45-degree angle from the front of the suspect's right hand to allow you to see his or her front and right sides. In doing so, you are making probability work for you. Most people are right-handed, and if a suspect attempts to assault you, the chances are that the attack will come from the right hand. Position yourself so that you can see the right side of his or her body but still be able to observe the left hand. Look for signs of objects that may be weapons. If you realize he or she is left-handed, simply move to his or her left side.

Make sure you stand at a distance beyond the suspect's leg reach as well as arm's reach. It takes only a moment for the suspect to reach you if attacking. Never be lulled into a false sense of security because you are beyond arm's reach.

The first thing an officer says to a suspect is usually, "Can I see some kind of identification?" Many officers are shot at this point. Make the subject lean far forward when handing you identification; do not lean forward yourself. This will cause the suspect to be off balance rather than you being in an awkward position and vulnerable to attack. If you are still suspicious, have the suspect place the identification on the ground and then back away before you pick it up. Do not overreact, but be cautious. Officers have mistakenly shot individuals because they appeared to be reaching for a handgun.

Rookies are taught to stand with their gun side away from a person standing next to them. This decreases accessibility to your sidearm. To avoid being kicked in the groin, stand at an angle to the suspect. This also limits vulnerability of other vital areas of your body. The sides of your thighs, arms, and shoulders can take a great deal more punishment than your abdomen, chest, and throat can. Your agility, balance, and ability to respond to an assault are also vastly improved while standing at an angle.

SHOOT-OUTS

NCIC, the National Crime Information Center, sends a notice to all agencies when an officer is killed in the line of duty. The notice contains a summary of the circumstances surrounding the officer's death, and many departments read it during roll call. As a result, most street cops learn the circumstances surrounding the death in the line of duty of every officer in America.

Only recently has the data concerning these deaths been used as the foundation for effective survival training. Prior to the 1980s, many misconceptions existed about how cops die. The history of firearms training is one of the saddest realities of our profession and directly reflects these misconceptions. Here are some of the most devastating facts.

- Most officers are shot less than four yards away from their assailant.
- The average time of a shoot-out is 2.5 to 2.7 seconds, very unlike what the movies portray.
- The number of rounds fired is usually fewer than three.
- Approximately 40 percent of the time when officers are in lethal shoot-outs, they will be facing more than one perpetrator.
- Two out of three times a police shoot-out will be during hours of darkness, even though most firearms training is still conducted in daylight.

Officers usually have little or no warning when they are being shot. Studies reveal that the mental and physical process for the assailant to fire a firearm takes approximately one-half of a second. Officers generally take slightly over one second to draw, point, and shoot. Cops who believe they will have the time to draw, aim, and shoot are more likely to die in a shoot-out; adding the time for aiming brings the total average time to almost three seconds.[1]

Target Center Mass

Most shoot-outs are over within a few seconds. The difference between life and death is measured in fractions of a second, and there is no time to aim. You must draw and point as one action and promptly fire as the second action. Your life is at stake, and you cannot be concerned with aiming for a leg or an arm rather than killing the suspect. You simply have no time to select a particular target area, and you cannot afford to hesitate while thinking about it.

The term *center mass* refers to the midtorso area of the body. Point your weapon at the perpetrator's midchest region, because firing into the center mass provides you with maximum stopping power. As projectiles enter the perpetrator's chest, their energy should stop the suspect by damaging the vital organs. You are not trying to kill the perpetrator, only to stop him or her, and the center mass strategy accomplishes the purpose most effectively.

Shoot to Stop

Advising officers to fire into a suspect's chest while stating that their purpose is not to kill may seem contradictory. No officer should intend to kill a perpetrator before, during, or after firing. Realistically, the probability of killing a suspect after placing two rounds into the chest is high, but killing should never be the intent.

To fully appreciate this point, think about the following scenario. A uniformed officer has been sued concerning an incident in which a homeowner was shot and killed. During cross-examination, the attorney for the plaintiff abruptly turns and stares at the officer. She asks, "Officer Jones, you just testified that the incident was a case of mistaken identity. You thought Mr. Johnson, the homeowner, was a burglar. You thought the flashlight he had in his hand was a gun. When he raised the flashlight, you thought he was going to shoot. You testified that at the moment you fired your intent was to kill him to save your own life. Isn't that correct? You wanted him to die, didn't you? Isn't that right, officer? Is that what you testified to? You testified your intent was to kill him, correct? Why? I am sure not only the jury but also his children and wife in the back of the courtroom would really like to hear your answer. So . . . what is it?"

As the scenario points out, civil liability is a stark reality to contemporary police work. The plaintiff's attorney was able to make the officer appear to be a monster during cross-examination. She was able to do this because the officer had been mentally conditioned to "shoot to kill" when firing is necessary. This attitude is merely a frame of mind.

When you must fire, do it speedily and accurately. Shoot into center mass, but do it with the intent of only stopping the person. Testifying that you only intended to stop the person because his or her actions forced you to fire could mean a great deal to you, your family, and even the perpetrator's family.

Every cop in America, regardless of his or her experiences, undergoes a split-second decision-making process when confronted with a potential shoot-out. The decision made during that fraction of a second will determine who lives or dies. Regardless of training, experiences, or attitudes, the probability of momentarily pausing because you are concerned with killing another person is greater with the shoot-to-kill attitude. In a shoot-out, you do not have time to pause; actions must be quick and decisive. When officers develop a shoot-to-stop viewpoint instead of shoot-to-kill, the possibility of a lethal pause is substantially reduced, and so is the probability of dying.

Training Methods

In a shoot-out, officers fire when, how, and the number of times they have been trained to, whether through hands-on, interactive training, simulations, or video-driven laser simulation training systems. Unfortunately, some trainers still do not understand the need to anchor desired responses into long-term memory through interactive firearms training. Sometimes the problem is not the trainer; rather, it is an administrator who will not acquire the firearms training program necessary for the trainer to do a sufficient job.

Some police survival trainers believe that firing two quick shots at a time is the best way to respond in a shoot-out. However, officers involved in shoot-outs must conserve ammunition. Approximately 40 percent of the time officers are in shoot-outs, they face two or more armed perpetrators. If they are not adequately trained, they may waste ammunition and perhaps be killed while trying to reload.

LEARN FROM NONSURVIVORS

Until the last two decades, few areas in American policing have been as lacking as police survival training. Training effectiveness improved dramatically during the 1980s, and law enforcement should be deeply grateful to those whose initiative and dedication made such tremendous improvement during the 1990s.

The way officers are trained is the way they will react in crises. The following facts are things we have learned from nonsurvivors in law enforcement. The tips provided with them will help you survive the street today.

Fact: Most police shoot-outs occur within 12 feet of the perpetrator. While we were being shot and killed at a distance of only a few feet, we were being trained for over a century only at distances of 21, 45, 75, and 150 feet.

Fact: You are always outwitted when facing a perpetrator if you have doubts about your abilities. Strengthen your skills with practice and intense training.

Fact: Always handcuff before you search! The reverse was taught for decades.

Fact: Approximately 40 percent of the time that a shoot-out occurs, the officer is facing more than one armed person. Until the last decade, most agencies conducted firearms training using a single, stationary silhouette target.

Fact: No matter what you have in your hands, when a perpetrator draws a gun, drop what is in your hands and draw your own firearm. Do not take the time to put away what you are holding; just drop it on the ground!

Fact: Two out of three shoot-outs occur during darkness or reduced lighting. Firearms training for most agencies has been deficient in this area. The proper training will include night firing in two out of three firing range practices. Logistics will make this difficult, but when you consider what is at stake, the obstacles must be overcome.

Fact: Never forget that anyone—no matter what size, height, age, or sex—has the ability to take your firearm away if you do not anticipate danger. Take every call you respond to seriously.

Fact: Sixty-five percent of all the officers murdered with their own firearm in 1997 had one handcuff on the suspect when they were attacked. Handcuff a suspect immediately.

Fact: In the past, officers were taught to fire six shots in succession, to unload the empty shells into their hand, and to turn around and throw the empty casings in a bucket. Training today simulates firing more realistically concerning when, how, and the number of rounds to fire. Drop the empty casings to the ground!

Fact: Many street and corrections officers have been attacked because prisoners have learned how to protect their faces from pepper spray. Use caution when approaching people you have sprayed; do not assume it has incapacitated them.

Fact: Making arrests of two people with no backup leaves one unsecured perpetrator. Carry a hidden plastic cuff or an extra pair of handcuffs at all times.

Fact: Helmets can be a brutal head-butt weapon. Always ask bikers and motorcyclists to remove their helmets and put them out of reach.

Training officers have done a good job of transforming the ineffective and sometimes dangerous instruction of past decades into much more professional internal training. Now that we have reached a new era in law enforcement, contemporary trainers are doing a great job of overcoming ineffective survival training. Today's trainers know that developing realistic in-service training is the key to keeping officers alive. Great survival training includes:

- Assessing your agency's survival training needs
- Writing a good lesson plan
- Keeping instruction standardized
- Using performance goals and objectives
- Instilling realism
- Conducting pretests and posttests
- Having instructors who are passionate about teaching
- Doing remedial training whenever it is needed
- Keeping accurate documentation

NEVER GIVE UP!

Good training helps to keep cops alive. Training, though, cannot give you the will to survive.

The street can be ugly and unforgiving, where officers see the worst of the worst. Many street officers have seen their own blood in the dirt. However, just because you are wounded does not mean you are going to die. Some officers have died only because they convinced themselves they were going to die once they were wounded, even though their wounds were superficial. If you become excited and hysterical, this can cause you to go into shock. Do not lose your will to survive or you may die needlessly.

The bad guys do not follow rules during a street fight. You will need defensive tactics, good physical conditioning, guts, and determination to survive. Keep thinking that your family is not going to lose you. If you realize you have just been injured, do not give up—fight back! Go home to your family by being mentally prepared to survive.

One final thing to remember is that officers die in the line of duty in ways that may not immediately come to mind (e.g., gunshots, car crashes, assaults), as Box 5-3 demonstrates.

Box 5-3
Line of Duty Death Statistics

2003 (JANUARY 1 THROUGH JUNE 7, 2003)

Total Line of Duty Deaths: 61

Aircraft accident: 1
Assault: 1
Automobile accident: 11
Drowned: 1
Electrocuted: 1
Fall: 1
Gunfire: 26
Gunfire (Accidental): 1
Heart attack: 4
Motorcycle accident: 1
Stabbed: 1
Struck by vehicle: 3
Vehicular assault: 5
Vehicle pursuit: 4

Totals by Month

January: 11
February: 8
March: 8

Box 5-3 *(continued)*

April: 14
May: 17
June: 3

Age

Average age: 38 (for officers whose ages are known)

Gender Breakdown

Female: 3
Male: 58

2002

Total Line of Duty Deaths: 152

Accident (Unclassified): 1
Aircraft accident: 7
Assault: 4
Automobile accident: 38
Drowned: 3
Duty related illness: 1
Gunfire: 54
Gunfire (Accidental): 3
Heart attack: 8
Motorcycle accident: 6
Stabbed: 2
Struck by train: 2
Struck by vehicle: 5
Training accident: 1
Vehicular assault: 12
Vehicle pursuit: 5

Totals by Month

January: 17
February: 8

(continued)

Box 5-3 *(continued)*

March: 10
April: 7
May: 13
June: 12
July: 12
August: 17
September: 14
October: 11
November: 19
December: 12

Age

Average age: 39 (for officers whose ages are known)

Gender Breakdown

Female: 15
Male: 137

2001

Total Line of Duty Deaths: 237

Accident (Unclassified): 2
Aircraft accident: 5
Animal related: 1
Assault: 2
Automobile accident: 34
Drowned: 1
Duty related illness: 3
Exposure: 2
Exposure to toxins: 1
Fall: 1
Gunfire: 63
Gunfire (Accidental): 6
Heart attack: 2
Heat exhaustion: 1

Box 5-3 *(continued)*

Motorcycle accident: 7
Struck by vehicle: 12
Terrorist attack: 72
Vehicular assault: 17
Vehicle pursuit: 5

Totals by Month

January: 11
February: 17
March: 19
April: 7
May: 12
June: 14
July: 12
August: 16
September: 90
October: 14
November: 13
December: 12

Age

Average age: 38 (for officers whose ages are known)

Gender Breakdown

Female: 10
Male: 227

2000

Total Line of Duty Deaths: 161

Accident (Unclassified): 2
Aircraft accident: 7
Animal related: 2
Assault: 2

(continued)

Box 5-3 *(continued)*

Automobile accident: 36
Bicycle accident: 2
Drowned: 2
Duty related illness: 1
Explosion: 1
Exposure to toxins: 2
Fall: 2
Gunfire: 50
Gunfire (Accidental): 3
Heart attack: 7
Motorcycle accident: 10
Stabbed: 2
Struck by vehicle: 9
Training accident: 1
Vehicular assault: 17
Vehicle pursuit: 3

Totals by Month

January: 16
February: 12
March: 12
April: 7
May: 13
June: 17
July: 20
August: 13
September: 14
October: 16
November: 8
December: 13

Age

Average age: 39 (for officers whose ages are known)

Box 5-3 *(continued)*

Gender Breakdown

Female: 5
Male: 156

OFFICERS KILLED IN THE LINE OF DUTY: BY STATE

From 1792 until April, 2003

Alabama	407
Alaska	40
Arizona	206
Arkansas	206
California	1,344
Colorado	219
Connecticut	127
Delaware	32
District of Columbia	116
Florida	608
Georgia	476
Hawaii	44
Idaho	52
Illinois	876
Indiana	335
Iowa	130
Kansas	218
Kentucky	324
Louisiana	337
Maine	77
Maryland	244
Massachusetts	282
Michigan	504
Minnesota	196
Mississippi	184
Missouri	586
Montana	109
Nebraska	83
Nevada	71
New Hampshire	29

(continued)

Box 5-3 *(continued)*

New Jersey	374
New Mexico	117
New York	1,156
North Carolina	375
North Dakota	46
N. Mariana Islands	3
Ohio	683
Oklahoma	322
Oregon	155
Puerto Rico	309
Pennsylvania	661
Railroad Agencies	101
Rhode Island	40
South Carolina	252
South Dakota	43
Tennessee	358
Texas	1,165
Tribal Agencies	37
U.S. Government	909
Utah	98
Vermont	15
Virgin Islands	6
Virginia	321
Washington	237
West Virginia	136
Wisconsin	231
Wyoming	44
Total	16,768

Source: The Officer Down Memorial Page, Inc., http://www.odmp.org.

The Officer Down Memorial Page (ODMP) was created in January 1996 with the purpose of honoring fallen law enforcement officers from the United States. The concept of the ODMP was thought of by Chris Cosgriff, a freshman at James Madison University, in Harrisonburg, Virginia. When the ODMP first went online, it honored only law enforcement officers who were killed or wounded in 1996, but it quickly expanded to include all law enforcement officers who were killed, going back to 1990. With the help of the National Law Enforcement Officers Memorial Fund, Inc. (NLEOMF), the ODMP was able to obtain the names of every law enforcement officer killed in the United States from 1792 through April 2003.

In law enforcement, to truly be successful you have to be able to know the difference between bravery and valor. Bravery is when things are at their worst yet you keep your presence of mind and act dynamically, according to the situation, having weighed the risks versus the benefits; deciding the right course of action; then doing it. Valor is when you stand tall and defy the dragons of the world armored with knowledge and integrity to withstand even the greatest personal attack with dignity and humbleness. A man or woman who possesses both bravery and valor in law enforcement is destined for success; be it great or small, in the end it is still success.

Lon Pepper
Chief of Police
Greenville, MS

QUESTIONS FOR DISCUSSION

1. The phrase "die in the line of duty" includes both officers who died from being murdered and those who were killed during accidents. How would you assess law enforcement's effectiveness at preventing officer murders and accidental deaths throughout the last century? Are we better at preventing officer deaths now than we were fifty years ago?

2. The Law Enforcement Officers Killed 2000 section of this chapter explains how the Uniform Crime Reporting program of the FBI responds when notified that an officer has died. Once the national program receives notification of a line-of-duty death, the staff sends inquiries through FBI field divisions to the victim officer's employing agency to obtain additional details concerning the circumstances surrounding the incident. Additionally, the national staff furnishes the agency with information concerning two federal programs that provide benefits to survivors of federal and nonfederal law enforcement officers killed in the line of duty. The national program staff also obtain pertinent criminal history data concerning the individuals

identified in connection with felonious killings from the FBI's Interstate Identification Index. How useful is this information, and do you think the program is being used by local agencies? Why do you think there is not a similar program about officers who commit suicide?

3. Which of the following facts about officers killed in 2000 is most surprising to you?

A total of 51 law enforcement officers fell victim to murder while performing their official duties.

City police departments employed 27 of the fallen officers.

County police and sheriffs' offices employed 21 victims, with state agencies employing three.

Law enforcement agencies in 21 states and Puerto Rico lost officers through line-of-duty felonious killings.

Fifty separate incidents, one of which occurred 43 years ago and another of which occurred 23 years ago, claimed the lives of the 51 officers.

Arrests or circumstances of exceptional means cleared 49 of these incidents.

The number of officers slain in 2000 increased 21.4 percent from the 42 officer fatalities of 1999.

Five- and 10-year trends show the number of officers slain in 2000 was 16.4 percent lower than in 1996 and 28.2 percent lower than in 1991.

4. What single change in law enforcement would most help to prevent officers from being killed?

5. The end of Chapter 5 includes a quote from Chief of Police Lon Pepper. Part of his quote states "Bravery is when things are at their worst yet you keep your presence of mind and act dynamically, according to the situation, having weighed the risks versus the benefits; deciding the right course of action; then doing it. Valor is when you stand tall and defy the dragons of the world armored with knowledge and integrity to withstand even the greatest personal attack with dignity and humbleness." Given these definitions of bravery and valor, describe a past situation in

which you displayed one or both of these qualities. Do you believe one is more important than the other for a policing career?

ENDNOTES

1. Ronald J. Adams, Thomas M. McTernan, and Charles Remsberg, *Street Survival Tactics for Armed Encounters* (Northbrook, IL: Caliber Press, 1980), pp. 24–39.

chapter 6

EMOTIONALLY SURVIVING

A great cop is a person who can be trusted to do the right thing even when no one is looking. It is a person who works hard and treats others as he or she wants to be treated.

Lee D. Donohue, Sr.
Chief of Police
Honolulu Police Department

Many people believe that being a cop is more dangerous emotionally than physically, and they may be right. Criminologists, police psychologists, law enforcement authors, police administrators, and seasoned officers have voiced their opinion time and time again that stress has a variety of severe detrimental effects. This view is different from the prevailing attitude of decades ago, when little or no concern was given to officers' emotional well-being.

Gradually law enforcement has come to realize the significance of the consequences of stress. Without deep appreciation, no effective remedies will occur. Law enforcement in general has done a poor job of taking care of its own, and psychological assistance varies greatly from agency to agency. Regardless of how much support an agency provides, nothing should prevent officers from learning how to successfully cope with the pressures of life as cops. They can live happier, healthier lives if they have the tools to help them cope with the job-associated emotions and stress.

LIFE PATTERNS

Gail Sheehy, a highly respected authority on adult development, shares her insight on the stages of adult development in the book *Passages*. Patterns exist in our lives, which, once understood, is a tremendous benefit. The patterns are comprised of predictable steps associated with age groups. During each time period there are crises that adults should expect to experience. Once understood, each crisis can be dealt with effectively. Individuals can then concentrate on reaching their greatest potential, instead of allowing emotions to create chaos and misery.

As adults pass through each of life's stages, they gradually experience subtle changes in their views: what is valuable, how much time should be devoted to work or entertainment, relationships with others, health and safety, religious beliefs, and financial concerns. As we grow older and mature, these stages are shaped by our life's experiences.

The Twenties

As opposed to the turmoil of adolescence, this period of life is more stable and may seem somewhat longer. It is a time of serious preparation for and beginning of a chosen career. To shape the vision of dreams and accomplishments yet to come gives tremendous personal satisfaction. Frequently, a lifestyle chosen during our twenties will follow us throughout life. The decisions, habits, and patterns established in this stage set in motion a pattern that is not easy to change.

One of the difficulties with this period is the belief that the choices we make are irrevocable. No one ever promised that life would be fair or things would always go our way. When tragedy strikes or serious mistakes are made, optimism and tenacity are crucial. The ability to view setbacks as only temporary and continue on does make a huge difference.

Intimate, long-term relationships are of major importance. To a large extent the values and beliefs developed as a child and modeled by parents will significantly affect the success of a marriage. The desire to "settle down" with a family is mixed with the need to establish one's self firmly within a career.

The Thirties

For many people their thirties are marked with impatience and a feeling of being too restricted. The decisions, choices, and preferences of the twenties often do not seem quite right. The return to relatively minor turbulence forces new commitments. Outgrowing careers or relationships with spouses sometimes leads to devastating problems. The need to improve professionally and personally continues. If single, the thought of living alone for the rest of their lives can create a great deal of anxiety.

To have a meaningful, financially rewarding career becomes very important as families grow and thoughts turn to the realities of retirement. Buying a home, raising children, and settling down becomes the norm.

The mid- to late thirties usually pose new challenges. Often the realization that life is now half over, reduced physical abilities, the loss of a youthful appearance, increased medical problems, and lost dreams are difficult to accept and deal with. Many people compensate for these feelings by reevaluating their immediate and long-range goals. Women usually become aware of this crossroad before men. A mixture of anxiety, exhilaration, and new assertiveness frequently result. For men, nearing forty means time is running out. Self-criticism, placing blame, and a general feeling of exasperation with their jobs frequently lead to difficulty within the family. Everything considered, however, this period of life can be very rewarding.

The Forties

Entering the forties is highlighted by the satisfaction of many accomplishments and continued feelings of restlessness and frustration. More years of concentrated effort on a career are ahead. Many men start developing second careers; others begin to shift their focus away from a career to personal or marriage-related matters.

People who understand the need for personal growth and change cope accordingly, and stability is regained. However, people refusing to take life in stride find failure. The midlife crisis is harder for individuals who withdraw within themselves. Support and assistance from close friends and relatives is crucial; alienating them can be devastating, as the value of family and friends increases with age.

The Fifties

For some people a personal crisis characterized by a feeling of stagnation may reoccur around fifty. If so, the remedy is the same as if it occurred during the forties—a revitalization and realignment of personal beliefs and goals is in order, and counseling is helpful.

Once the renewed purpose has occurred, individuals find a great deal more satisfaction and happiness. The fifties and beyond can be a very rewarding time of life. The key is being able to like yourself and accept life for what it is. A certain mellowing takes place in the fifties. Close friends and family become extremely important, and reminiscing on special memories prompts initiative to seek out the best the future has to offer.[1]

UNDERSTAND YOUR CAREER CHOICE

Considerable research has been conducted in criminal justice academic circles concerning the factors that influence individuals to choose a law enforcement career. It helps to understand why people become officers in order to appreciate the emotional trauma they often experience during a law enforcement career. Self-knowledge will help you get the most out of life. If you want to be a cop but do not know how to survive emotionally, the chances are great that you are in for more than your share of misery and a disappointing career.

Women and men enter law enforcement for similar reasons. Two primary reasons are the desire to help others and job security. Also frequently listed are doing something about crime, excitement, prestige, and an interesting life. Documented research shows that most people become cops because they have a sincere desire to help others. This sincerity toward a worthy purpose makes it difficult for officers when they realize that they cannot rid the world of all of its evil.

The belief that officers want to have power and authority over others is not substantiated by sound research. Studies indicate that such factors do not motivate most people who choose a law enforcement career. Nonetheless, experienced officers have seen more than one rookie with "John Wayne Syndrome."[2] This is a phenomenon whereby officers believe themselves to be indestructible. This feeling that nothing could happen to them often prompts foolhardy actions that may cause injury to themselves or others.

STRESS

The last decade has witnessed endless articles, books, and television specials about stress. The most commonly held notion is that stress is negative. However, stress can be either positive or negative. In general, it is defined as "the body's unspecific response to any demand placed upon it."[3]

Stress is derived from change, both positive and negative. Change is an inevitable aspect of life, so stress is just as certain. Positive stress triggers include events such as holidays, promotions, and reunions. Negative stress triggers include divorce, death of a spouse, and losing a job.

Massachusetts Institute of Technology psychologist Dean Ormish notes that the greatest cause of stress is the perceived mismatch between where and who people are and where and who they think they should be. In other words, people's expectations of themselves can produce devastating results. Some people were raised in households in which near perfection was expected of the children. These people as adults have difficulty coping with daily pressures. Hectic days, minor problems, and life's little irritations may be too much to handle unless they, like everyone else, learn to take things in stride. Even substantial disappointments have to be viewed as only temporary setbacks in a long line of accomplishments.[4]

Police behavior is a frequent topic of discussion these days. Their behavior is affected by numerous factors, such as negative and positive stress, society's expectations, personal aspects, management, ethics, and more. Cops must exercise care in all these areas in order to avoid tainting their behavior. Kevin M. Gilmartin and John J. Harris compiled an article (see Box 6-1) that helps us understand how the transition from a good, honest cop to a compromised officer can occur.

Understanding and Managing Stress

For most people stress at work is a significant concern regardless of their profession. Uncaring or demanding supervisors, unreasonable

Box 6-1

Law Enforcement Ethics ... The Continuum of Compromise

During the past few years, law enforcement behavior has been the subject of increased scrutiny across the country. Rodney King, Ruby Ridge, Waco, evidence planting in Philadelphia, Mark Furhman's testimony, Operation Big Spender, and the chase and apprehension of the illegal aliens in Southern California are just some of the incidents that have captured the nation's attention. With each new headline, mistrust of law enforcement increases; police/community relations suffer; and the reputations of good, hardworking and ethical law enforcement professionals and their organizations are tainted. Even the most avid supporters of law enforcement wonder what is happening and are asking, "Can the police be trusted to police themselves?" While high-profile cases capture the nation's attention, law enforcement agencies across the country spend an increasing amount of time investigating, disciplining and prosecuting officers for unethical or criminal behaviors that never make it to the front pages.

Is the concern over inappropriate police behavior just sensationalized media coverage; have a relatively few number of incidents been used to taint an entire profession or is this a real problem that needs close attention and immediate action? Unfortunately, the incidents that have made the headlines have tainted the reputation and called into question the behavior of the entire law enforcement community. These highly publicized incidents do not, however, address the more subtle ethical dilemmas that law enforcement agencies and their communities have to face each day. Law enforcement agencies across the country face issues of integrity that have to be examined and changed.

Concerns about police integrity, corruption and unethical behavior are not new. The Mollen, Knapp, Christopher and other commissions have examined issues in their respective jurisdictions. Suggestions and recommendations that have come from these and other commissions and investigations, although insightful or accurate, have not resulted in significant acceptance or change within law enforcement organizations nationwide.

(continued)

Box 6-1 *(continued)*

While departments may have increased the number of required ethics-related classes, the training itself has not changed dramatically. The information is still not internalized nor appreciated at the street level, or throughout the organization for that matter. For many officers, ethics training is seen as nothing more than a politically driven, knee-jerk reaction to the media attention that surrounds high-profile cases. Significant changes in the way law enforcement ethics is conceptualized, taught, and integrated throughout an organization are needed. Without these changes, it is doubtful any information will be accepted and internalized into the day-to-day lives of police officers and police organizations or result in meaningful change.

Ethics is typically taught during the basic academy or at in-service training after embarrassing situations erupt. It is often seen by instructors and students alike as a class that "has to be taught," but one which nobody really wants to talk about. While the training is necessary, its importance becomes diluted or rendered ineffective by the manner in which it is presented and/or the socialization process that occurs during a police officer's first year or two on the job.

Police corruption is often seen as a distant problem peculiar to "big city cops" or "other departments." Denial and refusal to accept the potential for ethical compromise and corruption at "our department" prevent administrators and officers from developing an in-depth understanding and appreciation of the issues. Without a clear understanding, adequate information and practical strategies, officers who are exposed to a risk-filled environment are more likely to engage in inappropriate behaviors that can destroy their organizations. The transformation from idealistic, highly ethical officer into a self-serving individual who believes "If we don't look out for ourselves, who will?" is a subtle process that usually occurs before the officer knows what has happened. For ethics training to be effective, officers have to see the information as relevant and credible. This approach, even when the information is interesting and enlightening, is rarely internalized by the officers nor incorporated into their day-to-day activities.

Box 6-1 *(continued)*

THE CONTINUUM OF COMPROMISE®

In this article, the authors explain the "continuum of compromise".[1] It is a framework for understanding and teaching how the transition from "honest cop" to "compromised officer" can occur. Law enforcement agencies can help prepare their officers for the ethical challenges they will face during their careers. However, that will require changing the way this topic is approached by the organization and teaching and integrating the information throughout the organization.

Officers live and work in a constantly changing and dynamically social context in which they are exposed to a myriad of ethical conflicts. When either unprepared or unaware, officers are more likely to "go with the flow" than they would be if they were adequately prepared to face potential ethical risks. Every day officers practice mental preparation as it relates to tactical situations. Officers who are mentally prepared to face a lethal encounter are more likely to be successful than officers who are tactically proficient but mentally unprepared. Just like lethal encounters, ethical dilemmas occur at the most inopportune times, frequently without warning and with little time to stop and think about the situation. When inadequately prepared, even the most honest, above-reproach officers can make inappropriate split-second ethical decisions ... decisions that can result in life-changing consequences. If officers are going to survive ethical dilemmas they need to be as mentally prepared as they would be for tactical encounters.

While police work is seductive and exhilarating, it can also lead officers down the path of ethical compromise. The "continuum of compromise" outlines the path of ethical compromise and can be used to help officers understand and mentally prepare for the ethical dilemmas they will face. Understanding the issues and being mentally prepared will help officers assume responsibility for and make more appropriate decisions. Compromising behavior has to be seen as something that can potentially affect all law enforcement officers ... not just those in "corruption rich" environments. Officers who view compromise or corruption as an "all or none" phenomenon will not see compromise as an unlikely event, training will be viewed as a waste of time and officers will

(continued)

Box 6-1 *(continued)*

not become mentally prepared. Understanding the continuum of compromise will allow officers to recognize the risks, assess their own potential for compromise and develop an effective strategy to ensure ethical integrity. When teaching ethics the goal must be to develop an understanding of the progression towards compromise and the development of self-monitoring strategies to prevent becoming embroiled in compromising events.

A Perceived Sense of Victimization Can Lead to the Rationalization and Justification of:

Acts of Omission

Acts of Commission–Administrative

Acts of Commission–Criminal

Entitlement Versus Accountability

Loyalty Versus Integrity

A Perceived Sense of Victimization

Officers frequently develop a perceived sense of victimization over time. Officers typically begin their careers as enthusiastic, highly motivated people. However, when these young officers over-invest in and over-identify with their professional role they will develop a sense of singular-identity based on their job and an increased sense of victimization. At greatest risk are officers whose jobs literally become their lives. For them, "I am a cop" is not just a cliché but rather a way of life. Over-identification and over-investment causes people to link their sense of self to their police role, a role they do not control. While this builds camaraderie, it can also cause officers to eventually hate and resent the job they once loved.

While officers have absolute control over their own integrity and professionalism, the rest of their police role is controlled by someone else. Department rules, procedures, policies, equipment, budget allocations, assignments, dress codes, and many other day-to-day and long-term activities are controlled by the chief, commanders, supervisors, prosecuting attorneys, the criminal justice system, laws, the courts, politicians, etc. Officers who over-identify with the job soon experience a loss of control over other aspects of their lives. Professional over-investment, coupled with a loss of personal control puts officers at serious risk, a risk that in some ways is more dangerous than

Box 6-1 *(continued)*

the physical risk they face on the street. "It doesn't matter how guilty you are, but how slick your lawyer is" can become the officers' cynical yet reality based perception of the legal system. These realities combine with over-investment to develop an "us versus them" perception in terms of how officers see the world.

The physical risks that officers are exposed to each day require them to see the world as potentially lethal. To survive, they have to develop a "hypervigilant"[2] mind-set. Hypervigilance coupled with over-investment leads officers to believe the only person you can really trust is another cop . . . a "real cop" that is, not some "pencil-neck in the administration." While officers first become alienated from the public, they can soon distance themselves from the criminal justice system and finally from their own department administration. "I can handle the morons on the street; I just can't handle the morons in the administration," is often heard among officers. It is ironic how quickly idealism and trust in the administration can change . . . oftentimes even before the first set of uniforms wears out. As a sense of perceived victimization intensifies, officers become more distrusting and resentful of anyone who controls their job role. At this point, without any conscious awareness and certainly without any unethical intent, unsuspecting officers can begin a journey down the continuum of compromise.

As the over-invested officer detaches from non-work-related interests or activities, a perceived sense of victimization will increase. Peer groups, friends, co-workers and potentially their entire frame of reference of life begins to change. By itself, feeling like a victim is by no means equivalent to being ethically compromised. However, feeling like a victim (whether real or imagined) is the first stop on the continuum of compromise.

Acts of Omission

When officers (or anyone for that matter) feel victimized, in their own mind they can rationalize and justify behaviors they may not normally engage in. "Acts of Omission" occur when officers rationalize and justify not doing things they are responsible for doing. At this point, officers can feel quite justified in not doing things that, from their own perspective, appear to "even the score." "If they (whomever it may be) don't care about us, why should we

(continued)

Box 6-1 *(continued)*

care about them." Acts of omission can include selective nonproductivity (ignoring traffic violations or certain criminal violations, etc.), "not seeing" or avoiding on-sight activity, superficial investigations, omitting paperwork, lack of follow-up, doing enough to just "get by" and many other activities which officers can easily omit. "You will never get in trouble for the stop you don't make!" typifies the mind-set of officers during this stage.

This results in decreased productivity and produces passive resistance to organizational mandates. "Acts of Omission" rarely face critical scrutiny from peers who themselves are frequently experiencing the same sense of victimization and socialization process. Peer acceptance and loyalty become more important than following some arbitrary set of professional principles. The perceived sense of being victimized can allow officers to rationalize and justify other acts of omission such as not reporting another officer's inappropriate behavior (sometimes regardless of how extreme or criminal the behavior may be).

Acts of Commission–Administrative

Once officers routinely omit job responsibilities, the journey to the next step is not a difficult one to make ... "Acts of Commission–Administrative." Instead of just omitting duties and responsibilities, officers commit administrative violations. Breaking small rules that seem inconsequential or which stand in the way of "real police work" is the first step. This can set the stage for continued progression down the continuum. Acts of administrative commission are seen in many ways ... carrying unauthorized equipment and/or weapons, engaging in prohibited pursuits and other activities, drinking on duty, romantic interludes at work, not reporting accidents and firing warning shots are just a few examples. Department sanctions are typically the only risk that officers will face at this point. For most officers this is the extent of their personal journey down the continuum of compromise. Acts of omission and acts of administrative commission are significant in terms of professional accountability and personal integrity. When discovered, they can erode community trust and damage police/community relations. However, they rarely place officers at risk for criminal prosecution. The initially honest and

Box 6-1 *(continued)*

highly motivated officers can now rationalize their behavior along the lines of "I'm not a naïve rookie out trying to change the world ... I know what it's really like on the streets and we (the police) have to look out for each other because no one else will."

Acts of Commission–Criminal

Unsuspecting officers can unwittingly travel to the next and final stage of the continuum ... "Acts of Commission–Criminal." In the final stage on the continuum of compromise officers engage in and rationalize behavior that just a few years before could not be imagined. At first, acts of criminal commission may appear benign and not terribly different from acts of administrative commission. Evidence that will never be of any use is thrown away instead of being turned in, overtime or payroll records are embellished, needed police equipment is inappropriately purchased with money seized from a drug dealer, expecting "a little something in the envelope" when the officers drop by are but a few examples that officers have easily rationalized. "What the hell, we put our lives on the line and they owe us." A gun not turned into evidence and kept by the officer can become "It's just a doper's; what's the big deal?" The "loyalty versus integrity" dilemma can permit criminal actions to develop into conspiracies ... whether other officers are actively involved or passively remain loyal and accept what takes place.

Now, the risks are far beyond just administrative reprimands or suspension ... officers face being fired and criminal sanctions when they are caught. The initially honest, dedicated, above reproach officers now ask, "Where did it all go wrong?" and "How did this happen?" as they face the realities of personal and professional devastation and criminal prosecution. Officers who reach the final stage did not wake up one day and take a quantum leap from being honest, hard working officers to criminal defendants.

Entitlement Versus Accountability.

Officers can develop an overwhelming sense of victimization and an intense resentment toward the supervisors and administrators who control their job-role. This can lead to another dilemma ... a sense of entitlement. Entitlement is a mindset

(continued)

Box 6-1 *(continued)*

that suggests "We stick together" and "We deserve special treatment." The off-duty officer who is driving 30 mph over the speed limit and weaving in and out of traffic who tells his passenger, a concerned co-worker, "Relax, I have Mastershields!" implies a sense of entitlement and feeling of impunity. Entitlement allows both on and off duty officers to operate with the belief that many of the rules don't apply to them. "Professional courtesy" goes far beyond just giving another officer a break on a traffic violation. Officers are constantly faced with the dilemma of "doing the right thing" or "doing what they know is right." The only way to change this sense of entitlement is to foster an environment of accountability . . . both organizational and personal accountability.

Loyalty Versus Integrity

Most officers want to be known as loyal and a man or woman of integrity. A problem occurs, however, when a sense of victimization and over-identification with the job sets into motion the dilemma of "loyalty versus integrity"[3] Here is where officers called in to Internal Affairs and asked questions about another officer lie, many times about a minor issue. When this occurs, the officer has traded his/her integrity for "loyalty" to a fellow officer.

Notes:

1. Kevin Gilmartin and John (Jack) Harris, The Continuum of Compromise, 1995, http://emotionalsurvival.com/lawenforcementethics.htm.

2. Kevin M. Gilmartin, Ph.D., Hypervigilance: A learned perceptual set and its consequences on police stress, Psychological Services to Law Enforcement, U.S. Dept. of Justice Federal Bureau of Investigation, Edited by Reese and Goldstein, Washington, D.C. 1986, Library of Congress Number 85–600538

3. *Commission to Investigate Allegations of Police Corruption and the Anti-Corruption Procedures of the Police Department*, July 7, 1994 (hereinafter Mollen Commission report), *The New York Times*, March 29, 1993, p. 8)

Source: Kevin M. Gilmartin and John J. Harris, "Law Enforcement Ethics . . . The Continuum of Compromise." *Police Chief Magazine* (January 1998).

deadlines, personality conflicts with coworkers, or a heavy workload can create burnout (see Box 6-2). Whether one is a cop, stylist, or insurance salesperson, this outcome is tragic, both physically and mentally. Many researchers feel that while major occurrences such as a divorce or death of a loved one create severe stress, it's life's little irritations that cause the most damage. In the long run, a continual dose of minor annoyances causes the most difficulty. We can all relate to losing things, having to watch our weight, car trouble, or disagreements with coworkers.

Box 6-2
Anger and Frustration about Your Agency

Most veteran officers feel far more stress from the operations and interactions within their own department than from carrying out their job responsibilities. This can be said with some certainty thanks to research conducted by the National Institute of Ethics. The research goal was to identify what circumstances cause officers throughout the nation to feel angry and frustrated about their job. Understanding what prompts these feelings is valuable for counteracting a wide assortment of undesirable behavior and poor morale.

Richard Mears is the Director of Community Justice Projects at the University of Maine and Assistant Professor of Criminal Justice. He is also the former Deputy Chief of Police, Brunswick, ME, and had a highly successful law enforcement career. Professor Mears shares his advice for how officers should deal with the frustration and stress from within their own department. Like most other officers, he begins by acknowledging that the stress from within was far worse that the aggravation from carrying out police duties.

> When I reflect on my police career and think about the really tough times (and there were a few) I can only say that I managed to survive them because of the support I got from my spouse and my peers when I had to make really difficult decisions. I would also suggest that the difficult decisions had to do with my

(continued)

Box 6-2 *(continued)*

fellow officers and police administrators and not with crime or criminals.

I tell people that I got promoted in spite of the police administrators I had, not because of them. When I say that, I mean that many of the police managers I met along the way put personal interests before professional interests. They were self centered, lacked any vision, and were not the best role models. Not very flattering comments to make. I did what I thought was the right thing to do in spite of the adversity.

Over time I think the quality of leadership has improved but there are still too many of the old guard still holding on. They see every progressive idea as a threat to them personally. Many are paranoid of someone looking better than them. They did everything they could to hold back people as opposed to developing talent. That's why very little in-service training was provided to staff.

When I entered law enforcement if you had a college degree you were shunned by the sergeants as a problem waiting to happen. They interpreted enforcing the law as harassing the public and causing them paperwork which they hated to do.

POLICE ANGER AND FRUSTRATION RESEARCH

Through 1999 and 2000 the National Institute of Ethics, America's largest provider of law enforcement ethics training, conducted research about what caused officers to become angry and frustrated. Data was collected by having participants of seminars they presented throughout the country complete a confidential written questionnaire.

The survey instructions were to place a number from zero to five in a space provided to the left of a list of categories. The number selected describes to what extent they felt they had been treated unfairly about that specific issue.

Box 6-2 *(continued)*

0	I don't feel any anger or frustration
1	Slightly angry or frustrated
2	Somewhat angry or frustrated
3	Moderately angry or frustrated
4	Substantially angry or frustrated
5	Extremely angry or frustrated

Total Surveys: 1,902
Gender: Male-1491; Female-326; Did not advise-85
Number of States: 20
Agency Type: Police-298; Sheriffs-144; State-01; Federal-01
Total Agencies: 444

The Top Twelve Anger and Frustration Causes

2.93	Accountability is unfair or inconsistent
2.93	Administration plays favoritism (promotions, transfers and discipline)
2.72	Motivation and morale is bad
2.65	Communication is very poor
2.65	Staffing levels are low
2.62	Discipline is unfair and inconsistent
2.62	Administration is "out of touch"
2.59	Administration does not support us
2.51	Fellow employees have bad attitudes
2.39	Supervisors play politics
2.34	Employees aren't listened to
2.31	Criminal justice system is frustrating

Remaining Causes (Random Order)

2.15	Respect isn't demonstrated
1.54	Safety is not high enough
2.06	Salary is not high enough
1.03	Sick days—I should get to use them
1.87	Supervisors are disrespectful
1.37	Supervisors never around in times of need

(continued)

Box 6-2 *(continued)*

1.72	Supplies are inadequate
0.98	Threats by supervisors
1.83	Don't go to enough training seminars
1.24	Writing too much of it
1.27	Assignments are unfair
1.61	Benefits are inadequate
0.71	Cars—others get to drive best ones
1.39	Compensation is unfair
1.06	Court—on my day off
2.03	Criticism—there's too much of it
1.77	Empathy—there's none of it
1.90	Goals and objectives are never used
1.17	Mission statement doesn't exist
1.02	No one else has to do it
1.74	Planning is non-existent
0.85	Race—I'm treated unfairly because of my race
1.49	Racism exists
1.54	Ridiculing supervisors
0.68	Shift work
1.84	Sincerity—a lack of it is prevalent
1.33	Supervisors always too critical
1.28	Supervisors don't answer my questions
2.07	Teamwork is pitiful
2.14	Training (internal) poor
0.69	Type of shift rotation
1.51	Background investigations are poor
2.29	Bias influences leaders' decisions
1.94	Cooperation among workers is poor
0.58	Day shift is too boring
1.73	Discrimination exists
0.37	Females—I don't like to work with
0.53	Hours of work are too long
1.64	Paperwork—too much of it
1.99	Unfair local media

Source: National Institute of Ethics, Anger and Frustration Research, Longwood, FL, 2001, www.ethicsinstitute.com.

The following thoughts can make a difference in dealing with irritations. Make a commitment to yourself to lighten up and enjoy life's little pleasures. Discover what irritations are bothering you, then carry out a plan of action to correct them.

- Establish long-range goals to put more direction and guidance in your life.
- Be an optimist; expect the best out of life!
- Make a things-to-do list every evening or the first thing in the morning.
- Do not ignore or try to forget about things that upset you. Instead, deal with them; overcome the things that make your life unhappy.
- Enjoy life. Savor the pleasurable, fun stuff that happens each day.

Religious leader Robert Schuller said it best when he talked about what to do when things go wrong. "When faced with a mountain, I will not quit. I will keep on striving until I climb over, find a pass through, tunnel underneath, or simply stay and turn the mountain into a gold mine."

Remember, some of life's greatest pleasures come from the ability to pause and appreciate the things that are really important. Do not get bogged down with self-imposed pressures that, in the long run, have very little meaning or importance. Promise yourself to take more time to watch sunsets, go for walks, have good conversations with your family, and even go fishing.

Medical Conditions

Many physical difficulties are often associated with negative stress, from headaches to serious coronary problems. Most controlled research about the relationship between stress and medical problems of the police has dealt with digestive disorders and heart disease. A 1950 study noted high rates of death due to heart disease among law enforcement officers relative to other occupations. Another study documented that 27 percent of the evaluated officers had medium-high- or high-risk coronary disease. Other research, conducted during the early 1970s, discovered that the police were admitted to hospitals for nonduty matters at a significantly higher rate than other individuals.

Almost two-thirds of the concerned officers were admitted for digestive or circulatory difficulties, compared to approximately one-half for other occupations.

Nationwide comparison research suggests officers experience ulcers and headaches more frequently than other people. Further data showed cops smoke more than the general population. Asthma, thyroid disorders, heartburn, high blood pressure, back-aches, and muscle cramps have also been associated with psychological stress.

Many studies generally substantiate that law enforcement careers are related to high instances of serious medical problems. However, there is a lack of data to pinpoint exactly how much more likely officers are to develop medical problems than workers from other occupations. Little data compares evidence of medical disorders in relation to different types of law enforcement agencies; it only overwhelmingly suggests that direct evidence proves a distinct relationship exists between the stress of police work and medical problems. Research must continue until there can be no doubt about the exact relationship.[5]

World-famous author and commentator Paul Harvey has cited law enforcement as "the most dangerous job." He wrote "Today's lawman is under more pressure than any of his predecessors. Individual officers are burdened with increasing legal, societal, and personal obligations, all negative. Dealing with stressful human conflicts every day, life-and-death decisions, survival decisions, policemen are every day 'wrung out.'"

Harvey further writes, "Routinely, the policeman sees the worst manifestation of human behavior. The sum total of an endless cacophony of such cruelty inevitably eventuates discouragement, depression, despair. Policemen are expected to epitomize manly qualities . . . to be tough, aggressive, dominating, unemotional. Some become gun freaks; others become super jocks, and sometimes super studs. No man can live up to this all the time."[6]

In his commentary, Paul Harvey emphasizes the emotional and medical toll of a police career. He refers to the police as "time bombs in blue." He points out that 1,500 cops received psychiatric aid or alcoholism counseling during 1985. Of that number, only 500 officers sought help on their own.

Fortunately, many agencies have or are now contemplating internal psychological counseling units, but only larger departments can afford these divisions. Several years ago the Federal

Bureau of Investigation announced that its highest training priority for state and local agencies is the handling of personal stress. Making stress manageable for the individual officer includes an emotional and medical ordeal that is grim, to say the least. Police experience a suicide rate six times higher than that of the general population. Forty percent of the police do not get help for their problems. Almost half of that 40 percent will assault their children or wives. Nearly ten percent of that half will either kill themselves or be killed by a member of their own family.

Paul Harvey was right when he spoke of the inherent danger of being a cop. Contrary to popular belief, stress harms more cops than criminals do. Few, if any, veteran officers have not been wounded by it. Divorce, drug abuse, alcoholism, physical disorders, and suicide are all consequences of the misery brought about from stress.

Some view stress as an occupational hazard of law enforcement. As such, it can be reduced or controlled through education and support from a concerned agency, friends, and relatives.

Agency Programs

Progressive police departments began to recognize and deal with stress problems during the 1950s and 1960s. These early attempts were aimed toward alcoholism and often associated with Alcoholics Anonymous. As occurred with much of America's workforce, the 1970s saw a dramatic increase of interest toward employee assistance programs by law enforcement.[7]

Is it fair to expect law enforcement agencies to provide effective employee assistance programs? If so, what should they consist of? What can you expect if they are already available? How much should you get involved? If a program is not provided, what can be done to assist in developing one? Yes, it is reasonable to expect your organization to provide an effective, formal program to help in dealing with work-related stress. Furthermore, it is not unreasonable to expect professional services. An employee assistance program usually includes counseling by mental health professionals.

Emotional problems can result from working the street, financial difficulties, postshooting trauma, internal management problems, or an assortment of other family and personal issues.

Whether the problems are related to work or family issues, the results are the same. No one goes through a divorce, death of a close friend, alcoholism, or other crisis and leaves their troubles completely at home.

Though police departments should provide assistance, effective programs are not inexpensive. The current cost for a program in a medium-size department varies from a couple thousand to nearly twenty thousand dollars annually. Regardless of the amount an agency has funded, there are many programs that may be offered. Several are very beneficial yet fairly inexpensive. Stress-related programs may include:

- Confidential counseling
- Stress-related needs assessment
- Physical fitness
- Nutritional/weight control
- Spouse training
- Stress management training
- Stress-related supervision training
- Postshooting trauma counseling
- Peer counseling
- Alcoholism counseling
- Drug abuse counseling

No matter what types of stress assistance are offered, they can be organized in several ways. An agency may choose to enter into a contract with an independent counseling agency. Another way is for the counselor to become an employee of the department. A third alternative is some variation of the first two.

Whichever method is chosen, officers must feel that they have an opportunity to voice their opinions in developing the program. A needs assessment should be conducted. Without input, the force may resist its implementation and view stress assistance as something being forced on them. Everyone must be educated on how the program will operate, and absolute confidentiality must be assured.

Crisis intervention, limited counseling, and alcoholism treatment are the most common services provided. Counseling services must be available for officers 24 hours a day every day. Marital problems often generate requests for assistance. Though most officers who receive counseling do so voluntarily, a system to provide necessary mandatory referrals is also important. While confidentiality is essential, a monitoring system that documents counseling must be established.

Any good stress or employee assistance program has an element of training. Everyone within the agency should participate in an orientation training class. Training developed specifically for supervisors should focus on their role and responsibilities in stress management. Seminars providing assistance to officers' spouses should be offered on a regular basis. As with all training, stress seminars must be thoroughly developed, based on a needs assessment and performance objectives, presented in a practical manner, and well documented.

Agency Management Style

Most officers agree that the pressures of their jobs can cause serious problems. Many feel that the majority of stress comes from within the department rather than on the street. If a department is riddled with backstabbing, power plays, internal politics, demeaning and ridiculing supervisors, lack of recognition for those who deserve it, and a constant feeling of tension, stress will take its toll.

Law enforcement agencies are structured in a semimilitary management style. Supervision is often authoritarian. Middle- and top-level managers have sometimes risen through the ranks under strict disciplinarian role models. They, in turn, are accustomed to a rigid, disciplined supervision style. Thus, the macho, tough cop image is perpetuated.

In a crisis situation, quick and immediate discipline is essential. There is no time for debate or discussion. At times like these, authoritarian leadership is crucial. In other ways and at times other than a crisis, a strict disciplinary leadership does little to improve an officer's self-esteem or feeling of achievement. It is past time for law enforcement to change its management style to that of the world's best run corporations. Enlightened leadership is people-oriented. Employees participate in decision making, and an atmosphere of respect, trust, and honesty must replace management ridicule, suspicion, and power struggles.

The ability of an administration to be sensitive to its employees' emotional needs is important. When management ignores the fact that officers need assistance with stress-related problems, they do an injustice to both the organization and its personnel. These situations frequently cause disgruntlement, absenteeism, discipline problems, or apathy. Police departments have been notorious for "not taking care of their own." This, in itself, has been a crime.

VETERAN OFFICER CONCERNS

As officers age, more than their physical appearance changes. If they have been in the same assignment for years without being promoted, especially the patrol division, feelings of frustration, depression, low self-esteem, and little sense of achievement may have been generated.

One extensive study of veteran officers identified a number of frequent complaints about internal operations:

- Veteran officers are not requested to provide their expertise
- Administrative insensitivity is a common perception of veteran officers
- Days off and shift selection do not take seniority into account
- Promotional processes are perceived to be unfair
- Supervisors show little respect for older officers' experience
- Measurement of productivity is unfair to veteran officers[8]

It is not difficult to understand why senior officers express these views. Most people, given the same situation, would share many of these feelings. It is difficult to understand, though, why some agencies ignore the problems.

Veteran officers should not be left to struggle alone with feelings of despair and frustration. Fighting the pressure from working the street, dealing with the judicial system, and departmental politics are more than enough for anyone to deal with. The administration of any agency should view its role as serving the department by removing obstacles that prevent employees from doing their jobs, not as supervisors who are served by subordinates. Officers, likewise, must be willing to be part of a cooperative team.

Emotional Detachment

He reported that one night during his routine patrol along the waterfront he happened to fall in behind a car being driven by a middle-age African-American man. Both cars drove the same route for several minutes, moving slowly past the industrial buildings, until the car in front suddenly stopped. The driver jumped out and strode back to the police car, which had also halted abruptly. "Why are you following me?" the man demanded angrily. "Can't a black person do anything around here without being harassed and treated like a criminal?"

"While he was raving at me for tailgating him," the officer explained, "I realized that my regular patrol had a whole different meaning for this man. Maybe he had been in trouble in the past; certainly he had been hassled—it sort of goes with the territory of being black in a rich white city. So I let him finish and then said in as offhand a way as I could, 'Do you think I have nothing better to do than follow you around? Why are you being so paranoid?' I added that I hadn't been following him but just happened to be going in the same direction, and he'd gotten there ahead of me. For a minute he didn't seem to believe me—it was like he wanted to stay mad— but he gradually calmed down and muttered something about looking for boxes because he was moving. 'Well,' I said, 'fine, good luck,' and backed up to pull around his car and finish my patrol."[9]

Anyone who has "worked the street" for any length of time can recall similar incidents. Snide remarks by someone an officer has stopped for a traffic citation, a rude business owner having just discovered that his or her business was burglarized, or the cold, frustrated comments of someone who has been a victim of abuse once too often—comments like these take their toll as the months and years pass. Dealing with the emotional turmoil caused by angry and frustrated citizens is easier said than done. It is aggravated by the fact that most people become cops because they are caring individuals; they want to help others.

Remember that good cops can detach themselves emotionally from street frustration. Do not "personalize" rude or angry comments that seem to be directed at you. Whether someone is a mean and nasty person or a good person who happens to be going through a bad time is something over which you have no control. You can, however, control how you react to the situation. Great cops learn to take everything in stride and remain detached.

The alternatives to emotional detachment could be alcoholism, marital problems, drug abuse, departmental discipline, suspension, termination, or suicide. Becoming emotionally involved will cause clouded judgment and decisions, and reacting out of anger or emotion instead of logic and reasoning can be fatal—for you or your career.

Exercise

Besides emotionally separating yourself from the mental roller coaster ride of life as an officer, other things can relieve the effects of stress. Documented, well-researched studies confirm that physical exercise is a great way of releasing stress. Running, racquetball, softball, tennis, swimming, and other sports are more than just fun. Officers must remember that rotating shifts, working weekends and holidays, unhealthy eating, long hours, bad weather, and boredom mixed with rare but intense physical exertion also can be a damaging burden. The benefits of staying healthy and physically fit, therefore, should be obvious to officers; people who stay in sound physical condition know the exhilarating sensation of exercise on their bodies, which also affects mental outlook.

Physical exercise can help relieve some of the negative aspects of stress and keep your body and mind prepared for survival. Imagine what your chances would be if you were overweight and totally out of shape. You have more than an obligation to yourself; you have a responsibility to the citizens you are sworn to protect.

Satisfaction from Helping Others

Eat nutritiously, get plenty of exercise, and "be a nice guy"—that is what more and more highly acclaimed research is confirming to be sound advice. Continued evidence has shown that helping others also has substantial health benefits. Neuroscientists, epidemiologists, sociologists, and psychiatrists continue to conclude that being of assistance to others provides an inner strength necessary to overcome one's own problems. Furthermore, increased life expectancy and improved vitality are documented results of giving long-term help to others.

Many studies have indicated that people need meaningful relationships for their own well-being. Nervous disorders, immune system problems, premature death, and deteriorating health have been disproportionately related to people who are unmarried, have few friends or relatives, and do not take part in community activities.

While researchers agree that social involvement provides health benefits, there is still controversy over why or how this occurs. Some researchers believe that a sense of satisfaction from helping others produces endorphins, the brain's natural proteins that induce pain relief, euphoria, and appetite modulation. This helps the nervous system.

Studies also indicate blood cells comprising the immune system are sensitive to neuropeptides, compounds produced by the brain. Nerve cells connect the brain to various parts of the body. Immune system cells are required to battle infection and are produced in several areas of the body. Though the debate continues, the possibilities are worth remembering and trying yourself.[10]

Disagreements

The proper way to disagree with others is important—whether you are at home or work, with family and friends, or discussing something with your supervisor. Often, needless hard feelings are created or friendships severed simply because those involved did not understand the importance of communicating effectively, especially when emotions run high.

The first ingredient of a successful formula for handling disagreements is to disagree without taking it personally. Becoming defensive and angry only escalates the negative aspects of a disagreement. Logical, intelligent people will always disagree on issues from time to time.

It is not wrong to disagree; it is very healthy to have a differing point of view. Do not become defensive. If you take the discussion personally and begin to attack the other person, no one will win. Your use of body language and choice of words can turn a mature, adult conversation into a bitter, childish argument. Remember to put yourself in the other person's place; think how you would feel if you were that person. Understand that the incident that prompted the discussion may not be the real issue. Maybe there is a hidden issue that must be resolved.

Everything does not have to be resolved during the disagreement. If emotions begin to flare, calm down. Agree that the discussion can be continued later in the day or on another day. Thinking things through has a way of resolving delicate situations. In addition, one of you may simply have had a rotten day or the entire situation may not be as gloomy as it appears at the moment.

Lastly, a few techniques may help. First, talking softly eases heated situations; it is very difficult to argue with someone who is calm and soft-spoken. Second, don't take cheap shots at the other person. Intentionally hurting someone's feelings does nothing but hurt everyone involved. You certainly won't feel good about yourself. Third, it is important to be able to forgive and forget. To harbor a grudge is of no benefit to anyone. Life is too short to handicap yourself emotionally.

> *Successful law enforcement officers possess good character, constantly pursue excellence, and enjoy working with people. They tend to be enterprising individuals committed to the profession with high expectations of themselves. They understand their role in society and cautiously exercise their authority in a respectful, equitable, and compassionate manner.*
>
> Donald Keith
> Assistant Director,
> Mississippi Police Corps

PERSONAL RELATIONSHIPS

From our childhood years until we become senior citizens, we have many relationships in our professional and personal lives. The ability to balance these relationships with our many other commitments can be challenging, especially in today's multitask, multirole society. Meeting that challenge is important to our well-being, happiness, and self-satisfaction.

Some of the most important relationships we have are those with our spouses, our children, and significant others. Keeping these relationships alive and well requires, from all parties involved, commitment, honesty, respect, communication, and, of course, love.

Spouses

Most people know that half of all marriages in the United States end in divorce. The divorce rate for police officers is even higher. Why are cops such poor risks when it comes to marriage?

Sometimes a spouse of an officer feels as though police work takes priority over the couple's relationship. Law enforcement has a way of becoming an obsession with some new officers. Veteran officers can look around the department and point out rookies who literally eat, breathe, and live for their jobs.

Obsession with police work, though not uncommon during the first few years on the force, is not healthy. Some officers work 30 to 40 hours off duty, without pay, every week. They would not consider being out sick and sometimes do not even want to take vacations. Even spending hour after hour around the station talking shop is common. Their husbands or wives would at first understand. Later they may feel hurt and rejected.

Rotating shifts and unpredictable work hours are additional causes of marital strain. They lead to nights sleeping alone, lack of sleep, and even more marital stress. Another reason for marital stress is the perceived or real sexual temptation that many officers face. Few spouses are comfortable with the thought of their better half driving around all night with someone of the opposite sex. Inevitably there are stories of men and women who throw themselves at officers in uniform. Officers' spouses often worry about the danger their loved ones face. The caring must be sincere and the commitment strong. It is no secret that marriage takes effort (for more information on the toll police work can take on relationships, see Box 6-3).

The most valuable asset to any police marriage is having the commitment to work through everyday problems. Take holidays as an example. Uniformed officers usually have to work on holidays. Changing work schedules to make your immediate family and relatives happy is not an easy task; everyone must learn how to compromise. Visiting several relatives at their homes may be necessary. Even an awkward schedule may be required. In any event, the key is to put yourself in your spouse's position.

Another ingredient for success is the ability to communicate. Once this art is lost you are both in trouble. Do whatever it takes to keep open, honest, and respectful communication alive. Make it a point to create situations that encourage talking. Go for walks. Go fishing, swimming, hiking, to the ball game, or to aerobics class together. Communicating is more than talking; it is body language and just being there for the other person. Remember, the best part of life is the here and now, so share it together.

Box 6-3

Law Officer Families

THE FAMILY OF A LAW ENFORCEMENT OFFICER

In 2001 Dr. Lorraine Greene and Dr. Ellen Kirschman conducted research in association with a federally funded project titled "On-Line Education, Resources and Support for Law Enforcement Families." The research conducted and report authored by Drs. Greene and Kirschman provide important insight for any officer. The following is from their final report to the U.S. Department of Justice.

Drs. Greene and Kirschman conducted important research as part of the project. Their study revealed the following facts about the importance of an officer's family.

Family Coherence

The family measure of coherence measures the degree to which family members believe they can control and manage their family responsibilities and work demands and predict and shape their future. It also assesses the respondents' commitment to the mission of the law enforcement agency and the support that they receive from the organization. All of these factors have a significant impact on family adaptation and longevity. Overall, the respondents scored high on the coherence measure. There was a strong commitment to the mission and they felt a sense of control over what was happening to them and thought that they could predict what was to occur in their immediate future. This was the perception of both sworn officers and spouses. There were no significant differences between their scores on the coherence measure.

Family Social Support

The social support index measured the degree to which family members provided support to each other, perceived support from the law enforcement community and their general sense of belonging. There were no statistically significant differences between spouses and sworn officers in the amount of social support they received. Overall, the entire group of respondents reported receiving considerable support from both family and the law enforcement communities.

Box 6-3 *(continued)*

There were differences among all respondents' perceptions of social support according to the size of their departments. Significant differences were found between large size and small size departments. Family members from large size agencies perceived themselves as having more family and community support than those from small size departments have.

Family Time and Routine

Spouses felt there was more family time and established routines than officers. Statistically significant differences were also found between spouses and officers on the relative connection subscale. Spouses found it more important than sworn officers to establish predictable routines to make connections with relatives. In addition, spouses more than sworn officers, found it important to establish predictable routines to promote a sense of family organization and accountability needed to maintain family order in the home.

Family Problem Solving Communication

Positive family communication patterns are essential for family problem solving, stability and hardiness. We examined family members' communication patterns using the Family Problem-solving Communication Index.[1] Overall, the respondents reported affirming communication patterns. There were no significant differences between sworn officers and spouses in overall problem-solving communication patterns.

Family Changes and Strains

The ability for the family to change and adapt over time is critical if it is to be resilient. The pile-up of strain and demands can adversely affect the family system. To determine the amount of strain and demands the family experiences, McCubbin's Family Changes and Strains Index was administered. Overall few stressors or demands were experienced by the study participants during the past twelve months; and there were no differences in the number of problems reported among sworn officers and spouses. There were differences in the number of

(continued)

Box 6-3 *(continued)*

strains and demands expressed by family members according to the size of their departments.

Family Coping

Participants were asked to rate how helpful specific coping strategies were to adjusting to the demands of family life. Three primary subscales were used: fitting into corporate life; developing self and interpersonal relationships; and establishing independence and self-sufficiency. Overall, most respondents found simply accepting the law enforcement life style demands as minimally helpful. Differences between spouses and sworn officers was approaching statistical significance, suggesting that sworn officers found the coping style more helpful than spouses did.

Work Climate, Organizational Issues, and Stress

Overall, respondents' perception of the work climate was rather unfavorable. Further, results revealed that large departments held more positive views of the work climate than small departments.

Some of the items for overall perception of the work climate were "Coworkers confront and embarrass each other in meetings" and "Command staff are respectful of each other at work." All items were coded in the positive direction in order to reflect a positive dimension of work climate.

Note:

1. Hamilton McCubbin, Hamilton McCubbin's Family Assessment, Family Coping Coherence Index, 1996, familymeasures.ksbe.edu/ TableOfContent.htm

Source: Lorraine Williams Greene and Ellen Freeman Kirschman, "On-Line Education, Resources and Support for Law Enforcement Families, Final Report," Washington, D.C., U.S. Department of Justice, Document No. 186749, 2001.

Understanding and compassion are important qualities. You are responsible for sharing and caring about your spouse's feelings. People worry because they care, and you must help your spouse through the rough moments. It is frustrating going to bed alone, having holidays disrupted, and feeling the insecurity of knowing sexual temptation may surround your mate. It is not difficult to understand how they feel. For the most part, you are the only one in a position to help. Officers have to show understanding and compassion for the problems their jobs create in their marriages. A defensive attitude only takes them further down the road to the marital war zone, and that is a battle no one wins. Don't fight it.

Force yourself not to become obsessed with work; you can still be a great cop. Even better, you will be a balanced person. Take time out. Go for minivacations whenever possible. Talk with each other. Enjoy life. Reach a healthy balance between work and your personal life. Otherwise, both your marriage and your career will suffer.

A happy marriage means you are more likely to be a better cop. It takes commitment, understanding, caring, and a lot of give and take.

Kind Words

Words of kindness between husband and wife help to keep a marriage from growing cold and bitter. Like most aspects of marriage, constant attention must be given to how and what we say to each other.

Time has a way of causing couples to take each other for granted. Sometimes people tend to be overly critical, and destructive criticism and verbal jabs are very damaging. To make matters worse, such a cycle feeds on itself, becoming only more vicious with time. On the other hand, if a couple makes a habit of giving praise, just the opposite is true. Warm, sincere compliments are priceless; they cost nothing and are invaluable in times of sadness. In fact, few things in life are as effective as a sincere smile and a kind remark.

People who have grown up in households where words of kindness were rare are unlikely to feel comfortable giving or receiving compliments. They simply are unaccustomed to it, leading to awkwardness or outright feelings of defensiveness. These feelings can overwhelm people who believe their spouse is pressuring them to pay more compliments.

These suggestions may help:

- Use a variety of ways to show your love and appreciation.
- Be creative.
- Give praise about the things that are most meaningful.
- Be spontaneous. Do not let yourself get in a rut.

- Be sincere in your compliments. Do not say things that are not true.
- Remember that the simplest deeds and remarks often mean the most.
- Romance can be a rewarding part of life.
- Express how much you enjoy your spouse's company. Learn to appreciate being with each other more and more, and tell each other how you feel.[11]

Significant Others

Much of the information presented for spouses also applies to officers considering serious relationship commitments or marriage. Like spouses, significant others, too, can find it difficult to understand or accept why officers must work long hours, miss some holidays, or rotate work schedules. They also worry when their loved ones face danger every day or meet other temptations. As an officer, you can be sensitive to your partner's concerns by communicating openly and honestly and having compassion for him or her.

In any serious love relationship, both partners need to clearly understand and communicate their level of commitment to one another. Perhaps one or both of you is ready for a further commitment. If so, it is wise before taking that next step for both of you to understand the type of work that you, as an officer, will be involved in and the commitment you must give to your job and to each other. A balance between your relationship and your work is possible with effort and understanding from both partners.

Children

As if growing up isn't hard enough, some kids are the children of police officers. Children of anyone in a high-visibility occupation occasionally will reap the benefits or burdens of their inherited situation. They need to be emotionally prepared to handle these situations, and parents are responsible for seeing that their children are emotionally ready for the future.

Every child looks to his parents for nurturing, advice, security, and role-modeling. Keep an open line of communication. Disagreements will be inevitable, especially as children mature into young adults, because then they begin to resist authority and strive for independence. You do not have to win every disagreement; if you feel you do, children will rebel. Have compassion for the emotional tornadoes they will experience during puberty and other stages of growing up.

Parenting is one of life's most difficult and rewarding challenges. Warmth, frustration, love, anger, caring, and endless memories are all part of being a parent. Some aspects of police work can make parenting an even greater challenge—long hours, missed holidays, potential danger—but do not miss the wonderful joys of raising children. Spend more time with them. Go fishing together, toss a ball around, go bowling, help them with homework, or simply sit and talk. You will cherish these times forever.

OH GOD

Give me wisdom of these that criticize me, so that I might not make wrong decisions again.
Give me patience with the young.
Give me compassion and understanding with the elderly.
Give me the wisdom to remain silent when I would rather express my thoughts loudly.
Give me the determination to keep on trying when plans fail, leads run out and information obtained is erroneous and all seems lost.
When the opinions of others differ from mine, let me listen with an open mind and consider the possible alternative.
Give me the humility to admit when I'm in error and the wisdom to stay silent when I'm right. Let me speak up for what is right and just.
Help me view and treat all persons as an equal, regardless of race, color, creed, sex or station in life.
Give me the courage to perform the duties of my job, even in the face of great danger or performing a task that is unpopular.
Let me put the safety of others ahead of my own safety.
When my job is finished and my head is hanging low, give me something else to do so I might show my love for you.

By an Old Lawman, Just a Cop to Quite a Few
In *Police Stress*, Edward C. Donovan, Editor,
The International Law Enforcement Association, Mattapan, MA
Winter 1987

QUESTIONS FOR DISCUSSION

1. Chapter 6 begins with Lee D. Donohue, Sr., the Honolulu police chief, stating, "A great cop is a person who can be trusted to do the right thing even when no one is looking. It is a person who works hard and treats others as he or she wants

to be treated." Think of situations when you have been tempted to do unethical things, knowing it would be very unlikely anyone would ever find out. What did you do, and how do you feel about it now?

2. Considering Gail Sheehy's research on the "passages" of life that adults move through, which stage of life do you believe will be most difficult for you, and what is the best approach for dealing with it? How will these influences impact your career?

3. Has law enforcement, as an occupation, done a good job of helping officers deal with the stress of their career? Justify your opinion.

4. The "Continuum of Compromise"[12] is a framework for understanding and teaching how the transition from "honest cop" to "compromised officer" can occur. Why is it important to know the Continuum of Compromise? What is the best way to help, if you know you are working with an officer who is progressing through the continuum?

5. According to recent nationwide research, the top ten reasons that officers feel anger and frustration are (ranked from one to ten):

Accountability is unfair or inconsistent.

Administration plays favoritism (promotions, transfers, and discipline).

Motivation and morale are bad.

Communication is very poor.

Staffing levels are low.

Discipline is unfair and inconsistent.

Administration is "out of touch."

Administration does not support us.

Fellow employees have bad attitudes.

Supervisors play politics.

You may notice that reasons such as the frustration caused by the judicial system and poor work hours are absent. Do you find this surprising? Why? What do you feel can be done to prevent these causes of anger and frustration? How important are these issues?

ENDNOTES

1. Gail Sheehy, *Passages* (New York: Bantam Books, 1976), pp. 39–46.

2. M. Steven Meagher and Nancy Yentes, "Choosing a Career in Policing: A Comparison of Male and Female Perceptions" (paper presented to the annual meeting of the Academy of Criminal Justice Sciences, March 20, 1986, Orlando, Florida).

3. John G. Stratton, "Police Stress: An Overview," *The Police Chief,* July 1978, pp. 58–61.

4. Robert A. Jud, "Making Stress Manageable," *Business Week*, July 1987, pp. 75–76.

5. Gail A. Goolkasian, Ronald W. Geddes, and William DeJong, *Coping with Police Stress* (Washington, DC: U.S. Government Printing Office, 1985), pp. 5–8.

6. Paul Harvey, "The Most Dangerous Job: Law Enforcement," *The Los Angeles Times*, 1986.

7. Gail A. Goolkasian, Ronald W. Geddes, and William DeJong, *Coping with Police Stress* (Washington, DC: U.S. Government Printing Office, 1985), p. 12.

8. Mark Pogrebin, "Alienation Among Veteran Police Officers," *The Police Chief,* 1987, pp. 38–40.

9. Edward E. Shev and Jeremy Joan Hewes, *Good Cops/Bad Cops* (San Francisco: San Francisco Book Co., 1977), p. 98.

10. Eileen Rockefeller Growald and Allan Luks, "The Good Guys Finish Healthier, Research Shows," *The Orlando Sentinel,* October 4, 1988, p. E-3.

11. Diane Hales, "Words That Can Warm Up Your Marriage," *McCalls Magazine*, April 1989, pp. 70–72.

12. Kevin Gilmartin and John (Jack) Harris, The Continuum of Compromise, 1995, http://emotionalsurvival.com/lawenforcementethics.htm.

chapter 7

STAYING PHYSICALLY FIT

Being a great cop is about being ethical and being a professional. It is about being a leader and not a follower, and setting an example as a highly skilled and dedicated individual. A great cop sets ethical standards others will want to emulate.

John Linn, Ph.D., Penn State University

In the last couple of decades the United States has witnessed a major shift toward physical fitness (see Box 7-1). We have been bombarded with exercise—television shows, magazines, books, spas, health clubs, aerobics, "prayercise," and more.

Most fitness information endorses a particular diet or exercise program. With the exception of fad diets, almost everything from a reputable source has merit. All fitness programs should begin with a physician's examination.

Americans lead the world in deaths from cardiovascular and respiratory difficulties. Staying physically fit is, literally, a matter of life and death. Understanding and appreciating the principles of cardiovascular health is not difficult, and it would be foolish not to do something to prevent heart disease. Most people exercise for appearance, health, and enjoyment. The following are heart disease risk factors that can be reduced through exercise:

- Obesity
- High blood pressure
- High blood sugar levels
- Stress

Box 7-1

Importance of Fitness

PHYSICAL ACTIVITY FUNDAMENTAL TO PREVENTING DISEASE

Regular physical activity, fitness, and exercise are critically important for the health and well-being of people of all ages. Research has demonstrated that virtually all individuals can benefit from regular physical activity, whether they participate in vigorous exercise or some type of moderate health-enhancing physical activity. Even among frail and very old adults, mobility and functioning can be improved through physical activity.[1] Therefore, physical fitness should be a priority for Americans of all ages. Regular physical activity has been shown to reduce the morbidity and mortality from many chronic diseases. Millions of Americans suffer from chronic illnesses that can be prevented or improved through regular physical activity:

- 12.6 million people have coronary heart disease[2];
- 1.1 million people suffer from a heart attack in a given year[2];
- 17 million people have diabetes; about 90% to 95% of cases are type 2 diabetes, which is associated with obesity and physical inactivity[3]; approximately 16 million people have "prediabetes";
- 107,000 people are newly diagnosed with colon cancer each year[4,5];
- 300,000 people suffer from hip fractures each year[6];
- 50 million people have high blood pressure[2]; and
- Nearly 50 million adults (between the ages of 20 and 74), or 27% of the adult population, are obese; overall more than 108 million adults, or 61% of the adult population, are either obese or overweight.[7,8]

In a 1993 study, 14 percent of all deaths in the United States were attributed to activity patterns and diet.[9] Another study linked sedentary lifestyles to 23 percent of deaths from major chronic diseases.[10] For example, physical activity has been shown to reduce the risk of developing or dying from heart disease, diabetes, colon cancer, and high blood pressure.

(continued)

Box 7-1 *(continued)*

On average, people who are physically active outlive those who are inactive.[11-16]

Despite the well-known benefits of physical activity, most adults and many children lead a relatively sedentary lifestyle and are not active enough to achieve these health benefits. A sedentary lifestyle is defined as engaging in no leisure-time physical activity (exercises, sports, physically active hobbies) in a two-week period. Data from the National Health Interview Survey shows that in 1997–1998 nearly four in 10 (38.3 percent) adults reported no participation in leisure-time physical activity.[17]

Approximately one-third of persons age 65 or older lead a sedentary lifestyle. Older women are generally less physically active than older men. Fifty-four percent of men and 66 percent of women age 75 and older engage in no leisure-time physical activity.[17] In general, African American older adults are less active than white older adults. In the mid-1990s, 37 percent of white men age 75 and older reported no leisure-time physical activity, compared to 59 percent of African-American men age 75 and older; 47 percent of white women age 75 and older reported no leisure-time physical activity, compared to 60 percent of African American women age 75 and older.[18]

More than one-third of young people in grades 9–12 do not regularly engage in vigorous physical activity. Furthermore, 43 percent of students in grades 9–12 watch television more than two hours per day.[19] Physical activity declines dramatically over the course of adolescence, and girls are significantly less likely than boys to participate regularly in vigorous physical activity.

ECONOMIC CONSEQUENCES OF INACTIVITY

Physical inactivity and its associated health problems have substantial economic consequences for the U.S. health care system. In the long run, physical inactivity threatens to reverse the decades-long progress that has been made in reducing the morbidity and mortality associated with many chronic conditions such as cardiovascular disease. A physically inactive population is at both medical and financial risk for

Box 7-1 *(continued)*

many chronic diseases and conditions including heart disease, stroke, colon cancer, diabetes, obesity, and osteoporosis.

The increasing prevalence of chronic medical conditions and diseases related to physical inactivity is associated with two types of costs. First, there are health care costs for preventative, diagnostic, and treatment services related to these chronic conditions. These costs may include expenditures for physician visits, pharmaceuticals, ambulance services, rehabilitation services and hospital and nursing home care. In addition, there are other costs associated with the value of wages lost by people unable to work because of illness and disability, as well as the value of future earnings lost by premature death. In 2000, the total cost of overweight and obesity was estimated to be $117 billion.[7] In addition, the total estimated cost from chronic diseases is substantial.

Individuals suffering from chronic diseases bear a substantial portion of these medical costs. A recent study demonstrated that obese individuals spend approximately 36 percent more than the general population on health services and 77 percent more on medications.[20] Furthermore, the study found that the effects of obesity on health spending were significantly larger than effects of current or past smoking.

Since regular physical activity helps prevent disease and promote health, it may actually decrease health care costs. A study performed by researchers at the Centers for Disease Control and Prevention found that physically active people had, on average, lower annual direct medical costs than did inactive people. The same study estimated that increasing regular moderate physical activity among the more than 88 million inactive Americans over the age of 15 years might reduce the annual national direct medical costs by as much as $76.6 billion in 2000 dollars.[21]

Further, the study found that physically active people had fewer hospital stays and physician visits and used less medication than physically inactive people. The cost savings were consistent for men and women, for those with and without physical limitations, and even for smokers and nonsmokers. In this study, the biggest difference in direct medical costs was

(continued)

Box 7-1 *(continued)*

among women 55 and older, supporting the belief that the potential gain associated with physical activity is especially high for older women. The researchers concluded that adoption of a population-wide physical activity strategy might produce health care cost savings among most adult age groups.

Employers can benefit too. Workplace physical activity programs can reduce short-term sick leave by six to 32 percent, reduce health care costs by 20 to 55 percent, and increase productivity by 2 to 52 percent.[22] In 1998, 93 percent of employers had programs that fostered employee health, up from 76 percent in 1992, according to Hewitt Associates. Such "wellness" programs typically offer help in smoking cessation, managing stress, prenatal care, nutrition, and fitness.[23]

PHYSICAL ACTIVITY AND GOOD PHYSICAL HEALTH

Participation in regular physical activity—at least 30 minutes of moderate activity on at least five days per week or 20 minutes of vigorous physical activity at least three times per week—is critical to sustaining good health. Youth should strive for at least one hour of exercise a day. Regular physical activity has beneficial effects on most (if not all) organ systems, and consequently it helps to prevent a broad range of health problems and diseases. People of all ages, both male and female, derive substantial health benefits from physical activity.

Regular physical activity reduces the risk of developing or dying from some of the leading causes of illness in the United States. Regular physical activity improves health in the following ways[22]:

- Reduces the risk of dying prematurely from heart disease and other conditions;
- Reduces the risk of developing diabetes;
- Reduces the risk of developing high blood pressure;
- Reduces blood pressure in people who already have high blood pressure;
- Reduces the risk of developing colon and breast cancer[5];
- Helps to maintain a healthy weight;

Box 7-1 *(continued)*

- Helps build and maintain healthy bones, muscles, and joints;
- Helps older adults to become stronger and better able to move about without falling;
- Reduces feelings of depression and anxiety; and
- Promotes psychological well-being.

Regular physical activity is associated with lower mortality rates for both older and younger adults.[22] Even those who are moderately active on a regular basis have lower mortality rates than those who are least active. Regular physical activity leads to cardiovascular fitness, which decreases the risk of cardiovascular disease mortality in general and coronary artery disease mortality in particular. High blood pressure is a major underlying cause of cardiovascular complications and mortality. Regular physical activity can prevent or delay the development of high blood pressure, and reduces blood pressure in persons with hypertension.

Regular physical activity is also important for maintaining muscle strength, joint structure, joint functioning, and bone health.[22] Weight-bearing physical activity is essential for normal skeletal development during childhood and adolescence and for achieving and maintaining peak bone mass in young adults. Among postmenopausal women, exercise, especially muscle strengthening (resistance) activity, may protect against the rapid decline in bone mass. However, data on the effects of exercise on postmenopausal bone loss are not clear-cut and the timing of the intervention (e.g., stage of menopausal transition) can influence the response. Regardless, physical activity including muscle-strengthening exercise appears to protect against falling and fractures among the elderly, probably by increasing muscle strength and balance.[22] In addition, physical activity may be beneficial for many people with arthritis.

Regular physical activity can help improve the lives of young people beyond its effects on physical health. Although research has not been conducted to conclusively demonstrate a direct link between physical activity and improved academic performance, such a link might be expected. Studies have

(continued)

Box 7-1 *(continued)*

found participation in physical activity increases adolescents' self-esteem and reduces anxiety and stress.[22] Through its effects on mental health, physical activity may help increase students' capacity for learning. One study found that spending more time in physical education did not have harmful effects on the standardized academic achievement test scores of elementary school students; in fact, there was some evidence that participation in a two-year health-related physical education program had several significant favorable effects on academic achievement.[24]

Participation in physical activity and sports can promote social well-being, as well as good physical and mental health, among young people. Research has shown that students who participate in interscholastic sports are less likely to be regular and heavy smokers or use drugs[25] and are more likely to stay in school and have good conduct and high academic achievement.[26] Sports and physical activity programs can introduce young people to skills such as teamwork, self-discipline, sportsmanship, leadership, and socialization. Lack of recreational activity, on the other hand, may contribute to making young people more vulnerable to gangs, drugs, or violence.

PHYSICAL ACTIVITY AND GOOD MENTAL HEALTH

Regular physical activity reduces morbidity and mortality from mental health disorders.[27] Mental health disorders pose a significant public health burden in the United States and are a major cause of hospitalization and disability. Mental health disorders cost approximately $148 billion per year.[22] Increasing physical activity levels in Americans could potentially reduce medical expenditures for mental health conditions.

In adults with affective disorders, physical activity has a beneficial effect on symptoms of depression and anxiety.[27] Animal research suggests that exercise may stimulate the growth of new brain cells that enhance memory and learning—two functions hampered by depression. Clinical studies have demonstrated the feasibility and efficacy of exercise as a treatment for depression in older men and women. Currently, National Institute of Mental

Box 7-1 *(continued)*

Health (NIMH) investigators are conducting research comparing the effectiveness of home-based and supervised aerobic exercise to the use of antidepressants in relieving depression and reducing relapse rates in these groups. Other NIMH researchers are studying whether greater exercise levels result in more symptom improvement. Regular physical activity also appears to enhance well-being.

The preventive effects of physical activity on mental disorders are less well studied. Some studies suggest physical activity prevents depressive illness. Future research will clarify the extent to which physical activity may actually protect against the development of depression.

Regular physical activity may also reduce risk of cognitive decline in older adults, though more research is needed to clarify the mechanism of this possible effect. Among people who suffer from mental illness, physical activity appears to improve the ability to perform activities of daily living.[27]

PHYSICAL ACTIVITY

Regular physical activity along with a nutritious diet is key to maintaining a healthy weight. In order to maintain a healthy weight, there must be a balance between calories consumed and calories expended through metabolic and physical activity. Although overweight and obesity are caused by many factors, in most individuals, weight gain results from a combination of excess calorie consumption and inadequate physical activity.

Even though a large portion of a person's total caloric requirement is used for basal metabolism and processing food, an individual's various physical activities may account for as much as 15 to 40 percent of the calories he or she burns each day. While vigorous exercise uses calories at a higher rate, any physical activity will burn calories. For example, a 140-pound person can burn 175 calories in 30 minutes of moderate bicycling and 322 calories in 30 minutes of moderate jogging. The same person can also burn 105 calories by vacuuming or raking leaves for the same amount of time.

(continued)

Box 7-1 *(continued)*

THE EPIDEMIC OF OVERWEIGHT AND OBESITY

As a result of lifestyle and dietary changes, overweight and obesity have reached epidemic proportions in the United States. The Body Mass Index (BMI) is the most commonly used measure to define overweight and obesity. BMI is a measure of weight in relation to height. BMI is calculated as weight in pounds divided by the square of the height in inches, then multiplied by 703.

According to the National Institutes of Health Clinical Guidelines, overweight in adults is defined as a BMI between 25 lbs/in^2 to 29.9 lbs/in^2; and obesity in adults is identified by a BMI of 30 lbs/in^2 or greater.[28] These definitions are based on evidence that suggests that health risks are greater at or above a BMI of 25 lbs/in^2 compared to those at a BMI below that level. The risk of premature death increases with an increasing BMI. This increase in mortality tends to be modest until a BMI of 30 lbs/in^2 is reached.

Overweight and obesity are increasing in both genders and among all population groups. In 1999, an estimated 61 percent of adults in the U.S. were overweight or obese; this contrasts with the late 1970s, when an estimated 47 percent of adults were overweight or obese.[7]

Among women, the prevalence of overweight and obesity generally is higher in women who are members of racial and ethnic minority populations than in non-Hispanic white women.[7] Among men, Mexican Americans have a higher prevalence of overweight and obesity than non-Hispanic whites or non-Hispanic blacks. For non-Hispanic men, the prevalence of overweight and obesity among whites is slightly greater than among blacks.

Disparities in prevalence of overweight and obesity also exist based on socioeconomic status.[7] For all racial and ethnic groups combined, women of lower socioeconomic status (income ≤ 130 percent of the poverty threshold) are approximately 50 percent more likely to be obese than those with higher socioeconomic status (income > 130 percent of the poverty threshold). Men are about equally likely to be obese whether they are in a low or high socioeconomic group.

Box 7-1 *(continued)*

The overweight and obesity epidemic is not limited to adults. What is particularly alarming is that the percentage of young people who are overweight has almost doubled in the last 20 years for children aged 6–11 and almost tripled for adolescents aged 12–19. In children and adolescents, overweight has been defined as a sex- and age-specific BMI at or above the 95th percentile for a reference population, based on Centers for Disease Control and Prevention (CDC) growth charts.

ASSOCIATED HEALTH RISKS OF NOT MAINTAINING A HEALTHY WEIGHT

Epidemiological studies show an increase in mortality associated with overweight and obesity. Approximately 300,000 deaths a year in this country are currently associated with overweight and obesity.[29] Morbidity from obesity may be as great as from poverty, smoking, or problem drinking.[20] Overweight and obesity are associated with an increased risk for developing various medical conditions including cardiovascular disease, certain cancers (endometrial, colon, postmenopausal breast, kidney, and esophageal),[5] high blood pressure, arthritis-related disabilities and type 2 diabetes.[7]

It is also important for individuals who are currently at a healthy weight to strive to maintain it since both modest and large weight gains are associated with significantly increased risk of disease. For example, a weight gain of 11 to 18 pounds increases a person's risk for developing type 2 diabetes to twice that of individuals who have not gained weight, while those who gain 44 pounds or more have four times the risk of developing type 2 diabetes.[30]

Recent research studies have shown that a gain of 10 to 20 pounds resulted in an increased risk of coronary heart disease (which can result in nonfatal heart attacks and death) of 1.25 times in women[31] and 1.6 times in men.[32] In these studies, weight increases of 22 pounds in men and 44 pounds in women resulted in an increased coronary heart disease risk of 1.75 and 2.65, respectively. In one study among women with a BMI of 34 or greater, the risk of developing endometrial cancer was increased

(continued)

Box 7-1 *(continued)*

by more than 6 times.[33] Overweight and obesity are also known to exacerbate many chronic conditions such as hypertension and elevated cholesterol. Overweight and obese individuals also may suffer from social stigmatization, discrimination, and poor body image.

Although obesity-associated morbidities occur most frequently in adults, important consequences of excess weight as well as antecedents of adult disease occur in overweight children and adolescents. Overweight children and adolescents are more likely to become overweight or obese adults. As the prevalence of overweight and obesity increases in children and adolescents, type 2 diabetes, high blood lipids, and hypertension as well as early maturation and orthopedic problems are occurring with increased frequency. A common consequence of childhood overweight is psychosocial—specifically, discrimination.[34]

Notes:

1. R. N. Butler, R. Davis, C. B. Lewis, et al., "Physical fitness: Benefits of exercising for the older patient." *Geriatrics* 53(10):46–62, 1998.

2. American Heart Association, *2002 Heart and Stroke Statistical Update* (Dallas: American Heart Association, 2001).

3. Centers for Disease Control and Prevention, *National Diabetes Fact Sheet: General Information and National Estimates on Diabetes in the United States, 2000* (Atlanta, GA: U.S. Department of Health and Human Services, Centers for Disease Control and Prevention, 2002).

4. American Cancer Society, *Cancer Facts & Figures 2002*. (Atlanta, GA: American Cancer Society, 2002).

5. H. Vainio and F. Bianchini (Eds.), *Weight Control and Physical Activity. IARC Handbooks of Cancer Prevention*, Vol. 6 (IARC Press, International Agency on Research for Cancer, Lyon, France, 2002).

6. J. R. Popovic, "1999 National Hospital Discharge Survey: Annual summary with detailed diagnosis and procedure data." *Vital Health Statistics* 13(151):2001.

7. U.S. Department of Health and Human Services, *The Surgeon General's Call to Action to Prevent and Decrease Overweight and Obesity* (Washington, DC: U.S. Government Printing Office, 2001), p.1.

8. U.S. Census Bureau, Resident population estimates of the United States by age and sex, July 1, 1999. http://eire.census.gov/popest/archives/national/nation2/intfile2–1.txt (Accessed June 17, 2002).

9. J. M. McGinnis and W. H. Foege, "Actual causes of death in the United States." *JAMA* 270(18):207–212, 1993.

Box 7-1 *(continued)*

10. R. A. Hahn, S. M. Teuesch, R. B. Rothenberg, et al., "Excess deaths from nine chronic diseases in the United States, 1986." *JAMA*, 264(20):2554–2459, 1998.

11. R. S. Paffenbarger, R. T. Hyde, A. L. Wing, et al., "The association of changes in physical-activity level and other lifestyle characteristics with mortality among men." *N Engl J Med* 328(8):538–545, 1993.

12. S. E. Sherman, R. B. D'Agostino, J. L. Cobb, et al., "Physical activity and mortality in women in the Framingham Heart Study." *Am Heart J* 128(5):879–884, 1994.

13. G. A. A. Kaplan, W. J. Strawbridge, R. D. Cohen, et al., "Natural history of leisure-time physical activity and its correlates: Associations with mortality from all causes and cardiovascular diseases over 28 years." *Am J Epidemiol* 144(8):793–797, 1996.

14. L. H. Kushi, R. M. Fee, A. R. Folsom, et al., "Physical activity and mortality in postmenopausal women." *JAMA* 277(16):1287–1292, 1997.

15. C. D. Lee, S. N. Blair, et al., "Cardiorespiratory fitness, body composition, and all-cause and cardiovascular disease mortality in men." *Am J Clin Nutr* 69(3):373–380, 1999.

16. M. Wei, J. B. Kampert, C. E. Barlow, et al., "Relationship between low cardiorespiratory fitness and mortality in normal-weight, overweight, and obese men." *JAMA* 282(16):1547–1553, 1999.

17. U.S. Department of Health and Human Services, *Leisure-time Physical Activity Among Adults: United States, 1997–98.* (Washington, DC: U.S. Department of Health and Human Services, Centers for Disease Control and Prevention, National Center for Health Statistics, U.S. Government Printing Office, 2002).

18. Centers for Disease Control and Prevention, "CDC Surveillance Summaries, December 17, 1999." *MMWR* 48(SS-8), 1999.

19. L. Kann, et al., "Youth risk behavior surveillance–United States, 1999." *MMWR* 49(SS-5):1–96, 2000.

20. R. Strum, "The effects of obesity, smoking and problem drinking on chronic medical problems and health care costs." *Health Affairs* 21(2):245–253, 2002.

21. M. Pratt, C. A. Macera, G. Wang, "Higher direct medical costs associated with physical inactivity." *The Physician and Sportsmedicine* 28:63–70, 2000.

22. U.S. Department of Health and Human Services, *Physical Activity and Health: A Report of the Surgeon General.* (Atlanta, GA: U.S. Department of Health and Human Services, Centers for Disease Control and Prevention, National Center for Chronic Disease Prevention and Health Promotion, 1996).

(continued)

Box 7-1 *(continued)*

23. M. Freudenheim, "Employers Focus on Weight as Workplace Health Issue," *New York Times*, Sept. 6, 1999.

24. J. F. Sallis, T. L. McKenzie, B. Kolody, et al., "Effects of health-related physical education on academic achievement: Project SPARK." *Research Quarterly for Exercise and Sport* 70(2):127–134, 1999.

25. L. G. Escobedo, S. E. Marcus, D. Holtzman, et al., "Sports participation, age at smoking initiation and the risk of smoking among US high school students." *JAMA* 269:1391–1395, 1993.

26. N. Zill, C. W. Nord, L. S. Loomis, *Adolescent Time Use, Risky Behavior and Outcomes: An Analysis of National Data* (Rockville, MD: Westat, 1995).

27. U.S. Preventive Services Task Force, *Guide to Clinical Preventive Services*, 2nd ed. (Baltimore: Williams and Wilkins, 1996), pp. 611–624.

28. U.S. Department of Health and Human Services, National Institutes of Health, National Heart, Lung, and Blood Institute, *Clinical Guidelines on the Identification, Evaluation, and Treatment of Overweight and Obesity in Adults* [Evidence Report]. (HHS, PHS; Pub. No. 98–4083, 1998).

29. D. B. Allison, K. R. Fontaine, J. E. Manson, et al., "Annual deaths attributable to obesity in the United States." *JAMA* 282(16):1530–1538, 1999.

30. E. S. Ford, D. F. Williamson, S. Liu, "Weight change and diabetes incidence: Findings from a national cohort of US adults." *Am J Epidemiol* 146(3):214–222, 1997.

31. W. C. Willett, J. E. Manson, M. J. Stampfer, et al., "Weight, weight change and coronary heart disease in women: Risk within the 'normal' weight range." *JAMA* 273(6):461–465, 1995.

32. D. J. Galanis, T. Harris, D. S. Sharp, et al., "Relative weight, weight change, and risk of coronary heart disease in the Honolulu Heart Program." *Am J Epidemiol* 147(4):379–386, 1998.

33. E. Weiderpass, I. Persson, H. O. Adami, et al., "Body size in different periods of life, diabetes, hypertension, and risk of postmenopausal endometrial cancer." *Cancer Causes Control* 11(2):185–192, 2000.

34. W. H. Dietz, "Health consequences of obesity in youth: Childhood predictors of adult disease." *Pediatrics* 101(3 Supp):518–525, 1998.

Source: U.S. Department of Health and Human Services Office of the Assistant Secretary for Planning and Evaluation of Physical Activity Fundamental to Preventing Disease, 2002.

- High cholesterol, LDL, and triglycerides levels
- Cardiovascular inactivity

Other major risk factors for heart disease are cigarette smoking and some inherited conditions.

Exercise allows you to live a more enjoyable, productive life. It helps you feel better, have more energy, and be much more resistant to injury. It relieves tension, improves attitude, and increases self-esteem naturally. Specifically, staying physically fit can:

- Result in more efficient use of the lungs
- Develop a stronger, more efficient heart
- Create improved digestion and bowel function
- Prevent lower back pain
- Reduce body fat
- Improve posture
- Reduce blood pressure
- Improve leg circulation
- Reduce the negative aspects of stress
- Enhance self-confidence
- Reduce health expenses
- Increase oxygen consumption
- Reduce resting pulse rate
- Improve athletic performance
- Enhance career achievement through role-modeling and appearance
- Improve family relationships[1]

Imagine pursuing someone on foot for several blocks then being assaulted by one or two suspects. Consider that you are 25 pounds overweight and never exercise and that they are athletic and fit. Imagine your numbness and exhaustion.

Make a commitment to stay in shape. (Box 7-2 lists a number of reasons why this is important, Box 7-3 lists recommendations on how to lose weight, and Box 7-4 gives obesity statistics by state.) Remember that you are not the only one who depends on your physical conditioning. Time and time again cops count on each other, and being unfit can get a fellow officer killed.

Box 7-2

U.S. Department of Health and Human Services Physical Activity and Health Fact Sheet

The following facts are based on information from publications prepared by agencies and offices of the Department of Health and Human Services.

- Physical inactivity contributes to 300,000 preventable deaths a year in the United States. Some 40% of deaths in the United States are caused by behavior patterns that could be modified. A sedentary lifestyle is a major risk factor across the spectrum of preventable diseases that lower the quality of life and kill Americans.

- Significant health benefits can be obtained by including a moderate amount of physical activity (e.g., 30 minutes of brisk walking or raking leaves, 15 minutes of running, 45 minutes of playing volleyball). Additional health benefits can be gained through greater amounts of physical activity.

- Physical activity has been identified as one of the Leading Health Indicators (LHI) in *Healthy People 2010*, the government's published health goals and objectives for the next decade.

- Moderate daily physical activity can reduce substantially the risk of developing or dying from cardiovascular disease, type 2 diabetes, and certain cancers, such as colon cancer. Daily physical activity helps to lower blood pressure and cholesterol, helps prevent or retard osteoporosis, and helps reduce obesity, symptoms of anxiety and depression, and symptoms of arthritis.

- Cardiovascular disease (heart attacks, strokes) is the number one killer of men and women in the United States. Physically inactive people are twice as likely to develop coronary heart disease as regularly active people. The health risk posed by physical inactivity is almost as high as risk factors such as cigarette smoking, high blood pressure, and high cholesterol.

- Nearly half of American adults (4 in 10) report that they are not active at all; 7 in 10 are not moderately active

Box 7-2 *(continued)*

for the recommended 30 minutes a day, 5 or more days a week.

- Poor diet and inactivity can lead to overweight/obesity. Persons who are overweight or obese are at increased risk for high blood pressure, type 2 diabetes, coronary heart disease, stroke, gallbladder disease, osteoarthritis, sleep apnea, respiratory problems and some types of cancer.

- Poor diet and inactivity can lead to diabetes. Seventeen million Americans have diabetes right now and 16 million more have pre-diabetes. Each year, there are 1 million new cases, and nearly 200,000 people die from diabetes. The cost to the economy is $100 billion annually in direct and indirect medical costs.

- The percentage of adults in the United States who were overweight or obese (body mass index greater than 25) in 1999 was 61%. Overweight and obesity cuts across all ages, racial and ethnic groups, and both genders.

- Overweight among children and teens has doubled in the past two decades; 13% of children aged 6 to 11 years and 14% of adolescents aged 12 to 19 years were overweight in 1999. This prevalence has nearly tripled for adolescents in the past 2 decades.

- The cost of overweight and obesity to the economy is $117 billion annually in direct and indirect medical costs.

- The major barriers most people face when trying to increase physical activity are time, access to convenient facilities, and safe environments in which to be active.

- School-based and workplace based interventions have been shown to be successful in increasing physical activity levels.

- Childhood and adolescence are pivotal times for preventing sedentary behavior among adults by maintaining the habit of physical activity throughout the school years.

- Type 2 diabetes, once called "adult onset" diabetes, and high blood pressure, once thought to be age-related, are now diagnosed in children and teens.

- Physical activity among children and adolescents is important because of the related health benefits (cardio-respiratory

(continued)

Box 7-2 *(continued)*

function, blood pressure control, weight management, cognitive and emotional benefits).

- Only about one-half of U.S. young people (ages 12–21 years) regularly participate in vigorous physical activity. One-fourth reported no vigorous physical activity. About 14 percent report no recent vigorous or light-to-moderate activity.

- A physically active lifestyle adopted early in life may continue into adulthood. Even among children aged 3 and 4 years, those who were less active tended to remain less active than most of their peers. According to a study done by the National Association of Sports and Physical Education (NASPE), infants, toddlers, and preschoolers should engage in at least 60 minutes of physical activity daily and should not be sedentary for more than 60 minutes at a time except when sleeping.

- One quarter of U.S. children spend 4 hours or more watching television daily.

- Young people are at particular risk for becoming sedentary as they grow older. Encouraging moderate and vigorous physical activity among youth is important. Because children spend most of their time in school, the type and amount of physical activity encouraged in schools are important.

- Only 20 percent of students in grades 9 through 12 engaged in moderate physical activity for at least 30 minutes on 5 or more of the previous 7 days in 1997.

- Only 29 percent of students in grades 9 through 12 participated in daily school physical education in 1999, down from 42 percent in 1991.

- Only 17 percent of middle and junior high schools and 2 percent of senior high schools require daily physical activity for all students.

Source: The President's Council on Physical Fitness and Sports (PCPFS) serves as a catalyst to promote, encourage and motivate Americans of all ages to become physically active and participate in sports. Assisted by elements of the U.S. Public Health Service, the PCPFS advises the President and the Secretary of Health and Human Services on how to encourage more Americans to be physically fit and active.

Box 7-3

Key Recommendations for Weight Loss

Expert Panel on the Identification, Evaluation, and Treatment of Overweight and Obesity in Adults

- Weight loss to lower elevated blood pressure in overweight and obese persons with high blood pressure.
- Weight loss to lower elevated levels of total cholesterol, LDL-cholesterol, and triglycerides, and to raise low levels of HDL-cholesterol in overweight and obese persons with dyslipidemia.
- Weight loss to lower elevated blood glucose levels in overweight and obese persons with type 2 diabetes.
- Use the BMI to assess overweight and obesity. Body weight alone can be used to follow weight loss, and to determine the effectiveness of therapy.
- Use the BMI to classify overweight and obesity and to estimate relative risk of disease compared to normal weight.
- The waist circumference should be used to assess abdominal fat content.
- The initial goal of weight loss therapy should be to reduce body weight by about 10 percent from baseline. With success, and if warranted, further weight loss can be attempted.
- Weight loss should be about 1 to 2 pounds per week for a period of 6 months, with the subsequent strategy based on the amount of weight lost.
- Low calorie diets (LCD) for weight loss in overweight and obese persons. Reducing fat as part of an LCD is a practical way to reduce calories.
- Reducing dietary fat alone without reducing calories is not sufficient for weight loss. However, reducing dietary fat, along with reducing dietary carbohydrates, can help reduce calories.
- A diet that is individually planned to help create a deficit of 500 to 1,000 kcal/day should be an integral part of any program aimed at achieving a weight loss of 1 to 2 pounds per week.

(continued)

Box 7-3 *(continued)*

- Physical activity should be part of a comprehensive weight loss therapy and weight control program because it: (1) modestly contributes to weight loss in overweight and obese adults, (2) may decrease abdominal fat, (3) increases cardiorespiratory fitness, and (4) may help with maintenance of weight loss.
- Physical activity should be an integral part of weight loss therapy and weight maintenance. Initially, moderate levels of physical activity for 30 to 45 minutes, 3 to 5 days a week, should be encouraged. All adults should set a long-term goal to accumulate at least 30 minutes or more of moderate-intensity physical activity on most, and preferably all, days of the week.
- The combination of a reduced calorie diet and increased physical activity is recommended since it produces weight loss that may also result in decreases in abdominal fat and increases in cardiorespiratory fitness.
- Behavior therapy is a useful adjunct when incorporated into treatment for weight loss and weight maintenance.
- Weight loss and weight maintenance therapy should employ the combination of LCD's, increased physical activity, and behavior therapy.
- After successful weight loss, the likelihood of weight loss maintenance is enhanced by a program consisting of dietary therapy, physical activity, and behavior therapy, which should be continued indefinitely. Drug therapy can also be used. However, drug safety and efficacy beyond 1 year of total treatment have not been established.
- A weight maintenance program should be a priority after the initial 6 months of weight loss therapy.
- According to the National Heart, Lung, and Blood Institute guidelines, assessment of overweight involves using three key measures:

Body mass index (BMI)

Waist circumference, and

Risk factors for diseases and conditions associated with obesity.

Box 7-3 *(continued)*

The BMI is a measure of your weight relative to your height and waist circumference measures abdominal fat. Combining these with information about your additional risk factors yields your risk for developing obesity-associated diseases.

WHAT IS YOUR RISK?

1. Body Mass Index (BMI). BMI is a reliable indicator of total body fat, which is related to the risk of disease and death. The score is valid for both men and women but it does have some limits. The limits are:

   - It may overestimate body fat in athletes and others who have a muscular build.
   - It may underestimate body fat in older persons and others who have lost muscle mass.

2. Waist Circumference. Determine your waist circumference by placing a measuring tape snugly around your waist. It is a good indicator of your abdominal fat, which is another predictor of your risk for developing risk factors for heart disease and other diseases. This risk increases with a waist measurement of over 40 inches in men and over 35 inches in women.

3. Other Risk Factors. Besides being overweight or obese, there are additional risk factors to consider.

   - High blood pressure (hypertension)
   - High LDL-cholesterol ("bad" cholesterol)
   - Low HDL-cholesterol ("good" cholesterol)
   - High triglycerides
   - High blood glucose (sugar)
   - Family history of premature heart disease
   - Physical inactivity
   - Cigarette smoking

4. Assessment. For people who are considered obese (BMI greater than or equal to 30) or those who are overweight (BMI of 25 to 29.9) and have two or more risk factors, the

(continued)

Box 7-3 *(continued)*

guidelines recommend weight loss. Even a small weight loss (just 10 percent of your current weight) will help to lower your risk of developing diseases associated with obesity. Patients who are overweight, do not have a high waist measurement, and have less than 2 risk factors may need to prevent further weight gain rather than lose weight.

Talk to your doctor to see if you are at an increased risk and if you should lose weight. Your doctor will evaluate your BMI, waist measurement, and other risk factors for heart disease. People who are overweight or obese have a greater chance of developing high blood pressure, high blood cholesterol or other lipid disorders, type 2 diabetes, heart disease, stroke, and certain cancers, and even a small weight loss (just 10 percent of your current weight) will help to lower your risk of developing those diseases.

Source: The facts are based on information from publications prepared by agencies and offices of the Department of Health and Human Services: the Centers for Disease Control and Prevention; the National Center for Health Statistics; the Office of the Surgeon General of the United States (*Physical Activity and Health*, 1996; *Call to Action to Prevent and Decrease Overweight and Obesity*, 2001); and the Office of Disease Prevention and Health Promotion (*Healthy People 2010*, 2001).

Box 7-4

National Center for Chronic Disease Prevention and Health Promotion

PERCENTAGE OF ADULTS WHO REPORT BEING OBESE,* BY STATE

- States where there were no data available: None
- States where less than 10% of adults report being obese: None
- States where 10%–14% of adults report being obese: Colorado
- States where 15%–19% of adults report being obese: Arizona, Connecticut, Florida, Hawaii, Maine, Maryland, Massachusetts, Minnesota, Montana, Nevada, New

Box 7-4 *(continued)*

Hampshire, New Jersey, New Mexico, North Dakota, Rhode Island, South Dakota, Utah, Vermont, Washington, Wyoming
- States where 20%–24% of adults report being obese: Alabama, Alaska, Arkansas, California, Delaware, Georgia, Idaho, Illinois, Indiana, Iowa, Kansas, Kentucky, Louisiana, Michigan, Missouri, Nebraska, New York, North Carolina, Ohio, Oklahoma, Oregon, Pennsylvania, South Carolina, Tennessee, Texas, Virginia, West Virginia, Wisconsin
- States where greater than 25% of adults report being obese: Mississippi

*Body mass index greater than or equal to 30 or about 30 pounds overweight for a 5'4" person.

Source: CDC, Behavioral Risk Factor Surveillance System, National Center for Chronic Disease Prevention and Health Promotion, Department of Health and Human Services. http://apps.nccd.cdc.gov/BurdenBook/index.asp, access date 4-12-04.

YOUR FITNESS LIFESTYLE

Fitness should be viewed as a continual lifestyle, not a program or diet. A commitment to good health must be lifelong, not short-term. It should be based on common sense and reputable research. Fad diets are often not worthwhile. Height/weight tables are frequently misleading. In addition, there is no need to buy a lot of athletic clothing or join an expensive spa. Anyone with a dedicated attitude will find the necessary requirements simple and straightforward.

Establish Goals and Objectives

Decide what you want to accomplish and then establish meaningful goals. Perhaps you want to lose a specific amount of weight, increase strength or endurance, improve cardiovascular activity, or lower cholesterol levels. Once you establish goals, set specific objectives. For example, if your overall goal is to lose 40 pounds within one year, the objective might be to lose 3–4 pounds each month. Objectives can show your progress and motivate you to continue in pursuit of a goal.[2]

Physical Examination and Assessment

Begin your evaluation with a physical examination and assessment by a physician. This will help you avoid overworking yourself and endangering your health unknowingly. Tell the physician that you intend to develop a fitness lifestyle. He or she should give special attention to your circulatory and heart conditions, cholesterol levels, and joint and skeletal conditions. In addition, the physician should evaluate your fitness lifestyle in terms of medical conditions you may have, such as diabetes or back trouble. The exam may also alert you to previously undetected medical conditions or problems.

After a physician explains the results of the exam, reassess your lifestyle. Do you smoke or drink? Are you overweight? What kind of and how much exercise do you do? How much stress are you under? Are your eating habits of concern? Relate the answers to the goals and objectives you established. Then decide whether lifestyle changes are necessary to meet and sustain your goals.

Assess Your Physical Fitness

An objective evaluation of your physical fitness can be eye-opening. Once the physician's exam is complete, appraise your abdominal conditioning, upper body strength, and cardiovascular system.

Abdominal Conditioning   To assess abdominal conditioning, do as many sit-ups as you can in two minutes without stopping.

1. Lie flat on your back with knees bent, feet held down on the floor by a partner.
2. With your arms straight out in front of your body, raise yourself forward until your elbows reach your knees.
3. Lower yourself back to the floor.
4. Repeat the entire process. If you stop for more than a second at any point, the test is over.

You should be able to do at least 30 sit-ups in the allotted time without stopping.

Upper Body Strength   To assess your upper body strength, do as many push-ups as you can within two minutes.

1. Assume the standard push-up position: body and head nearly parallel to the floor, arms almost straight up and placed at a width equal to your shoulders, legs together and propped up on toes. Ensure that your body is as straight as possible.
2. Lower your body to within three inches of the ground. Keep your entire body totally straight during the test.
3. Raise your body until arms are straight again.
4. Repeat the entire process. If you stop for more than a second at any point, the test is over. You should be able to do at least twenty-five push-ups.

Cardiovascular Condition   To assess cardiovascular fitness, do the step test for three minutes.

1. Use a stool or a similar sturdy object that is 8 inches high. Stand in front of the stool and step up and down with both feet every five seconds, alternating the first foot each time.
2. Thirty seconds after stopping, take your pulse rate for 30 seconds, then multiply that number by two.

The most important element of fitness is the cardiovascular system. To a street cop, muscular strength is important, as is the ability to sustain physical exertion without fatigue. The key to superior endurance is a cardiovascular system developed to the extent that it supplies enough oxygen to muscles in motion while improving their ability to use additional oxygen. An officer who is in poor condition will produce an excess of the chemical lactic acid, which tends to induce fatigue, which destroys the ability to defend oneself.

Measuring your heart's pulse rate immediately after exercise is a good way to check cardiovascular fitness. Place the index and the middle fingers together on your neck beside the Adam's apple and count the number of beats you feel for thirty seconds, then multiply the result by two. This is your resting heart rate. Most people have a rate between 50 and 90 beats a minute. A lower rate usually means good cardiovascular conditioning.

An individual in good cardiovascular condition can expect to have a pulse rate in the 120s. Someone in poor cardiovascular condition will have a rate in the 160s or 170s, generally speaking.

These tests should give you a fairly good idea of your physical condition. Begin a fitness diary; write the date and scores of these three tests. Each time you take the tests, record the same information. It is motivating and fun to track your improvement.[3]

Choose Your Exercise

Like the general public, some officers get virtually no exercise. For the most part, it is because they just do not enjoy it. Many people think of exercise as something that causes them pain and anguish and is not much fun. Most of these people push themselves too hard while beginning. The key to remember is that if exercising hurts, slow down! Do not try to get in condition in a couple of weeks. The results could be dangerous to your health.

Understand discomfort before beginning. The basic guideline is do not ignore discomfort or pain, particularly if it is in the chest or left arm or if you have a sensation of numbness or dizziness. Pain in these areas could be a sign of heart difficulty or attack. Also take into account high temperatures. Seek medical assistance immediately if you have a high temperature or numbness or dizziness in your chest or left arm.

Keep in mind these additional factors:

- If you have stopped exercising for more than a week, begin at a reduced level.
- Be patient—getting in shape takes time.
- Do not exercise on a full stomach.
- During warm months, drink 6–8 ounces of fluid before exercising.[4]

There are many ways to get and stay in shape, so choose something you like; otherwise, you will eventually quit. Some people have more fun participating in team sports while others prefer solitary pursuits such as running, hiking, or cycling. Remember to consider the goals that you initially set. Some exercises will help you reach your goals better than others.

Consider also the cost of equipment. If you are faced with not having enough money to select your favorite sport or exercise, start with an exercise or sport you can afford. Do not use lack of money as an excuse for inactivity.

STRETCHING

The first step of every workout should be stretching, also called the warm-up. It is the vital transition between a sedentary and active state that helps to prepare you for exertion, keeps muscles supple, and prevents stress and strain throughout the body.

Some physical activities, such as bicycling, racquetball, and running, generate particular muscle tightness. Stretching before and after each workout affords maximum flexibility of your muscles and prevents injuries. Achilles tendonitis, shin splints, and pulled muscles can be very painful. When these types of injuries occur, you may have to face the frustration of having to get in shape all over again.

Stretching is easy, but many people do not know the proper techniques. If it is done incorrectly, it can do more harm than if it were never done at all. The basic rule is to remember that stretching feels good when it is done properly and hurts if it is done improperly. Relax when you stretch and establish a regular stretching routine. If you find that the stretched muscles hurt, you have gone too far and should reduce the stretch.

Stretching should be enjoyable, because it relaxes and energizes. Remember, no one gets in shape within a few days. Long-term commitment, patience, and a good attitude will make your workout a pleasure.

Stretching should become a habit for several reasons:

- It increases blood circulation.
- It improves your range of motion.
- It makes you feel good.
- It improves your awareness of different body areas.
- It decreases the possibility of injury.
- It enhances coordination.
- It reduces tension and stress.
- It helps give you confidence and self-esteem.

Convenience

Anyone can enjoy stretching. It makes no difference if you work in an office, operate out of a squad car, or ride a motorcycle. Unlike many types of exercise, stretching can be done whenever you want: at your desk, walking through a parking lot, at home, even while in a car. In addition to stretching before and after exercise, there are several other times when it is particularly helpful:

- Whenever you feel tight or stiff.
- During or after standing or sitting for long periods.
- When you want to release nervous tension.
- As soon as you get up to begin the day.
- When you need to relieve a tension headache.

Technique

Bouncing and stretching until it hurts is an incorrect stretching technique. Stretching should be a sustained, relaxed process. Loosening up tense muscles cannot be accomplished quickly. It becomes easier after time if done properly and on a regular basis.

Hold each muscle stretch for 10 to 30 seconds. Nationally recognized stretching and fitness authority Bob Anderson describes the sensation you should feel as a "mild tension." He goes on to say, "The feeling of tension should subside as you hold the position. If it does not, ease off slightly and find a degree of tension that is comfortable." Never bounce!

Breathing should be slow and systematic. Holding your breath is not recommended. If you are unable to breathe slowly and naturally, you should relax more. Take everything slow and easy and teach yourself to breathe naturally.[5]

Use a book for reference that illustrates stretching in detail. The text *Stretching* by Bob Anderson is highly recommended. It is published by Shelter Publications, Bolinas, California. Box 7-5 lists specifics regarding exercise.

One of the most important attributes to having a successful career in Law Enforcement, I believe, is to develop a strong passion for wanting to make a difference and truly believing that you have the ability to make a difference. I also believe it is important to take the initiative and not wait for things to happen. We all also need to understand that we are not perfect, that we all will make mistakes at every level of our careers and when that mistake occurs, we need to take responsibility and learn and grow from it.

Gary L. Bullard
Executive Director
Northern Virginia Criminal Justice Academy

Box 7-5
Guidelines for Personal Fitness Programs— Fitness Fundamentals

MAKING A COMMITMENT

You have taken the important first step on the path to physical fitness by seeking information. The next step is to decide that you are going to be physically fit. This pamphlet is designed to help you reach that decision and your goal.

The decision to carry out a physical fitness program cannot be taken lightly. It requires a lifelong commitment of time and effort. Exercise must become one of those things that you do without question, like bathing and brushing your teeth. Unless you are convinced of the benefits of fitness and the risks of unfitness, you will not succeed.

Patience is essential. Don't try to do too much too soon and don't quit before you have a chance to experience the rewards of improved fitness. You can't regain in a few days or weeks what you have lost in years of sedentary living, but you can get it back if you persevere. And the prize is worth the price.

In the following pages you will find the basic information you need to begin and maintain a personal physical fitness program. These guidelines are intended for the average healthy adult. It tells you what your goals should be and how often, how long and how hard you must exercise to achieve them. It also includes information that will make your workouts easier, safer and more satisfying. The rest is up to you.

CHECKING YOUR HEALTH

If you're under 35 and in good health, you don't need to see a doctor before beginning an exercise program. But if you are over 35 and have been inactive for several years, you should consult your physician, who may or may not recommend a graded exercise test. Other conditions that indicate a need for medical clearance are:

- High blood pressure.
- Heart trouble.

(continued)

Box 7-5 *(continued)*

- Family history of early stroke or heart attack deaths.
- Frequent dizzy spells.
- Extreme breathlessness after mild exertion.
- Arthritis or other bone problems.
- Severe muscular, ligament or tendon problems.
- Other known or suspected disease.

Vigorous exercise involves minimal health risks for persons in good health or those following a doctor's advice. Far greater risks are presented by habitual inactivity and obesity.

DEFINING FITNESS

Physical fitness is to the human body what fine-tuning is to an engine. It enables us to perform up to our potential. Fitness can be described as a condition that helps us look, feel and do our best. More specifically, it is:

> The ability to perform daily tasks vigorously and alertly, with energy left over for enjoying leisure-time activities and meeting emergency demands. It is the ability to endure, to bear up, to withstand stress, to carry on in circumstances where an unfit person could not continue, and is a major basis for good health and well-being.[1]

Physical fitness involves the performance of the heart and lungs, and the muscles of the body. And, since what we do with our bodies also affects what we can do with our minds, fitness influences to some degree qualities such as mental alertness and emotional stability.

As you undertake your fitness program, it's important to remember that fitness is an individual quality that varies from person to person. It is influenced by age, sex, heredity, personal habits, exercise and eating practices. You can't do anything about the first three factors. However, it is within your power to change and improve the others where needed.

Box 7-5 *(continued)*

KNOWING THE BASICS

Physical fitness is most easily understood by examining its components, or "parts." There is widespread agreement that these four components are basic:

1. Cardiorespiratory Endurance—the ability to deliver oxygen and nutrients to tissues, and to remove wastes, over sustained periods of time. Long runs and swims are among the methods employed in measuring this component.
2. Muscular Strength—the ability of a muscle to exert force for a brief period of time. Upper-body strength, for example, can be measured by various weight-lifting exercises.
3. Muscular Endurance—the ability of a muscle, or a group of muscles, to sustain repeated contractions or to continue applying force against a fixed object. Pushups are often used to test endurance of arm and shoulder muscles.
4. Flexibility—the ability to move joints and use muscles through their full range of motion. The sit-and-reach test is a good measure of flexibility of the lower back and backs of the upper legs.

Body composition is often considered a component of fitness. It refers to the makeup of the body in terms of lean mass (muscle, bone, vital tissue and organs) and fat mass. An optimal ratio of fat to lean mass is an indication of fitness, and the right types of exercises will help you decrease body fat and increase or maintain muscle mass.

A WORKOUT SCHEDULE

How often, how long and how hard you exercise, and what kinds of exercises you do should be determined by what you are trying to accomplish. Your goals, your present fitness level, age, health, skills, interest and convenience are among the factors you should consider. For example, an athlete training for high-level competition would follow a different program than a person whose goals are good health and the ability to meet work and recreational needs.

(continued)

Box 7-5 *(continued)*

Your exercise program should include something from each of the four basic fitness components described previously. Each workout should begin with a warmup and end with a cooldown. As a general rule, space your workouts throughout the week and avoid consecutive days of hard exercise.

Here are the amounts of activity necessary for the average healthy person to maintain a minimum level of overall fitness. Included are some of the popular exercises for each category.

- WARMUP—5–10 minutes of exercise such as walking, slow jogging, knee lifts, arm circles or trunk rotations. Low intensity movements that simulate movements to be used in the activity can also be included in the warmup.
- MUSCULAR STRENGTH—a minimum of two 20-minute sessions per week that include exercises for all the major muscle groups. Lifting weights is the most effective way to increase strength.
- MUSCULAR ENDURANCE—at least three 30-minute sessions each week that include exercises such as calisthenics, pushups, situps, pullups, and weight training for all the major muscle groups.
- CARDIORESPIRATORY ENDURANCE—at least three 20-minute bouts of continuous aerobic (activity requiring oxygen) rhythmic exercise each week. Popular aerobic conditioning activities include brisk walking, jogging, swimming, cycling, rope-jumping, rowing, cross-country skiing, and some continuous action games like racquetball and handball.
- FLEXIBILITY—10–12 minutes of daily stretching exercises performed slowly, without a bouncing motion. This can be included after a warmup or during a cooldown.
- COOLDOWN—a minimum of 5–10 minutes of slow walking or low-level exercise, combined with stretching.

A MATTER OF PRINCIPLE

The keys to selecting the right kinds of exercises for developing and maintaining each of the basic components of fitness are found in these principles:

Box 7-5 *(continued)*

- SPECIFICITY—pick the right kind of activities to affect each component. Strength training results in specific strength changes. Also, train for the specific activity you're interested in. For example, optimal swimming performance is best achieved when the muscles involved in swimming are trained for the movements required. It does not necessarily follow that a good runner is a good swimmer.

- OVERLOAD—work hard enough, at levels that are vigorous and long enough to overload your body above its resting level, to bring about improvement.

- REGULARITY—you can't hoard physical fitness. At least three balanced workouts a week are necessary to maintain a desirable level of fitness.

- PROGRESSION—increase the intensity, frequency and/or duration of activity over periods of time in order to improve.

Some activities can be used to fulfill more than one of your basic exercise requirements. For example, in addition to increasing cardiorespiratory endurance, running builds muscular endurance in the legs, and swimming develops the arm, shoulder and chest muscles. If you select the proper activities, it is possible to fit parts of your muscular endurance workout into your cardiorespiratory workout and save time.

MEASURING YOUR HEART RATE

Heart rate is widely accepted as a good method for measuring intensity during running, swimming, cycling, and other aerobic activities. Exercise that doesn't raise your heart rate to a certain level and keep it there for 20 minutes won't contribute significantly to cardiovascular fitness.

The heart rate you should maintain is called your target heart rate. There are several ways of arriving at this figure. One of the simplest is: maximum heart rate $(220 - age) \times 70\%$. Thus, the target heart rate for a 40-year-old would be 126. Some

(continued)

Box 7-5 *(continued)*

methods for figuring the target rate take individual differences into consideration. Here is one of them:

1. Subtract age from 220 to find maximum heart rate.
2. Subtract resting heart rate from maximum heart rate to determine heart rate reserve.
3. Take 70% of heart rate reserve to determine heart rate raise.
4. Add heart rate raise to resting heart rate to find target rate.

Resting heart rate should be determined by taking your pulse after sitting quietly for five minutes. When checking heart rate during a workout, take your pulse within five seconds after interrupting exercise because it starts to go down once you stop moving. Count pulse for 10 seconds and multiply by six to get the per-minute rate.

Controlling Your Weight

The key to weight control is keeping energy intake (food) and energy output (physical activity) in balance. When you consume only as many calories as your body needs, your weight will usually remain constant. If you take in more calories than your body needs, you will put on excess fat. If you expend more energy than you take in you will burn excess fat.

Exercise plays an important role in weight control by increasing energy output, calling on stored calories for extra fuel. Recent studies show that not only does exercise increase metabolism during a workout, but it causes your metabolism to stay increased for a period of time after exercising, allowing you to burn more calories.

How much exercise is needed to make a difference in your weight depends on the amount and type of activity, and on how much you eat. Aerobic exercise burns body fat. A medium-sized adult would have to walk more than 30 miles to burn up 3,500 calories, the equivalent of one pound of fat. Although that may seem like a lot, you don't have to walk the 30 miles all at once. Walking a mile a day for 30 days will achieve the same result, providing you don't increase your food intake to negate the effects of walking.

Box 7-5 *(continued)*

If you consume 100 calories a day more than your body needs, you will gain approximately 10 pounds in a year. You could take that weight off, or keep it off, by doing 30 minutes of moderate exercise daily. The combination of exercise and diet offers the most flexible and effective approach to weight control.

Since muscle tissue weighs more than fat tissue, and exercise develops muscle to a certain degree, your bathroom scale won't necessarily tell you whether or not you are "fat." Well-muscled individuals, with relatively little body fat, invariably are "over-weight" according to standard weight charts. If you are doing a regular program of strength training, your muscles will increase in weight, and possibly your overall weight will increase. Body composition is a better indicator of your condition than body weight.

Lack of physical activity causes muscles to get soft, and if food intake is not decreased, added body weight is almost always fat. Once-active people who continue to eat as they always have after settling into sedentary lifestyles tend to suffer from "creeping obesity."

CLOTHING

All exercise clothing should be loose-fitting to permit freedom of movement, and should make the wearer feel comfortable and self-assured.

As a general rule, you should wear lighter clothes than temperatures might indicate. Exercise generates great amounts of body heat. Light-colored clothing that reflects the sun's rays is cooler in the summer, and dark clothes are warmer in winter. When the weather is very cold, it's better to wear several layers of light clothing than one or two heavy layers. The extra layers help trap heat, and it's easy to shed one of them if you become too warm.

In cold weather, and in hot, sunny weather, it's a good idea to wear something on your head. Wool watch or ski caps are recommended for winter wear, and some form of tennis or sailor's hat that provides shade and can be soaked in water is good for summer. Never wear rubberized or plastic clothing; such garments interfere with the evaporation of perspiration

(continued)

Box 7-5 *(continued)*

and can cause body temperature to rise to dangerous levels. The most important item of equipment for the runner is a pair of sturdy, properly-fitting running shoes. Training shoes with heavy, cushioned soles and arch supports are preferable to flimsy sneakers and light racing flats.

WHEN TO EXERCISE

The hour just before the evening meal is a popular time for exercise. The late afternoon workout provides a welcome change of pace at the end of the work day and helps dissolve the day's worries and tensions.

Another popular time to work out is early morning, before the work day begins. Advocates of the early start say it makes them more alert and energetic on the job.

Among the factors you should consider in developing your workout schedule are personal preference, job and family responsibilities, availability of exercise facilities and weather. It's important to schedule your workouts for a time when there is little chance that you will have to cancel or interrupt them because of other demands on your time.

You should not exercise strenuously during extremely hot, humid weather or within two hours after eating. Heat and/or digestion both make heavy demands on the circulatory system, and in combination with exercise can be an overtaxing double load.

Note:
1. U.S. Department of Health and Human Services: the Centers for Disease Control and Prevention; the National Center for Health Statistics; *Call to Action to Prevent and Decrease Overweight and Obesity*, 2001.

Source: President's Council on Physical Fitness and Sports, Guideline for Personal Fitness Programs, 2003, Website Publications, PCPFS. Department W, 200 Independence Ave., SW, Room 738-H, Washington, D.C.

NUTRITION AND EATING HABITS

Contrary to popular belief, dieting is not recommended, even for those with a weight problem. Diets are usually meant to be temporary. After most people complete a diet, they usually put the weight back on, sometimes more weight than they lost.

The best method for weight control and a healthy body is nutritional eating habits and a healthy lifestyle (see Box 7-6). Frustration and disappointment are inevitable unless the right nutrition, eating habits, and exercise exist. The proper blend of these makes a healthier, happier life possible and allows your body to maintain, repair, and develop itself.

Box 7-6

Nutrition Facts—U.S. Department of Agriculture and the U.S. Department of Health and Human Services

Fats supply energy and essential fatty acids, and they help absorb the fat-soluble vitamins A, D, E, and K, and carotenoids. You need some fat in the food you eat, but choose sensibly. Some kinds of fat, especially saturated fats, increase the risk for coronary heart disease by raising the blood cholesterol. In contrast, unsaturated fats (found mainly in vegetable oils) do not increase blood cholesterol. Fat intake in the United States as a proportion of total calories is lower than it was many years ago, but most people still eat too much saturated fat. Eating lots of fat of any type can provide excess calories.

KNOW THE DIFFERENT TYPES OF FATS

Saturated Fats

Foods high in saturated fats tend to raise blood cholesterol. These foods include high-fat dairy products (like cheese, whole milk, cream, butter, and regular ice cream), fatty fresh and processed meats, the skin and fat of poultry, lard, palm oil, and coconut oil. Keep your intake of these foods low.

Dietary Cholesterol

Foods that are high in cholesterol also tend to raise blood cholesterol. These foods include liver and other organ meats, egg yolks, and dairy fats.

(continued)

Box 7-6 *(continued)*

Trans Fatty Acids

Foods high in trans fatty acids tend to raise blood cholesterol. These foods include those high in partially hydrogenated vegetable oils, such as many hard margarines and shortenings. Foods with a high amount of these ingredients include some commercially fried foods and some bakery goods.

Unsaturated Fats

Unsaturated fats (oils) do not raise blood cholesterol. Unsaturated fats occur in vegetable oils, most nuts, olives, avocados, and fatty fish like salmon. Unsaturated oils include both monounsaturated fats and polyunsaturated fats. Olive, canola, sunflower, and peanut oils are some of the oils high in monounsaturated fats. Vegetable oils such as soybean oil, corn oil, and cottonseed oil and many kinds of nuts are good sources of polyunsaturated fats. Some fish, such as salmon, tuna, and mackerel, contain omega-3 fatty acids that are being studied to determine if they offer protection against heart disease. Use moderate amounts of food high in unsaturated fats, taking care to avoid excess calories.

FOOD CHOICES LOW IN SATURATED FAT AND CHOLESTEROL AND MODERATE IN TOTAL FAT

Keep Total Fat Intake Moderate

- Aim for a total fat intake of no more than 30 percent of calories, as recommended in previous editions of the Guidelines. If you need to reduce your fat intake to achieve this level, do so primarily by cutting back on saturated and trans fats. For example, at 2,200 calories per day, your suggested upper limit on fat intake would be about 73 grams. If you are at a healthy weight and you eat little saturated fat, you'll have leeway to eat some plant foods that are high in unsaturated fats. Get most of your calories from plant foods (grains, fruits, vegetables). If you eat foods high in saturated fat for a special occasion, return to foods that are low in saturated fat the next day.

Box 7-6 *(continued)*

Fats and Oils

- Choose vegetable oils rather than solid fats (meat and dairy fats, shortening). If you need fewer calories, decrease the amount of fat you use in cooking and at the table.

Meat, Poultry, Fish, Shellfish, Eggs, Beans, and Nuts

- Choose 2 to 3 servings of fish, shellfish, lean poultry, other lean meats, beans, or nuts daily. Trim fat from meat and take skin off poultry. Choose dry beans, peas, or lentils often.
- Limit your intake of high-fat processed meats such as bacon, sausages, salami, bologna, and other cold cuts. Try the lower fat varieties (check the Nutrition Facts Label).
- Limit your intake of liver and other organ meats. Use egg yolks and whole eggs in moderation. Use egg whites and egg substitutes freely when cooking since they contain no cholesterol and little or no fat.

Dairy Products

- Choose fat-free or low-fat milk, fat-free or low-fat yogurt, and low-fat cheese most often. Try switching from whole to fat-free or low-fat milk. This decreases the saturated fat and calories but keeps all other nutrients the same.

Prepared Foods

- Check the Nutrition Facts Label to see how much saturated fat and cholesterol are in a serving of prepared food. Choose foods lower in saturated fat and cholesterol.

Foods at Restaurants or Other Eating Establishments

- Choose fish or lean meats as suggested above. Limit ground meat and fatty processed meats, marbled steaks, and cheese.
- Limit your intake of foods with creamy sauces, and add little or no butter to your food.

(continued)

Box 7-6 *(continued)*

- Choose fruits as desserts most often.
- Choose beverages and foods to moderate your intake of sugars.
- Sugars are carbohydrates and a source of energy (calories). Dietary carbohydrates also include the complex carbohydrates starch and dietary fiber. During digestion all carbohydrates except fiber break down into sugars. Sugars and starches occur naturally in many foods that also supply other nutrients. Examples of these foods include milk, fruits, some vegetables, breads, cereals, and grains.

Sugars and Tooth Decay

- Foods containing sugars and starches can promote tooth decay. The amount of bacteria in your mouth and lack of exposure to fluorides also promote tooth decay. These bacteria use sugars and starches to produce the acid that causes tooth decay. The more often you eat foods that contain sugars and starches, and the longer these foods remain in your mouth before you brush your teeth, the greater your risk for tooth decay. Frequent eating or drinking sweet or starchy foods between meals is more likely to harm teeth than eating the same foods at meals and then brushing. Daily dental hygiene, including brushing with fluoride toothpaste and flossing, and adequate intake of fluorides will help prevent tooth decay.

Added Sugars

- Added sugars are sugars and syrups added to foods in processing or preparation, not the naturally occurring sugars in foods like fruit or milk. The body cannot tell the difference between naturally occurring and added sugars because they are identical chemically. Foods containing added sugars provide calories, but may have few vitamins and minerals. In the United States, the number one source of added sugars is nondiet soft drinks (soda or pop). Sweets and candies, cakes and cookies, and fruit drinks and fruitades are also major sources of added sugars.

Box 7-6 *(continued)*

Sugar Substitutes

- Sugar substitutes such as saccharin, aspartame, acesulfame potassium, and sucralose are extremely low in calories. Some people find them useful if they want a sweet taste without the calories. Some foods that contain sugar substitutes, however, still have calories. Unless you reduce the total calories you eat or increase your physical activity, using sugar substitutes will not cause you to lose weight.

Sugars and Other Health Issues

- Behavior. Intake of sugars does not appear to affect children's behavior patterns or their ability to learn. Many scientific studies conclude that sugars do not cause hyperactivity in children.

Weight Control

- Foods that are high in sugars but low in essential nutrients primarily contribute calories to the diet. When you take in extra calories and don't offset them by increasing your physical activity, you will gain weight. As you aim for a healthy weight and fitness, keep an eye on portion size for all foods and beverages, not only those high in sugars.

ADVICE FOR TODAY

- Choose sensibly to limit your intake of beverages and foods that are high in added sugars.
- Get most of your calories from grains (especially whole grains), fruits and vegetables, low-fat or non-fat dairy products, and lean meats or meat substitutes.
- Take care not to let soft drinks or other sweets crowd out other foods you need to maintain health, such as low-fat milk or other good sources of calcium.
- Drink water often.

(continued)

Box 7-6 *(continued)*

Intake of a lot of foods high in added sugars, like soft drinks, is of concern. Consuming excess calories from these foods may contribute to weight gain or lower consumption of more nutritious foods. Identify the most commonly eaten foods that are high in added sugars (unless they are labeled "sugar free" or "diet"). Limit your use of these beverages and foods. Drink water to quench your thirst, and offer it to children.

Some foods with added sugars, like chocolate milk, presweetened cereals, and sweetened canned fruits, also are high in vitamins and minerals. These foods may provide extra calories along with the nutrients and are fine if you need the extra calories.

The Nutrition Facts Label gives the content of sugars from all sources. You can use the Nutrition Facts Label to compare the amount of total sugars among similar products. To find out if sugars have been added, you also need to look at the food label ingredient list.

More Advice

- Choose sensibly to moderate your salt intake.
- Choose fruits and vegetables often. They contain very little salt unless it is added in processing.
- Read the Nutrition Facts Label to compare and help identify foods lower in sodium—especially prepared foods.
- If you eat restaurant foods or fast foods, choose those that are prepared with only moderated amounts of salt or salty flavorings.

If you drink alcoholic beverages, do so in moderation. Alcoholic beverages supply calories but few nutrients. Alcoholic beverages are harmful when consumed in excess, and some people should not drink at all. Excess alcohol alters judgment and can lead to dependency and a great many other serious health problems. Taking more than one drink per day for women or two drinks per day for men can raise the risk for motor vehicle crashes, other injuries, high blood pressure, stroke, violence,

Box 7-6 *(continued)*

suicide, and certain types of cancer. Even one drink per day can slightly raise the risk of breast cancer. Alcohol consumption during pregnancy increases risk of birth defects. Too much alcohol may cause social and psychological problems, cirrhosis of the liver, inflammation of the pancreas, and damage to the brain and heart. Heavy drinkers also are at risk of malnutrition because alcohol contains calories that may substitute for those in nutritious foods. If adults choose to drink alcoholic beverages, they should consume them only in moderation.

Drinking in moderation may lower risk for coronary heart disease, mainly among men over age 45 and women over age 55. However, there are other factors that reduce the risk of heart disease, including a healthy diet, physical activity, avoidance of smoking, and maintenance of a healthy weight.

Moderate consumption provides little, if any, health benefit for younger people. Risk of alcohol abuse increases when drinking starts at an early age. Some studies suggest that older people may become more sensitive to the effects of alcohol as they age.

SPORTS NUTRITION

Water, Water Everywhere

You can survive for a month without food, but only a few days without water.

- Water is the most important nutrient for active people.
- When you sweat, you lose water, which must be replaced. Drink fluids before, during, and after workouts.
- Water is a fine choice for most workouts. However, during continuous workouts of greater than 90 minutes, your body may benefit from a sports drink.
- Sports drinks have two very important ingredients— electrolytes and carbohydrates.
- Sports drinks replace electrolytes lost through sweat during workouts lasting several hours.

(continued)

Box 7-6 *(continued)*

- Carbohydrates in sports drinks provide extra energy. The most effective sports drinks contain 15 to 18 grams of carbohydrate in every 8 ounces of fluid.

Rev Up Your Engine with Carbohydrates

Carbohydrates are your body's main source of energy.

- Carbohydrates are sugars and starches, and they are found in foods such as breads, cereals, fruits, vegetables, pasta, milk, honey, syrups and table sugar.
- Sugars and starches are broken down by your body into glucose, which is used by your muscles for energy.
- For health and peak performance, more than half your daily calories should come from carbohydrates.
- Sugars and starches have 4 calories per gram, while fat has 9 calories per gram. In other words, carbohydrates have less than half the calories of fat.
- If you regularly eat a carbohydrate-rich diet you probably have enough carbohydrate stored to fuel activity. Even so, be sure to eat a precompetition meal for fluid and additional energy. What you eat as well as when you eat your precompetition meal will be entirely individual.

Flexing Your Options to Build Bigger Muscles

It is a myth that eating lots of protein and/or taking protein supplements and exercising vigorously will definitely turn you into a big, muscular person.

- Building muscle depends on your genes, how hard you train, and whether you get enough calories.
- The average American diet has more than enough protein for muscle building. Extra protein is eliminated from the body or stored as fat.

Score with Vitamins and Minerals

Eating a varied diet will give you all the vitamins and minerals you need for health and peak performance.

Box 7-6 *(continued)*

- Exceptions include active people who follow strict vegetarian diets, avoid an entire group of foods, or eat less than 1800 calories a day. If you fall into any of these categories, a multivitamin and mineral pill may provide the vitamins and minerals missing in your diet.
- Taking large doses of vitamins and minerals will not help your performance and may be bad for your health. Vitamins and minerals do not supply the body with energy and therefore are not a substitute for carbohydrates.

Popeye and All That Spinach

Iron supplies working muscles with oxygen.

- If your iron level is low, you may tire easily and not have enough stamina for activity.
- The best sources of iron are animal products, but plant foods such as fortified breads, cereals, beans and green leafy vegetables also contain iron.
- Iron supplements may have side effects, so take them only if your doctor tells you to.

No Bones About It, You Need Calcium Every Day

Many people do not get enough of the calcium needed for strong bones and proper muscle function.

- Lack of calcium can contribute to stress fractures and the bone disease osteoporosis.
- The best sources of calcium are dairy products, but many other foods such as salmon with bones, sardines, collard greens, and okra also contain calcium. Additionally, some brands of bread, tofu, and orange juice are fortified with calcium.

A Weighty Matter

Your calorie needs depend on your age, body size, sport and training program.

(continued)

Box 7-6 *(continued)*

- The best way to make sure you are not getting too many or too few calories is to check your weight from time to time.
- If you're keeping within your ideal weight range, you're probably getting the right amount of calories.

Source: President's Council on Physical Fitness and Sports, Guideline for Personal Fitness Programs, 2003, Website Publications, PCPFS. Department W, 200 Independence Ave., SW, Room 738-H, Washington, D.C.

In addition to the performance we all seek, preventing illness is a major goal. People usually do not appreciate good health until they no longer have it. Following nutritional guidelines will help to prevent many things, from a heart attack to digestive trouble. Maintenance of the body is similar to that of a well-operating vehicle. Investing the relatively small price of exercising and eating right will prevent you from having to pay the devastating price of losing your health.

Stay Motivated

If you are not staying in shape, check your attitude; it could be the only thing preventing you from having better fitness. People who are not physically fit usually lack the motivation necessary to live a healthy lifestyle. For the officer who refuses to stay in shape, a lack of commitment can mean someone may be hurt because the officer did not have the physical abilities required at the moment.

Consider these aspects:

- You may not be the strongest or fastest, but you can make the most of your natural abilities. Making the best of your capabilities is one of life's greatest responsibilities and satisfactions.
- Imagine the arteries of your body literally clearing each time you exercise.
- Whether your goal is losing weight or reaching new athletic heights, there will be plateaus, times when it appears you are making little progress. Your body is catching up with the

change it is undergoing. View these periods as merely stepping stones toward better things to come.

- Pick up a 10-pound weight and carry it around for 20 minutes. Imagine how much easier everyday life will be once you have lost those ten pounds.
- Think about the greatest accomplishments that have been achieved throughout history. Ask yourself what your greatest achievements have been. All great endeavors take sacrifice and determination. Having a healthy body, good marriage, or great law enforcement career all demand an enormous amount of hard work and commitment, but they are worth it.
- Remember, every time you work out and eat right, you are increasing the length of your life.
- Think about how much more confident you will be with your new, toned body.
- Consider what it will feel like to get back into your favorite pair of pants, shirt, skirt, or blouse.[6]

The best commitment you can make in becoming physically fit is to believe in yourself. The rewards will be invaluable, and your body will appreciate the special treatment it deserves. For a list of resources, see Box 7-7.

Box 7-7
Resources

Center for Nutrition Policy and Promotion, USDA
1120 20th Street, NW, Suite 200, North Lobby
Washington, DC 20036
Internet: www.usda.gov/cnpp

Food and Nutrition Information Center
National Agricultural Library, USDA
10301 Baltimore Boulevard, Room 304
Beltsville, MD 20705–2351
Internet: www.fns.usda.gov/fns

(continued)

Box 7-7 *(continued)*

healthfinder®—Gateway to Reliable Consumer Health Information
National Health Information Center
U.S. Department of Health and Human Services
P.O. Box 1133
Washington, DC 20013–1133
Internet: www.healthfinder.gov

Cancer Information Service
Office of Cancer Communications
National Cancer Institute
Building 31, Room 10A16
9000 Rockville Pike
Bethesda, MD 20892
Internet: www.cis.nci.nih.gov

National Heart, Lung, and Blood Institute Information Center
P.O. Box 30105
Bethesda, MD 20824–0105
Internet: www.nhlbi.nih.gov

Food Safety and Inspection Service, USDA
Food Safety Education Staff
1400 Independence Avenue, SW, Room 2942S
Washington, DC 20250
Internet: www.fsis.usda.gov

Gateway to Government Food Safety Information
Internet: www.foodsafety.gov

National Institute of Diabetes and Digestive and Kidney Diseases
Office of Communications and Public Liaison
31 Center Drive, MSC 2560
Bethesda, MD 20892–2560
Internet: www.niddk.nih.gov

Box 7-7 *(continued)*

National Institute on Alcohol Abuse and Alcoholism
600 Executive Boulevard, Suite 409
Bethesda, MD 20892–7003
Internet: www.niaaa.nih.gov

National Institute on Aging Information Center
Building 31, Room 5C27
Bethesda, MD 20892
Internet: www.aoa.gov/elderpage.html#ap

Food and Drug Administration
200 C Street, SW
Washington, DC 20204
Internet: www.fda.gov

Centers for Disease Control and Prevention
1600 Clifton Road
Atlanta, GA 30333
Internet: www.cdc.gov

Source: The U.S. Department of Agriculture and the U.S. Department of Health and Human Services, Dietary Guidelines Advisory Committee. The committee consisted of Cutberto Garza, M.D., Ph.D. (chair), Suzanne P. Murphy, Ph.D., R.D. (vice-chair), Richard J. Deckelbaum, M.D., Johanna Dwyer, D.Sc., R.D., Scott M. Grundy, M.D., Ph.D., Rachel K. Johnson, Ph.D., M.P.H., R.D., Shiriki K. Kumanyika, Ph.D., Alice H. Lichtenstein, D.Sc., Meir Stampfer, M.D., Dr.P.H., Lesley Fels Tinker, Ph.D., and Roland L. Weinsier, M.D., Dr.P.H. Carol Suitor, D.Sc., R.D., served as the committee's technical writer/editor. The Departments also acknowledge the staff work of the executive secretaries to the committee: Shanthy Bowman, Ph.D., and Carole Davis, M.S., R.D., from USDA; Kathryn McMurry, M.S., and Joan Lyon, M.S., R.D., L.D., from HHS.

The greatest quality for any law enforcement or corrections officer to posses is moral courage. Although there are endless challenges, temptations and dilemmas throughout a criminal justice career, the ones that test your honor and integrity will be defining moments. Whether you are a police officer, deputy, state trooper or work in a corrections facility, when it is all over all you will have is your integrity. Then again, people only have that, if they did the right thing in those defining moments.

Don Cabana, Criminal Justice Chair, University of Southern Mississippi

QUESTIONS FOR DISCUSSION

1. The beginning of this chapter presents a summary about how devastating being unfit can be. What is the greatest weakness of your own physical condition? How can this weakness be dangerous, considering a law enforcement career?

2. List the specific types and amounts of exercise you engage in each week.

3. Chapter 7 notes that the cost of overweight and obesity to the economy is $117 billion annually in direct and indirect medical costs. What are the nonmonetary direct and indirect costs of officers who are not in shape to their agency? To their fellow officers? To their community?

4. Several sections of Chapter 7 include a component on self-assessment. How would your fellow officers or classmates assess your physical condition? How would you most likely assess your condition?

5. Gary L. Bullard, Executive Director of the Northern Virginia Criminal Justice Academy, states "One of the most important attributes to having a successful career in Law Enforcement, I believe, is to develop a strong passion for wanting to make a difference and truly believing that you have the ability to make a difference. I also believe it is important to take the initiative and not wait for things to happen." Considering Director Bullard's belief that individuals have to take the initiative to makes things happen, what do you think should be done about officers who refuse to stay in shape? Do you believe every agency should have mandatory physical fitness employment tests and an in-service fitness program?

ENDNOTES

1. J. Boyce Davis and E. Leslie Knight, *CVR Fitness* (Dubuque, IA: Kendall/Hunt Publishing Co.), pp. 1–27.

2. Frank I. Katch, William D. McArdle, and Brian Richard Boylan, *Getting In Shape* (Boston, MA: Houghton Mifflin Co., 1979), pp. 1–8.

3. Ibid.

4. J. Boyce Davis and E. Leslie Knight, *CVR Fitness* (Dubuque, IA: Kendall/Hunt Publishing Co.), pp. 1–27.

5. Bob Anderson, *Stretching* (Bolinas, CA: Shelter Publications, 1984), pp. 8–12.

6. Bob Wolff, "Motivation." *Muscle and Fitness*, August 1989, pp. 177–178.

appendix ***A***

FEDERAL LAW
ENFORCEMENT AGENCIES

DEPARTMENT OF HOMELAND SECURITY

The creation of the Department of Homeland Security (DHS) is the most significant transformation of the U.S. government since 1947, when Harry S Truman merged the various branches of the U.S. Armed Forces into the Department of Defense to better coordinate the nation's defense against military threats.

The DHS represents a similar consolidation, both in style and substance. In the aftermath of the terrorist attacks against America on September 11, 2001, President George W. Bush decided 22 previously disparate domestic agencies needed to be coordinated into one department to protect the nation against threats to the homeland.

The new department's first priority is to protect the nation against further terrorist attacks. Component agencies will analyze threats and intelligence, guard our borders and airports, protect our critical infrastructure, and coordinate the response of our nation for future emergencies.

Besides providing a better-coordinated defense of the homeland, the DHS is also dedicated to protecting the rights of American citizens and enhancing public services, such as natural disaster assistance and citizenship services, by dedicating offices to these important missions.

The DHS has five major divisions, or "directorates":

Border and Transportation Security (BTS)

BTS is led by Under Secretary Asa Hutchinson and is responsible for maintaining the security of our nation's borders and transportation systems. The largest of the directorates, it is home to agencies such as the Transportation Security Administration, U.S. Customs Service, the border security functions of the Immigration and Naturalization Service, Animal & Plant Health Inspection Service, and the Federal Law Enforcement Training Center.

Securing Our Borders   Securing our nation's air, land, and sea borders is a difficult yet critical task. The United States has 5,525 miles of border with Canada and 1,989 miles with Mexico. Our maritime border includes 95,000 miles of shoreline and a 3.4 million-square-mile exclusive economic zone. Each year, more than 500 million people cross the borders into the United States, some 330 million of whom are noncitizens.

On March 1st, the Department of Homeland Security, through the Directorate of Border and Transportation Security, assumed responsibility for securing our nation's borders and transportation systems, which straddle 350 official ports of entry and connect our homeland to the rest of the world. BTS also assumed responsibility for enforcing the nation's immigration laws.

The department's first priority is to prevent the entry of terrorists and the instruments of terrorism while simultaneously ensuring the efficient flow of lawful traffic and commerce. BTS manages and coordinates port of entry activities and leads efforts to create a border of the future that provides greater security through better intelligence, coordinated national efforts, and unprecedented international cooperation against terrorists, the instruments of terrorism, and other international threats.

To carry out its border security mission, BTS incorporates the United States Customs Service (previously part of the Department of Treasury), the enforcement division of the Immigration and Naturalization Service (INS) (Department of Justice), the Animal and Plant Health Inspection Service (Department of Agriculture), the Federal Law Enforcement Training Center (Department of Treasury) and the Transportation Security Administration (Department of Transportation). BTS will also incorporate the Federal Protective Service (General Services Administration) to perform the additional function of protecting government buildings, a task closely related to the department's infrastructure protection responsibilities.

The BTS Directorate is also responsible for securing our nation's transportation systems, which move people from our borders to anywhere in the country within hours. The recently created Transportation Security Administration (TSA), which is now part of the BTS Directorate, has statutory responsibility for security of all of the airports. Tools it uses include intelligence, regulation, enforcement, inspection, and screening and education of carriers, passengers and shippers. The incorporation of TSA into the new department allows the Department of Transportation to remain focused on its core mandate of ensuring that the nation has a robust and efficient transportation infrastructure that keeps pace with modern technology and the nation's demographic and economic growth.

Another important function of BTS's border management mission is enforcing the nation's immigration laws—both in deterring illegal immigration and pursuing investigations when laws are broken. BTS absorbed the enforcement units of the Immigration and Naturalization Service, such as the Border Patrol and investigative agents of the INS. Working together with agents from other agencies that comprise the BTS Directorate, such as the U.S. Customs Service and Transportation Security personnel, these well-trained law enforcement professionals provide a coordinated defense against unlawful entry into the United States.

Emergency Preparedness and Response (EP&R)

This Directorate, which is headed by Under Secretary Mike Brown, ensures that our nation is prepared for, and able to recover from, terrorist attacks and natural disasters.

Preparing America   As September 11 showed, the consequences of terrorism can be far-reaching and diverse. As part of the Department of Homeland Security, the Directorate of Emergency Preparedness and Response (EP&R) will ensure that our nation is prepared for catastrophes—whether natural disasters or terrorist assaults. Not only will the directorate coordinate with first responders, it will oversee the federal government's national response and recovery strategy.

To fulfill these missions, the Department of Homeland Security will build upon the Federal Emergency Management Agency (FEMA), which has a long and solid track record of aiding the nation's recovery from emergency situations. The EP&R Directorate will continue FEMA's efforts to reduce the loss of life and property and to protect our nation's institutions from all types of hazards through a comprehensive, risk-based emergency management program of preparedness, prevention, response, and recovery. And it will further the evolution of the emergency management culture from one that reacts to disasters to one that proactively helps communities and citizens avoid becoming victims. In addition, the directorate will develop and manage a national training and evaluation system to design curriculums, set standards, evaluate, and reward performance in local, state, and federal training efforts.

The directorate will also continue FEMA's practice of focusing on risk mitigation in advance of emergencies by promoting the concept of disaster-resistant communities, including providing federal support for local governments that promote structures and communities that reduce the chances of being hit by disasters. EP&R will coordinate with private industry, the insurance sector, mortgage lenders, the real estate industry, homebuilding associations, citizens, and others to create model communities in high-risk areas.

The directorate will also lead the DHS response to any sort of biological or radiological attack and also coordinate the involvement of other federal response teams, such as the National Guard, in the event of a major incident. Building upon the successes of FEMA, the DHS will lead the nation's recovery from catastrophes and help minimize the suffering and disruption caused by disasters.

Science and Technology (S&T)

Under the direction of Under Secretary Dr. Charles McQueary, this directorate coordinates the Department's efforts in research and development, including preparing for and responding to the full range of terrorist threats involving weapons of mass destruction.

Developing Technology The Directorate of Science and Technology (S&T) will become the primary research and development arm of the Department of Homeland Security. The S&T Directorate will organize the vast scientific and technological resources of the United States to prevent or mitigate the effects of catastrophic terrorism against the United States or its allies. It will unify and coordinate much of the federal government's efforts to develop and implement scientific and technological countermeasures, including channeling the intellectual energy and extensive capacity of important scientific institutions, such as the national laboratories and academic institutions.

One priority of the directorate will be to sponsor research, development, and testing to invent new vaccines, antidotes, diagnostics, and therapies against biological and chemical warfare agents.

In the war against terrorism, America's already existent science and technology base provides us with a key advantage. The department will press this advantage with a national research and development enterprise for homeland security comparable in emphasis and scope to that which has supported the national security community for more than fifty years. This is appropriate, given the scale of the mission and the catastrophic potential of the threat. Many of the needed systems are potentially continental in scope, and thus the technologies must scale appropriately, in terms of complexity, operation, and sustainability.

This research and development emphasis will be driven by a constant examination of the nation's vulnerabilities, constant testing of our security systems, and a thorough evaluation of the threats and their weaknesses. The emphasis within this enterprise will be on catastrophic terrorism—threats to the security of our homeland that could result in large-scale loss of life and major economic impact. It will be aimed at both evolutionary improvements to current capabilities as well as the development of revolutionary new capabilities.

Information Analysis and Infrastructure Protection (IAIP)

IAIP merges the capability to identify and assess a broad range of intelligence information concerning threats to the homeland, issue timely warnings, and take appropriate preventive and protective action under one roof.

Synthesizing and Disseminating Information The Department of Homeland Security, through the Directorate of Information

Analysis and Infrastructure Protection (IAIP) will merge under one roof the capability to identify and assess current and future threats to the homeland, map those threats against our vulnerabilities, issue timely warnings, and take preventive and protective action.

Intelligence Analysis and Alerts   Actionable intelligence—that is, information which can lead to stopping or apprehending terrorists—is essential to the primary mission of the DHS. The timely and thorough analysis and dissemination of information about terrorists and their activities will improve the government's ability to disrupt and prevent terrorist acts and to provide useful warning to the private sector and our population. The directorate will fuse and analyze information from multiple sources pertaining to terrorist threats. The department will be a full partner and consumer of all intelligence-generating agencies, such as the National Security Agency (NSA), the CIA and the FBI.

The department's threat analysis and warning functions will support the President and, as he directs, other national decision-makers responsible for securing the homeland from terrorism. It will coordinate and, as appropriate, consolidate the federal government's lines of communication with state and local public safety agencies and with the private sector, creating a coherent and efficient system for conveying actionable intelligence and other threat information. The IAIP Directorate will also administer the Homeland Security Advisory System.

As designed, IAIP fully reflects the President's commitment to safeguard our way of life, including the integrity of our democratic political system and the essential elements of our individual liberty. To further ensure such protections, the DHS will establish an office for a Chief Privacy Officer.

Critical Infrastructure Protection   The attacks of September 11 highlighted the fact that terrorists are capable of causing enormous damage to our country by attacking our critical infrastructure: food, water, agriculture, and health and emergency services; energy sources (electrical, nuclear, gas and oil, dams); transportation (air, road, rail, ports, waterways); information and telecommunications networks; banking and finance systems; postal and other assets and systems vital to our national security, public health and safety, economy, and way of life.

Protecting America's critical infrastructure is the shared responsibility of federal, state, and local governments, in active partnership with the private sector, which owns approximately 85 percent of our nation's critical infrastructure. IAIP will take the lead in coordinating the national effort to secure the nation's infrastructure. This will give state, local, and private entities one primary contact instead of many for coordinating protection activities within the federal government, including vulnerability assessments, strategic planning efforts, and exercises.

Cyber Security Our nation's information and telecommunications systems are directly connected to many other critical infrastructure sectors, including banking and finance, energy, and transportation. The consequences of an attack on our cyber infrastructure can cascade across many sectors, causing widespread disruption of essential services, damaging our economy, and imperiling public safety. The speed, virulence, and maliciousness of cyber attacks have increased dramatically in recent years. Accordingly, the directorate places an especially high priority on protecting our cyber infrastructure from terrorist attack by unifying and focusing the key cyber security activities performed by the Critical Infrastructure Assurance Office (currently part of the Department of Commerce) and the National Infrastructure Protection Center (FBI). The directorate will augment those capabilities with the response functions of the Federal Computer Incident Response Center (General Services Administration). Because our information and telecommunications sectors are increasingly interconnected, the DHS will also assume the functions and assets of the National Communications System (Department of Defense), which coordinates emergency preparedness for the telecommunications sector.

Indications and Warning Advisories In advance of real-time crisis or attack, IAIP will provide:

- Threat warnings and advisories against the homeland including physical and cyber events.
- Processes to develop and issue national and sector-specific threat advisories through the Homeland Security Advisory System.
- Terrorist threat information for release to the public, private industry, or state and local governments.

Partnerships   The IAIP team will establish:

- Partnerships with key government, public, private, and international stakeholders to create an environment that enables them to better protect their infrastructures.
- Awareness programs, development of information sharing mechanisms, and sector-focused best practices and guidelines.

National Communications System   The IAIP team will provide:

- Coordination of planning and provision of National Security and Emergency Preparedness (NS/EP) communications for the Federal government.

Management

The Undersecretary of Management, Janet Hale, will be responsible for budget, management, and personnel issues in the DHS.

Building a Team of Professionals   The Undersecretary of Management is responsible for budget, appropriations, expenditure of funds, accounting, and finance; procurement; human resources and personnel; information technology systems; facilities, property, equipment, and other material resources; and identification and tracking of performance measurements relating to the responsibilities of the department.

Key to the success of the department overall is the success of its employees, and the Directorate for Management is responsible for ensuring that employees have clear responsibilities and means of communication with other personnel and management. An important resource for communications will be the office of the Chief Information Officer, who is responsible for maintaining the information technology necessary to keep the more than 170,000 employees of the DHS connected to and fully a part of the goals and mission of the Department.

Besides the five Directorates of the DHS, several other critical agencies are folding into the new department or being newly created:

- *United States Coast Guard (USCG):* The Commandant of the Coast Guard reports directly to the Secretary of Homeland Security. However, the USCG also works closely with the

Undersecretary of Border and Transportation Security as well as maintains its existing independent identity as a military service. Upon declaration of war or when the President so directs, the Coast Guard would operate as an element of the Department of Defense, consistent with existing law.

- *United States Secret Service:* The primary mission of the Secret Service is the protection of the President and other government leaders, as well as security for designated national events. The Secret Service is also the primary agency responsible for protecting U.S. currency from counterfeiters and safeguarding Americans from credit card fraud.

- *Bureau of Citizenship and Immigration Services:* While BTS is responsible for enforcement of our nation's immigration laws, the Bureau of Citizenship and Immigration Services dedicates its full energies to providing efficient immigration services and easing the transition to American citizenship. The Director of Citizenship and Immigration Services will report directly to the Deputy Secretary of Homeland Security.

- *Office of State and Local Government Coordination:* A truly secure homeland requires close coordination between local, state, and federal governments. This office ensures that close coordination takes place with state and local first responders, emergency services, and governments.

- *Office of Private Sector Liaison:* The Office of Private Sector Liaison provides America's business community a direct line of communication to the Department of Homeland Security. The office works directly with individual businesses and through trade associations and other non-governmental organizations to foster dialogue between the Private Sector and the Department of Homeland Security on the full range of issues and challenges faced by America's business sector in the post 9–11 world.

- *Office of Inspector General:* The Office of Inspector General serves as an independent and objective inspection, audit, and investigative body to promote effectiveness, efficiency, and economy in the Department of Homeland Security's programs and operations and to prevent and detect fraud, abuse, mismanagement, and waste in such programs and operations. To contact Acting Inspector General Clark Kent Ervin, or his staff, call (202) 254-4100. To report waste, fraud or abuse, call the Hotline at 1-800-323-8603.

Agencies Department of Homeland Security agencies are housed in one of four major directorates: Border and Transportation Security, Emergency Preparedness and Response, Science and Technology, and Information Analysis and Infrastructure Protection.

The Border and Transportation Security Directorate will bring the major border security and transportation operations under one roof, including:

- U.S. Customs Service (Treasury)
- Immigration and Naturalization Service (part) (Justice)
- Federal Protective Service (GSA)
- Transportation Security Administration (Transportation)
- Federal Law Enforcement Training Center (Treasury)
- Animal and Plant Health Inspection Service (part) (Agriculture)
- Office for Domestic Preparedness (Justice)

The Emergency Preparedness and Response Directorate will oversee domestic disaster preparedness training and coordinate government disaster response. It will bring together:

- Federal Emergency Management Agency (FEMA)
- Strategic National Stockpile and the National Disaster Medical System (HHS)
- Nuclear Incident Response Team (Energy)
- Domestic Emergency Support Teams (Justice)
- National Domestic Preparedness Office (FBI)

The Science and Technology directorate will seek to utilize all scientific and technological advantages when securing the homeland. The following assets will be part of this effort:

- CBRN Countermeasures Programs (Energy)
- Environmental Measurements Laboratory (Energy)
- National BW Defense Analysis Center (Defense)
- Plum Island Animal Disease Center (Agriculture)

The Information Analysis and Infrastructure Protection Directorate will analyze intelligence and information from other agencies (including the CIA, FBI, DIA and NSA) involving threats to homeland security and evaluate vulnerabilities in the nation's infrastructure. It will bring together:

- Critical Infrastructure Assurance Office (Commerce)
- Federal Computer Incident Response Center (GSA)
- National Communications System (Defense)
- National Infrastructure Protection Center (FBI)
- Energy Security and Assurance Program (Energy)

The Secret Service and the Coast Guard will also be located in the Department of Homeland Security, remaining intact and reporting directly to the Secretary. In addition, the INS adjudications and benefits programs will report directly to the Deputy Secretary as the Bureau of Citizenship and Immigration Services.

Bureau of Alcohol, Tobacco and Firearms
650 Massachusetts Ave., N.W.
Washington, D.C. 20226
(202) 927-8700   Fax (202) 927-8876

www.atf.treas.gov

Drug Enforcement Administration
Washington, D.C. 20537
(202) 307-8000   Fax (202) 307-7335

www.usdoj.gov/dea

Federal Bureau of Investigation
J. Edgar Hoover Building
Washington, D.C. 20535
(202) 324-3000   Fax (202) 324-4705

www.fbi.gov

Financial Crime Enforcement Network
2070 Chain Bridge Rd.
Vienna, VA 22182
(703) 905-3591   Fax (703) 905-3690

www.ustreas.gov/fincen

National Park Service—U.S. Park Police
Ohio Dr., S.W.
Washington, D.C. 20242
(202) 619-7350   Fax (202) 205-7981

www.di.gov/u.s.park.police

U.S. Customs Service
1300 Pennsylvania Ave., N.W., Suite 44A
Washington, D.C. 20229
(202) 927-1010   Fax (202) 927-1380

www.customs.treas.gov

U.S. Department of Treasury
1500 Pennsylvania Ave., N.W.
Washington, D.C. 20220
(202) 622-1100   Fax (202) 622-0073

www.ustreas.gov

U.S. Fish and Wildlife Service
4401 N. Fairfax Dr.
Arlington, VA 22203
(703) 358-1949   Fax (703) 358-2271

www.fws.gov

U.S. Marshals Service
600 Army Navy Dr.
Arlington, VA 22202
(202) 307-9001   Fax (202) 557-9788

www.usdoj-gov/marshals

Source: Department of Homeland Security Website

appendix **B**

LAW ENFORCEMENT TRAINING ORGANIZATIONS

**American Society of Law Enforcement
Trainers (ASLET)**
P.O. Box 361
Lewes, DE 19958
(302) 645-4080   Fax (302) 645-4084

www.aslet.com

**Association of Public Safety Communications
Officials International, Inc.**
2040 S. Ridgeway Ave.
South Daytona, FL 32119
(904) 322-2500   Fax (904) 322-2501

www.apcointl.org

Canada Association of Chiefs of Police (CACP)
130 Albert St., Suite 1710
Ottawa, Canada K1P 5G4
(613) 233-1106   Fax (613) 233-6960

www.cacp.org

Federal Law Enforcement Training Center
Glynco, GA 31524
(912) 267-2224   Fax (912) 267-2495

www.fas.org

Institute of Police Technology and Management
12000 Alumni Dr.
Jacksonville, FL 32224
(904) 620-4786   Fax (904) 620-2453

www.unf.edu

International Association of Arson
300 S. Broadway, Suite 100
St. Louis, MO 63102
(314) 739-4224   Fax (314) 621-5125

www.fire-investigators.org

International Association of Bomb Technicians and Investigators
P.O. Box 8629
Naples, FL 34101
(941) 353-6843   Fax (941) 353-6841

www.iabti.org

International Association of Chiefs of Police (IACP)
515 N. Washington St.
Alexandria, VA 22314
(800) 843-4227   Fax (703) 836-4543

www.theiacp.org

International Association of Ethics Trainers
P.O. Box 388191
Chicago, IL 60638-8191
(773) 284-1326

www.ethicstrainers.com

International Association of Financial Crimes Investigators
385 Bel Marin Keys, Suite H
Novato, CA 94949
(415) 884-6600   Fax (415) 884-6605

www.iafci.org

International Association of Fire Chiefs
4025 Fair Ridge Rd., Suite 300
Fairfax, VA 22033
(703) 273-0911   Fax (703) 273-9363

www.iafc.org

International Association of Women Police
P.O. Box 15207
Seattle, WA 98115
(206) 625-4465

www.iawp.org

International Narcotic Enforcement Officers Association Inc.
112 State St., Suite 1200
Albany, NY 12207
(518) 253-2874   Fax (518) 253-3378

www.ineoa.org

National Association of School Resource Officers
2714 S.W. 5th St.
Boynton Beach, FL 33435
(561) 736-1736   Fax (561) 736-1736

www.nasro.org

National Institute of Ethics
2301 14th St., Suite 606
P.O. Box 116
Gulfport, MS 39502
1-800-273-2559   Fax (228) 867-2044

www.ethicsinstitute.com

National Institute of Justice Resources
Office of the Director
810 7th St., N.W.
Washington, D.C. 20531
(202) 307-2942   Fax (202) 307-6394

www.ojp.usdoj.gov/nij

National Criminal Justice Reference Service
Office of the Director
P.O. Box 6000
Rockville, MD 20849
(800) 851-3420   Fax (301) 519-5212

www.ncjrs.org

Bureau of Justice Assistance Clearinghouse
(800) 688-4252   Fax (410) 953-3848

www.ncjrs.org/task16.htm

Juvenile Justice Clearinghouse
(800) 638-8736   Fax (301) 519-5212

www.fsu.edu/~crimedo/jjclearinghouse

Victims of Crimes Resource Center
(800) 627-6872   Fax (410) 953-3848

www.avp.org/resources.htm

appendix **C**

LAW ENFORCEMENT—
RELATED ASSOCIATIONS

AAA Foundation for Traffic Safety
1440 New York Ave. N.W., Suite 201
Washington, D.C. 20005
(202) 638-5944   Fax (202) 638-5943

www.aaafts.org

Air Force Security Police Association
818 Willow Creek Cir.
San Marcos, TX 78666-5060
(800) 782-7653   Fax (512) 396-7328

www.uts.cc.utexas.edu/~ehre/AFSPA.html

Air Incident Research
P.O. Box 4745
East Lansing, MI 48826
(517) 336-9375   Fax (517) 336-9375

www.airsafety.com

Airborne Law Enforcement Association Inc.
14268 Linda Vista Dr.
Whittier, CA 90602
(213) 485-2011   Fax (213) 485-2073

www.alea.org

American Association of Railroads
P.O. Box 11130
Pueblo, CO 81001
(719) 584-0701   Fax (719) 585-1819

www.aar.org

American Association of Retired Persons (AARP)
601 E St., N.W.
Washington, D.C. 20049
(202) 434-2222   Fax (202) 434-6466

www.aarp.org

**American Association of State Highway
and Transportation Officials**
444 N. Capitol St., N.W., Suite 249
Washington, D.C. 20001
(202) 434-2222   Fax (202) 434-6466

www.aashto.org

American Correctional Association
4380 Forbes Blvd.
Lanham, MD 20706
(301) 918-1800   Fax (301) 918-1900

www.correctional.com/aca

American Criminal Justice Association
P.O. Box 601047
Sacramento, CA 95860
(916) 484-6553   Fax (916) 488-2227

www.acjalae.org

American Federation of Police and Concerned Citizens
3801 Biscayne Blvd.
Miami, FL 33137
(305) 573-0070   Fax (305) 573-9819

www.aphf.org

American Jail Association
2053 Day Rd., Suite 100
Hagerstown, MD 21740
(301) 790-3930   Fax (301) 790-2941

www.corrections.com/aja

American Planning Association
1776 Massachusetts Ave. N.W., Suite 400
Washington, D.C. 20036
(202) 872-0611   Fax (202) 872-0643

www.planning.org

American Police Hall of Fame and Museum
3801 Biscayne Blvd.
Miami, FL 33137
(305) 573-0070   Fax (305) 573-9819

www.aphf.org

American Police Officers Association
2173 Embassy Dr.
Lancaster, PA 17603
(888) 644-8022

www.apai.org

American Polygraph Association
P.O. Box 8037
Chattanooga, TN 37414
(423) 892-3992   Fax (423) 894-5435
1-800-APA-8037

www.polygraph.org

American Probation and Parole Association
2760 Research Park Dr.
Lexington, KY 40578
(606) 244-3216   Fax (606) 244-8001

www.csom.org

American Psychiatric Association
1400 K St., N.W.
Washington, D.C. 20005
(202) 682-6000   Fax (202) 682-6850

www.psych.org

American Society of Law Enforcement Trainers (ASLET)
P.O. Box 361
Lewes, DE 19958
(302) 645-4080   Fax (302) 645-4084

www.aslet.org

Americans for Effective Law Enforcement Inc.
5519 W. Cumberland Ave., Suite 1008
Chicago, IL 60656
(800) 763-2802   Fax (800) 763-3221

www.aele.org

Association of Public Safety Communications Officials International Inc.
2040 S. Ridgeway Ave.
South Daytona, FL 32119
(904) 322-2500   Fax (904) 322-2501

www.apcointl.org

Canada Association of Chiefs of Police (CACP)
130 Albert St., Suite 1710
Ottawa, Canada K1P 5G4
(613) 233-1106   Fax (613) 233-6960

www.cacp.ca

Child Find of America, Inc.
243 Main St.
New Paltz, NY 12561
(845) 255-1848   Fax (845) 255-5706

www.childfindofamerica.org

Child Shield USA
103 W. Spring St.
Titusville, PA 16354
(800) 652-4453   Fax (814) 827-6977

www.childshieldusa.com

Commission on Accreditation for Law Enforcement Agencies
10306 Eaton Pl., Suite 320
Fairfax, VA 22030
(800) 368-3757   Fax (703) 591-2206

www.calea.org

Concerns of Police Survivors Inc. (COPS)
South Highway 5
Camdenton, MO 65020
(573) 346-4911   Fax (573) 346-1414

www.nationalcops.org

Congressional Fire Services Institute
900 Second St., N.E., Suite 303
Washington, D.C. 20002
(202) 371-1277   Fax (202) 682-3473

www.cfsi.org

Council of International Investigators
2150 N. 107th, Suite 205
Seattle, WA 98133-9009

www.cii2.org

Crime Stoppers International, Inc.
P.O. Box 614
Arlington, TX 76004-0614
Phone: (800) 245-0009 or 817-446-6253, Fax: (817) 446-6253

D-A-R-E America
P.O. Box 512090
Los Angeles, CA 90051
(310) 215-0575   Fax (310) 215-0180

www.dare-America.com

Eastern Armed Robbery Conference, Ltd.
P.O. Box 5772
Wilmington, DE 19808
(516) 852-6271   Fax (516) 852-6478

www.earc.org

Federal Law Enforcement Officers Association
P.O. Box 508
East Northport, NY 11731
(717) 938-2300   Fax (717) 932-2262

www.fleoa.org

Federal Pretrial Services Agency
500 Pearl St., Room 550
New York, NY 10007
(212) 805-0015   Fax (212) 805-4172

Hostage Negotiators of America
2072 Edinburgh Dr.
Montgomery, AL 36116
(334) 244-7411

Institute of Police Technology and Management
University of North Florida
12000 Alumni Dr.
Jacksonville, FL 32224-2678
(904) 620-4786   Fax (904) 620-2453

www.iptm.org

International Association for Identification
2535 Pilot Knob Rd., Suite 117
Mendota Heights, MN 55120
(651) 681-8566   Fax (651) 681-8443

www.theiai.org

International Association for Property and Evidence
903 N. San Fernando Blvd., Suite 4
Burbank, CA 91504-4327
(800) 449-4273   Fax (818) 846-4543

www.iape.org

International Association of Bomb Technicians and Investigators
P.O. Box 8629
Naples, FL 34101
(941) 353-6843   Fax (941) 353-6841

www.iabti.org

International Association of Campus Law Enforcement Administrators (IACLEA)
342 N. Main St.
West Hartford, CT 06117
(860) 586-7517   Fax (860) 586-7550

www.iaclea.org

International Association of Chiefs of Police (IACP)
515 N. Washington St.
Alexandria, VA 22314
(800) 843-4227   Fax (703) 836-4543

www.theiacp.org

International Association of Correctional Officers
3900 Industrial Ave.
Lincoln, NE 68504
(402) 464-0602   Fax (402) 464-5931

International Association of Ethics Trainers
1620 West State Route 434, Suite 164
Longwood, FL 32750
(407) 339-0322 Fax (407) 339-7139
www.ethicstrainers.com

International Association of Financial Crimes Investigators
385 Bel Marin Keys Blvd., Suite H
Novato, CA 94949
(415) 884-6600 Fax (415) 884-6605

www.iatci.org

International Association of Fire Chiefs
4025 Fair Ridge Rd., Suite 300
Fairfax, VA 22033
(703) 273-0911 Fax (703) 273-9363

www.iafc.org

International Association of Law Enforcement Planners
1300 Executive Center Dr., Suite 450
Tallahassee, FL 32301-5025
(850) 878-7254 Fax (850) 656-7944

www.ialep.org

International Association of Personal Protection Agents
458 W. Kenwood
Brighton, TN 38011-6294
(901) 837-1915 Fax (901) 837-4949

www.tiac.net/users/jmking

International Association of Women Police
P.O. Box 15207
Seattle, WA 98115
(206) 625-4465

www.iawp.org

International City/County Management Association (ICMA)
777 N. Capitol St., N.E., Suite 500
Washington, D.C. 20002
(202) 289-4262   Fax (202) 962-3500

www.icma.org

International Conference of Police Chaplains
P.O. Box 5590
Destin, FL 32540
(850) 654-9736   Fax (850) 654-9742

www.members.tripod.com/~FSG3/icpc.htm

International Fire Marshals Association
One Batterymarch Park
Quincy, MA 02269
(617) 984-7424   Fax (617) 984-7056

International Foundation for Art Research
500 5th Ave., Suite 1234
New York, NY 10101
(212) 391-6234   Fax (212) 391-8794

www.ifar.com

International Foundation for Protection Officers
3106 Tami Annie Trail
Naples, FL 34103
(941) 430-0534   Fax (941) 430-5333

www.ifpo.com

International Juvenile Officers Association Inc.
P.O. Box 56
Easton, CT 06612
(203) 377-4424

International Law Enforcement Stress Association
5485 David Blvd.
Port Charlotte, FL 33981
(813) 697-8863

International Narcotic Enforcement Officers Association Inc.
112 State St., Suite 1200
Albany, NY 12207
(518) 253-2874   Fax (518) 253-3378

www.ineoa.org

International Police Association–U.S. Section
P.O. Box 43-1822
Miami, FL 33243
(305) 253-2874   Fax (305) 253-3568

www.ipausa.org

International Police Mountain Bike Association
28 E. Ostend St.
Baltimore, MD 21230
(410) 685-2220   Fax (410) 685-2240

www.ipmba.org

International Prisoners Aid Association
Dept. of Sociology, University of Louisville
Louisville, KY 40292
(502) 241-7831   Fax (502) 241-7831

International Union of Police Association AFL/CIO
1421 Prince St., Suite 330
Alexandria, VA 22314
(703) 549-7434   Fax (703) 549-9048

Jewelers Security Alliance
6 E. 45th St.
New York, NY 10017
(800) 537-0067   Fax (212) 808-9168

www.jsa.polygon.net

Law Enforcement Alliance of America
7700 Leesburg Pike, Suite 421
Falls Church, VA 22043
(703) 847-2677   Fax (703) 556-6485

www.leaa.org

Law Enforcement and Emergency Services Video Association
P.O. Box 126167
Fort Worth, TX 76126
(817) 249-4002   Fax (817) 249-4002

Law Enforcement Memorial Association Inc.
P.O. Box 72835
Roselle, IL 60172
(847) 795-1547   Fax (847) 795-2469

www.w8ca.com/lema/

Military Police Regimental Association
P.O. Box 5278
Anniston, AL 36205
(256) 848-5014   Fax (256) 848-6691

Missing Children Society of Canada
3501 23rd St., N.E. Suite 219
Calgary, Canada T2E 6V8
(403) 291-0705   Fax (403) 291-9728

www.mcsc.ca/

Narcotic Enforcement Officers Association
29 N. Plains Highway Phoenix Park, Suite 10
Wallingford, CT 06492
(203) 269-8940   Fax (203) 284-9103

www.neoa.org

National Association Against Gang and Domestic Violence
P.O. Box 775186
St. Louis, MO 63177
(314) 631-3723

National Association of Chiefs of Police
1000 Connecticut Ave. N.W., Suite 9
Washington, D.C. 20036
(202) 293-9088   Fax (305) 573-9819

www.bluegrass.net/~n2try/nacop.htm

National Association of Counties
440 First St. N.W., 8th Floor
Washington, D.C. 20001
(202) 393-6226   Fax (202) 393-2630

www.naco.org

National Association of Drug Court Professionals
901 N. Pitt St., Suite 370
Alexandria, VA 22314
(703) 706-0576   Fax (703) 706-0577

www.drugcourt.org/home.cfm

National Association of Field Training Officers (NAFTO)
Sage Valley Rd.
Longmont, CO 80503
(303) 442-0482   Fax (303) 546-6791

www.nafto.org

National Association of Medical Examiners (N.A.M.E.)
1402 S. Grand Blvd.
St. Louis, MO 3104
(314) 577-8298

www.thename.org

National Association of Police Athletic Leagues
618 N. U.S. Hwy. 1, Suite 201
N. Palm Beach, FL 33408
(561) 844-1823   Fax (561) 863-6120

www.reeusda.gov/pavnet/cj/cjnatass.htm

National Association of Police Organizations (NAPO)
750 First St., Suite 920
Washington, D.C. 20002
(202) 842-4420   Fax (202) 842-4396

www.napo.org

National Association of School Resource Officers (NASRO)
2714 S.W. 5th St.
Boynton Beach, FL 33435
(561) 736-1736   Fax (561) 736-1736

www.nasro.org

National Association of Town Watch (NATW)
One Wynnewood Rd., Suite 102
Wynnewood, PA 19096
(610) 649-7055   Fax (610) 649-5456

www.nationaltownwatch.org

National Center for Missing and Exploited Children
2101 Wilson Blvd., Suite 550
Arlington, VA 22201
(703) 235-3900   Fax (703) 235-4067

www.missingkids.com

National Child Safety Council
4065 Page Ave.
P.O. Box 1368
Jackson, MI 49204
(517) 764-6070   Fax (517) 764-4140
(800) 222-1464

National Constables Association
16 Stonybrook Dr.
Levittown, PA 19055
(215) 547-6400   Fax (215) 943-0907

www.angelfire.com/la/nationalconstable

National Council on Crime and Delinquency (NCCD)
685 Market St., Suite 620
San Francisco, CA 94105
(415) 896-6223   Fax (415) 896-5109

www.nccd-crc.org

National Crime Prevention Council
1700 K St., 2nd Floor
Washington, D.C. 20006
(202) 466-6272   Fax (202) 296-1356

www.ncpc.org

National Crime and Punishment Learning Center
623 Sarazen Dr.
Gulfport, MS 39507
(228) 896-5280   Fax (228) 896-8696

www.crimeandpunishment.net

National Criminal Justice Association
444 N. Capitol St., N.W., Suite 618
Washington, D.C. 20001
(202) 624-1440   Fax (202) 508-3859

www.sso.org/ncja/default.htm

National District Attorneys Association
99 Canal Center Plaza, Suite 510
Alexandria, VA 22314
(703) 549-9222   Fax (703) 836-3195

www.ndaa.org

National Family Legal Foundation (NFLF)
11000 N. Scottsdale Rd., Suite 144
Scottsdale, AZ 85254
(602) 922-9731   Fax (602) 922-7240

www.nflf.com

National Fire Protection Association
One Batterymarch Park
Quincy, MA 02269
(617) 770-3000   Fax (617) 770-0700

www.nfpa.org

National Fraternal Order of Police
1410 Donelson Pike, Suite A17
Nashville, TN 37217
(615) 339-0900   Fax (615) 339-0400

www.grandlodgefop.org

National Institute of Ethics
1610 West State Route 434, Suite 164
Longwood, FL 32750
(407) 339-0322   Fax (407) 339-7139

www.ethicsinstitute

National Institute on Economic Crime
P.O. Box 7186
Fairfax, VA 22039
(703) 250-8706   Fax (703) 860-8449

National Insurance Crime Bureau (NICB)
10330 S. Roberts Rd.
Palos Hills, IL 60465
(708) 430-2430   Fax (708) 430-2446

www.nicb.org

National Law Enforcement Council
888 Sixteenth St., N.W., Suite 700
Washington, D.C. 20006
(202) 835-8020   Fax (202) 331-4291

National Law Enforcement Officers Memorial Fund Inc.
605 E St., N.W.
Washington, D.C. 20004
(202) 737-3400   Fax (202) 737-3405

www.nleomf.com

National Law Enforcement Research Center
P.O. Box 70966
Sunnydale, CA 94086
(408) 245-2037   Fax (408) 245-2037

National League of Cities (NLC)
1301 Pennsylvania Ave., N.W., Suite 550
Washington, D.C. 20004
(202) 626-3000   Fax (202) 626-3043

www.nlc.org

National Legal Aid and Defender Association
1625 K St., N.W., Suite 800
Washington, D.C. 20006
(202) 452-0620   Fax (202) 872-1031

www.nlada.org

National Organization for Victim Assistance
1757 Park Rd., N.W.
Washington, D.C.
(202) 232-6682   Fax (202) 462-2255

www.try-nova.org

National Organization of Black Law Enforcement Executives
1757 Park Rd., N.W.
Washington, D.C. 20010
(703) 658-1529   Fax (703) 658-9479

www.noblenatl.org

National Police Institute
Central Missouri State University
200 Main St.
Warrensburg, MO 22312
(660) 543-4091   Fax (660) 543-83306

National Recreation and Park Association
DuPage County Forest Preserve District
Glen Ellyn, IL 60138
(630) 933-7239   Fax (630) 790-1071

National Reserve Law Officers Association
P.O. Box 6505
San Antonio, TX 78209
(210) 820-0478   Fax (210) 804-2463

National Rifle Association
11250 Waples Mill Rd.
Fairfax, VA 22030
(703) 267-1000   Fax (703) 267-3989

www.nra.org/

National Safety Council
1025 Connecticut Ave., N.W., Suite 1200
Washington, D.C. 20036
(202) 974-2480   Fax (202) 293-0032

www.nsc.org

National Sheriffs Association
1450 Duke St.
Alexandria, VA 22314
(703) 836-7827   Fax (703) 683-6541

www.sheriffs.org

National Tactical Officers Association (NTOA)
P.O. Box 529
Doylestown, PA 18901
(800) 279-9127   Fax (215) 230-7552

www.ntoa.org

National Technical Investigators Association
6933 N. 26th St.
Falls Church, VA 22046
(703) 237-9388   Fax (703) 241-0353

www.natia.org

National Traffic Law Center
99 Canal Center Plaza, Suite 510
Alexandria, VA 22314
(703) 549-4253   Fax (703) 836-3195

National Troopers Coalition
Andrea Lane
La Plata, MD 20646
(410) 653-3885   Fax (410) 653-0929

www.nat-trooperscoalition.com

National United Law Enforcement Officers Association Inc.
265 E. McLemore Ave.
Memphis, TN 38106
(901) 774-1118   Fax (901) 774-1139

National White Collar Crime Center
7401 Beausant Springs Dr.
Richmond, VA 23225
(804) 323-3563   Fax (804) 323-3566

www.nw3c.org

National Wildlife Federation
8925 Leesburg Pike
Vienna, VA 22184
(703) 790-4000   Fax (703) 790-4330

www.nwf.org

National Youth Gang Center (NYGC)
2894 Remington Green Circle
Tallahassee, FL 32308
(850) 385-0600   Fax (850) 385-5356

www.iir.com/nygc

Nine Lives Associates Executive Protection Institute
Rural Route 1, Box 332
Bluemont, VA 26135
(540) 955-1128   Fax (540) 955-0255

Office of International Criminal Justice (OICJ)
1033 W. Van Burden St.
Chicago, IL 60607
(312) 996-9595   Fax (312) 312-0458

www.acsp.uic.edu/

Office of Law Enforcement Standards (OLES)
National Institute of Standards and Technology Building, Room 225

Gaithersburg, MD 20899
(800) 975-2757   Fax (301) 948-0978
www.oles.org

Operation Lifesaver
1420 King St., Suite 401
Alexandria, VA 22314
(800) 537-6224   Fax (703) 519-8267

www.oli.org

Operation Lookout National Center for Missing Youth
6320 Evergreen Way, Suite 201
Everett, WA 98203
(800) 782-7335   Fax (425) 438-4111

www.operationlookout.org

Organized Crime Task Force
143 Grand St.
White Plains, NY 10601
(914) 422-8780   Fax (914) 422-8795

Police Chiefs Spouses—Worldwide
1521 Sixth Ave. East
Menomonie, WI 54751
(715) 235-9749

www.gtesupersite.com/pcsw/

Police Communication Center
215 Church Ave. S.W.
Roanoke, VA 24011
(540) 853-2411   Fax (540) 853-1599

Police Executive Research Forum (PERF)
1120 Connecticut Ave., N.W., Suite 930
Washington, D.C. 20036
(202) 466-7820   Fax (202) 466-7826

www.inca.net/perf

Police and Fireman's Insurance Association
101 E. 116th St.
Carmel, IN 46032
(317) 581-1913   Fax (317) 571-5946

Police Marksman Association
6000 E. Shirley Lane
Montgomery, AL 36117
(334) 271-2010   Fax (334) 279-9267

www.policemarksman.com

Pretrial Services Resource Center
1325 G St., N.W., Suite 770
Washington, D.C. 20005
(202) 638-3080   Fax (202) 347-0493

www.pretrial.org

**Reserve Law Officers Association
of America (RESLAW)**
San Antonio, TX 78217
(210) 653-5754   Fax (210) 653-9655

www.reslaw.com

Retired and Disabled Police of America
1900 S. Harbor City Blvd., Suite 328
Melbourne, FL 32901
(800) 395-7376   Fax (407) 779-8046

The Police Supervisors Group
1401 Johnson Ferry Rd., Suite 328-F42
Marietta, GA 30062
(770) 321-5018   Fax (770) 321-5019

www.policesupervisors.org

Transportation Research Board
2101 Constitution Ave., N.W.
Washington, D.C. 20418
(202) 334-2936   Fax (202) 334-2003

www.nas.edu.trb

U.S. Conference of Mayors
1620 I St., N.W.
Washington, D.C. 20006
(202) 293-7330   Fax (202) 293-2352

www.USmayors.org

United States Fire Administration (USFA)
National Emergency Training Center
16825 S. Seton
Emmitsburg, MD 21727
(301) 447-1200   Fax (301) 447-1102

www.usfa.fema.gov

STATE TRAINING COUNCILS AND POLICE STANDARDS COMMISSIONS

Contact your state training council or police standards commission to learn of upcoming training opportunities or for questions about the hiring or training requirements in your state.

R. Alan Benefield, Chief Director
Alabama Peace Officer Standards and Training Board
P.O. Box 300075
Montgomery, AL 35130-0075
(334) 242-4045   Fax (334) 242-4633

www.apostc.state.al.us

Jim Meehan, Executive Director
Alaska Police Standards Council
P.O. Box 111200
Juneau, AK 99811-1200
(907) 465-4378   Fax (907) 465-3263

www.dps.state.ak.us/aps

Rod Covey, Executive Director
Arizona Peace Officer Standards and Training Board
2643 East University
P.O. Box 6638
Phoenix, AZ 85005
(602) 223-2514   Fax (602) 244-0477

www.azpost.state.az.us

Terry Bolton, Director
Arkansas Commission on Law Enforcement
Standards and Training
P.O. Box 3106
East Camden, AR 71711
(870) 574-1810   Fax (870) 574-2706

www.law/enforcement.org/CLEST

Kenneth O'Brien, Executive Director
California Commission on Peace Officer Standards
and Training
1601 Alahambra Blvd.
Sacramento, CA 95816-7053
(916) 227-2802   Fax (916) 227-2801

www.POST.ca.gov

John Kammerzell, Director
Colorado Peace Officer Standards and Training Board
1525 Sherman St., 6th Floor
Denver, CO 80203
(303) 866-5692   Fax (303) 866-5671

www.ago.state.co.us/post/pst

T. William Knapp, Executive Director
Connecticut Police Officer Standards and Training Council
285 Preston Ave.
Meridan, CT 06450
(203) 238-6505   Fax (203) 238-6503

www.post.state.ct.us

Col. James Ford, Jr. (Ret.), Chairman
Delaware Council on Police Training
1453 DuPont Highway
P.O. Box 430
Dover, DE 19903
(302) 739-5903   Fax (302) 739-5945

A. Leon Lowry, II, Director
Florida Dept. of Law Enforcement
P.O. Box 1489
Tallahassee, FL 32302-1489
(850) 410-8600   Fax (850) 410-8606

Steve Black, Executive Director
Georgia Peace Officer Standards and Training Council
2175 Northlake Parkway, Suite 144
Tucker, GA 30084
(770) 414-3313   Fax (770) 414-3332

www.gapost.org

Eugene Vemura, Assistant Chief
Honolulu Police Department
801 S. Beretania St.
Honolulu, HI 96813
(808) 677-1474   Fax (808) 677-7394

www.honolulupd.org

Michael N. Becar, Executive Director
Idaho Peace Officer Standards and Training
P.O. Box 700
Meridian, ID 83680-0700
(208) 884-7250   Fax (208) 884-7295

www.idaho.post.org

Thomas J. Jurkanin, Executive Director
Illinois Law Enforcement Training and Standards Board
600 S. 2nd St.
Springfield, IL 62704-2542
(217) 782-4540   Fax (217) 524-5711

www.ptb.state.il.us

Charles C. Burch, Executive Director
Indiana Law Enforcement
Training Board
P.O. Box 313
Plainfield, IN 46168-0313
(317) 839-5191 ext. 212   Fax (317) 839-9741

www.state.in.us/iu

Gene W. Shepard, Director
Iowa Law Enforcement Academy
P.O. Box 130
Johnston, IA 50131-0130
(515) 242-5357   Fax (515) 242-5471

www.state.ia.us/ilea

Ed H. Pavey, Director
Kansas Law Enforcement
Training Center
P.O. Box 647
Hutchinson, KS 67504
(316) 662-3378   Fax (316) 662-4720

www.kletc.org

John Bizzack, Commissioner
Kentucky Dept. of Criminal
Justice Training
Kit Carson Dr., Funderbach Bldg., EKU
Richmond, KY 40475
(606) 622-1328   Fax (606) 622-2740

www.docjt.jus.state.ky.us

Michael Ranatza, Director
Louisiana Commission on
Law Enforcement
1885 Wooddale Blvd., Room 208
Baton Rouge, LA 70806
(225) 925-4942   Fax (225) 925-1998

www.cole.state.la.us

Steven R. Giorgetti, Director
Maine Criminal Justice Academy
93 Silver St.
Waterville, ME 04901
(207) 877-8000   Fax (207) 877-8027

www.state.maine.us

Donald Hopkins, Executive Director
Maryland Police and Correctional
Training Commission
3085 Hemwood Rd.
Woodstock, MD 21163
(410) 750-6500   Fax (410) 203-1010

www.dpscs.state.md.us/pct

**Massachusetts Criminal Justice
Training Council**
411 Waverly Oaks Rd., Suite 250
Waltham, MA 02154
(617) 727-7827   Fax (617) 642-6898

www.state.ma.us/cjtc

**Raymond Beach, Jr.,
Executive Director**
Michigan Commission on Law
Enforcement Standards
7426 N. Canal Rd.
Lansing, MI 48913
(517) 322-1946   Fax (517) 322-6439

www.coles-online.org

John T. Laux, Executive Director
Minnesota Board of Police Officers
Standards and Training
1600 University Ave., Suite 200
St. Paul, MN 55104
(612) 543-3060   Fax (612) 643-3072

James B. Walker, Director
Mississippi Office on Law Enforcement
Standards and Training
401 Northwest St.
P.O. Box 23039
Jackson, MS 39204
(601) 359-7880   Fax (601) 359-7832

Chris Egbert, Program Administrator
Missouri Peace Officer Standards
and Training
P.O. Box 749
Jefferson City, MO 65102
(573) 751-4819   Fax (573) 517-5399

www.dps.state.mo/us

Jim Oberhofer, Executive Director
Montana Peace Officer Standards
and Training Council
303 N. Roberts
Helena, MT 59620
(406) 444-3604   (406) 444-4722

www.adlest.org/montana

Steve Lamken, Director
Nebraska Law Enforcement
Training Center
3600 North Academy Rd.
Grand Island, NE 68801
(308) 385-6030   Fax (308) 385-6032

www.nletc.state.ne.us

Richard Clark, Executive Director
Nevada Commission of Peace
Officer's Standards and Training
3476 Executive Pointe Way
Carson City, NV 89706
(775) 684-7678   Fax (775) 687-4911

www.leg.state.nv.us/nac

Earl M. Sweeney, Director
New Hampshire Police Standards
and Training Council
17 Fan Rd.
Concord, NH 03301
(603) 271-2133   Fax (603) 271-1785

www.justiceworks.unh.edu

Wayne Fisher, Deputy Director
New Jersey Police Training Commission
P.O. Box 085
Trenton, NJ 07039
(609) 984-0960   Fax (609) 984-4473

www.state.nj.us/lps/dcj

Darrel G. Hart, Director
New Mexico Law Enforcement
Academy Board
4491 Cerrillos Rd.
Santa Fe, NM 87505
(505) 827-9255   Fax (505) 827-3449

www.dps.nm.org/training

Jerry Burrell, Deputy Commissioner
New York Office of Public Safety—Division
of Criminal Justice Services
4 Tower Place
Albany, NY 12203
(518) 457-6101   Fax (518) 457-0145

www.criminaljust.state.ny.us

David D. Cashwell, Director
North Carolina Criminal Justice
Standards Division
P.O. Drawer 149
(919) 716-6470   Fax (919) 716-6752
Raleigh, NC 27602

www.jus.state.nc.us/justice

Mark Gilbertson, Executive Secretary
North Dakota Peace Officer Standards
and Training
Law Enforcement Academy
600 East Blvd., Dept. 504
Bismarck, ND 58505
(701) 328-9968   Fax (701) 328-9988

www.iadlest.org/ndakota

Vernon Chenevey, Executive Director
Ohio Peace Officer Training Commission
1650 State Route 56 N.W.
P.O. Box 309
London, OH 43140
(614) 466-7771   Fax (614) 728-5150

www.ag.state.oh.us

Jeanie Nelson, Ph.D., Director
Oklahoma Council on Law Enforcement
Education and Training
P.O Box 11476
Oklahoma City, OK 73136
(405) 425-2750   Fax (405) 425-2773

www.dps.state.ok.us/clete

Dianne Middle, Director
Dept. of Public Safety Standards
and Training
550 N. Monmouth Ave.
Monmouth, OR 97361
(503) 378-2100   Fax (503) 378-3330

www.oregonvof.net/dpsst

Richard Mooney, Executive Director
Pennsylvania Municipal Police Officer's
Education and Training Commission
75 E. Derry Rd.
Hershey, PA 17033
(717) 533-5987   Fax (717) 787-1650

www.mpoetc.org

Steven D. Weaver, Director
Rhode Island Municipal Police Training Academy,
Community College of Rhode Island—Flanagan Campus
Lincoln, RI 02865
(401) 222-3755   Fax (401) 726-5720

William Gibson, Deputy Director
South Carolina Criminal Justice Academy
5400 Broad River Rd.
Columbia, SC 29210
(803) 896-7777   Fax (803) 896-8347

www.iadlest.org/scaa

Kevin Thorn, Director
South Dakota Law Enforcement Standards and Training
Commission
E. Hwy. 34, 500 East Capital
Pierre, SD 57501
(605) 773-3584   Fax (605) 773-4629

Mark Bracy, Executive Secretary
Tennessee Peace Officer Standards
and Training Commission
3025 Lebanon Rd.
Nashville, TN 37214
(615) 741-3361   Fax (615) 532-0502

Jim Dozier, Executive Director
Texas Commission on Law Enforcement Officer
Standards and Education
6300 U.S. Hwy. 290 E., Suite 200
Austin, TX 78723
(512) 936-7700   Fax (512) 406-3614

www.tcjeose.state.tx.us

Sidney Groll, Executive Director
Utah Peace Officer Standards and Training
4525 S. 2700 West
Salt Lake City, UT 84119
(801) 965-4731   Fax (801) 965-4619

www.ps.ex.state.ut.us/pos

Gary L. Bullard, Executive Director
Vermont Criminal Justice Training Council
Rural Rd. 2, Box 2160
Pittsford, VT 05487
(802) 483-6225　　　　Fax (802) 483-2343

www.vcjt.state.vt.us

George Gotschalk, Deputy Director
Virginia Dept. of Criminal Justice Services
805 E. Broad St.
Richmond, VA 23219
(804) 786-4000　　　　Fax (804) 786-0588

www.dcjs.state.va.us

Michael Parsons, Ph.D., Executive Director
Washington State Criminal Justice Training Commission
19010 1st Ave. S.
Seattle, WA 98148
(206) 439-3740　　　　Fax (206) 439-3752

www.wa.gov/cjt

Don Davidson, Training Coordinator
West Virginia Criminal Justice Services
1204 Kanawha Blvd. E.
Charleston, WV 25301
(304) 558-8814 ext. 214　　　Fax (304) 558-0391

www.wvdjs.com

Dennis Hanson, Director
Wisconsin Dept. of Justice, Training and Standards Bureau
P.O. Box 7070
Madison, WI 53707
(608) 266-8800　　　　Fax (608) 266-7869

Donald Pierson, Executive Director
Wyoming Peace Officer Standards and Training
1710 Pacific Ave.
Cheyenne, WY 82002
(307) 777-6619　　　　Fax (307) 638-9706

www.iadlest.org/wyoming

INDEX